Terrorism, Instability, and Democracy
in Asia and Africa

Northeastern Series on Democratization and Political Development
AMILCAR ANTONIO BARRETO, EDITOR

For a complete list of books that are available in this series,
see www.upne.com

Terrorism, Instability, and Democracy in Asia and Africa

Dan G. Cox, John Falconer,
and Brian Stackhouse

Northeastern University Press
BOSTON

PUBLISHED BY UNIVERSITY PRESS OF NEW ENGLAND
HANOVER AND LONDON

NORTHEASTERN UNIVERSITY PRESS
Published by
University Press of New England
One Court Street, Lebanon, NH 03766
www.upne.com
© 2009 by Northeastern University Press
Printed in U.S.A.
Text design by Joyce Weston
5 4 3 2 1

Library of Congress Cataloging-in-Publication Data
Cox, Dan G.
  Terrorism, instability, and democracy in Asia and Africa / Dan G. Cox, John Falconer, and Brian Stackhouse.
     p.   cm. — (Northeastern series on democratization and political development)
  Includes bibliographical references and index.
  ISBN 978-1-55553-705-0 (cloth : alk. paper)
  1. Political stability — Asia. 2. Terrorism — Asia. 3. Democracy — Asia.
  4. Political stability — Africa. 5. Terrorism — Africa. 6. Democracy — Africa.
  7. Asia — Politics and government — 21st century. 8. Africa — Politics and government — 21st century. I. Falconer, John. II. Stackhouse, Brian. III. Title.
  JQ24.C69 2009
  363.325095 — dc22   2008049863

University Press of New England is a member of the
Green Press Initiative. The paper used in this book
meets their minimum requirement for recycled paper.

This book is dedicated to Stephanie and Sienna.—*DGC*

This book is dedicated to Tracy, Lauren, and Megan.—*JF*

This book is dedicated to Dee.—*BKS*

Contents

Illustrations

Figures

Tables

Acknowledgments

The authors wish to thank the Western Institute for its grant in the summer of 2006 supporting this project.

We would also like to thank Natalie Bailey, Scott Bensyl, Drew Jurgensen, Natasha Price, Michael Stevens, and Kassandra Norris for their help in obtaining and preparing the data for this project.

We would also like to thank Stephanie Cox for her amazing support and editorial comments.

Terrorism, Instability, and Democracy
in Asia and Africa

CHAPTER I

Introduction

Most Americans did not recognize terrorism as a threat to the United States or their personal interests until the 11 September 2001 attacks on the Pentagon in Washington, D.C., and the World Trade Center buildings in New York City. While the Al-Qaeda terror attacks were a shocking introduction to the frightening power of terrorism, many states throughout the world had already been fighting domestic, regional, and international terror groups for decades. The false invulnerability felt by the U.S. government and its citizens was in stark contrast to most states' historical experience with terrorism. Even Europe had to contend with a very well organized and sometimes deadly left-wing terror campaign thirty years ago. In Italy, the Red Brigades conducted a terror campaign from 1970 until the mid-1980s, aimed at installing a communist regime through violence, and a similarly Marxist-oriented Baader-Meinhof Gang in Germany engaged in terror from 1968 to 1977. In fact, one can trace terrorism back thousands of years to the first century A.D. when a Jewish terror group—the Sicarii (Alexander, 2002: 4)—attempted to expel the Roman occupiers with tactics such as poisoning public wells (Weinberger, 2003: 64).

Sustained, deadly, decades-long terror campaigns are the norm for most regions in the world with the exception of North America. Thus it comes as no surprise that only after the September 11th attacks has the U.S. government committed serious resources and political clout to fighting many of these terrorist campaigns. Adding to the challenge is the fact that terror groups have had many years to learn from their mistakes, build upon their successes, and fortify their positions and local support in many regions vital to United States and world interests. In fact, the data on terror events (Memorial Institute for the Prevention of Terrorism–Terrorism Knowledge Base, hereafter referred to as the MIPT-TKB) show a broadening campaign of terror that continues to escalate in both frequency and deadliness.

Researchers in the social sciences have recently begun, in earnest, the quest to find a solution that will fell the fearsome specter of terrorism. There are three main potential causes of terrorism that have been examined with any frequency: democracy, cultural or civilizational factors, and poverty. But even with scholars and policymakers beginning to focus on causes surrounding terrorism, the literature remains quite thin and attention to solutions is almost nonexistent.

Much of the current research is being driven by past examinations of the correlation between democracy and peace that arose out of the University of Michigan's *Correlates of War* project. In fact, one could argue that much of the foreign policy used by both President Bill Clinton and President George W. Bush was driven by the democratic peace research. President Bill Clinton responded to the deadly Al-Qaeda attacks on the United States embassies in Nairobi, Kenya, and Dar es Salaam, Tanzania, by arguing that the United States is sometimes the target of terrorists because we spread peace and democracy. He argued further that we cannot stop attempting to spread freedom and democracy, as that is what will ultimately weaken terrorist groups and movements (Lippman, 1998: A25). The direct influence of the findings contained in the democratic peace literature on President Clinton's thinking becomes more apparent when one combines his statements about terrorism in Africa with his 1994 State of the Union speech, as he specifically related the main finding of the democratic peace research—namely, that "democracies don't attack each other."

President George W. Bush picked up on this foreign policy theme and launched a campaign for democratization in the Middle East, which is seen as the region at the heart of international terrorism by the Bush administration (Wright and Kessler, 2004: A1). He, too, saw the lack of war between democracies as being an infallible truth, and therefore democracy, in this light, becomes an "unstoppable force for good" (Curl, 2005: A1). This thinking prompted President Bush to engage in war in an attempt to force democracy on two Muslim states simultaneously, while pressuring Middle Eastern and Central Asian neighbors to adopt freedom and democracy as well.

The problem with basing a counterterrorism foreign policy on democratic peace is that the democratic peace applies only to interstate war and, even there, it exists largely as a statistical finding that was discovered decades ago (and admittedly is still true today) but that has no theoretical explanation behind it. As we discuss in Chapter 3, democracies are no more pacific than nondemocracies, and no element in democracy has been shown to be the foundational impetus prohibiting democracies from warring with one another. In other words, a very dangerous set of foreign policy initiatives currently pursued by the United States in both Iraq and Afghanistan is poised on shaky theoretical ground. Unfortunately, recent research focusing specifically on democracy and terrorism has found no evidence that democracy lessens terrorism within a state (see, for example, Everyman, 1998; Eubank and Weinberg, 1998; Li and Schaub, 2004).

Democracy is not the only variable that researchers are interested in examining in attempting to explain terrorism. Cultural differences have been used by various authors to explain, in part or in whole, many international and domestic terror campaigns. The events of 11 September 2001, often called in shorthand 9/11, were portrayed by Al-Qaeda as an attack on Western imperialism. The choice of targets was symbolic of Al-Qaeda's struggle against Western capitalism and Western military intervention, which is perceived as enslaving Middle Easterners and diluting true or fundamental Islamic culture. But this clash of Eastern and Western culture is nothing new. When America first formed, pirates from the northern African state of Morocco and the semi-autonomous Ottoman provinces of Tripoli, Tunis, and Algiers regularly attacked American vessels, often enslaving and torturing the Christians they captured (Oren, 2007: 18). After several failed diplomacy missions to Northern Africa, the Tripolitan Army formally declared and engaged in war with America starting in 1801 (Oren, 2007: 55). This was to be the first of many civilizational confrontations between the United States and the Islamic world.

Samuel Huntington's seminal works on clashing civilizations has served as a foundation for multiple research endeavors, several of which have concluded that terrorism is largely driven by differences in religion, ethnicity, language, culture, and history (Morgan, 2004; Olcott and Bahajanov, 2003; Voeten, 2000). While his findings and claims are not without controversy, there is some truth to this conclusion, and one can certainly find civilizational aspects fueling terrorist groups throughout Asia and Africa. However, our research shows that differences in civilizations are rarely the only impetus for terrorists and terror groups, especially domestic terror groups. In fact, these cultural differences seem to be tools that terrorist and governmental leaders use to foment hatred among specific populaces within a state, usually within the larger context of injustice perpetrated by the central government. Without other impetuses, either from within or from outside the state, civilizational differences do not automatically spark terrorism. Still, there is an aspect of conflicting civilizations in many of the cases we examined and there is a long history of violence between the Islamic and Western world.

Poverty is a culprit that is often blamed for terrorism (Benjamin and Simon, 2002; Bueno de Mesquita, 2005; Haleem, 2005). But there is no consensus in the literature, nor a pattern that conclusively links poverty with terrorism. While some terrorist movements in Asia and Africa do have a significant poverty component attached to them, the poverty is almost always linked to a governmental regime that has historically mistreated a minority out-group in society. Poverty, in and of itself, does not appear to be a catalyst for terrorism. Extreme poverty in Mongolia, for example, has produced no terrorism. Poverty linked to human and social rights abuses by the government and aimed at a specific population within a state, like the Central Communist Party treatment of the Uyghur minority in China or the Sinhalese-dominated government's treatment of the Tamil minority in Sri Lanka, does seem to create a good foundation for terrorist activity.

This book is aimed at examining all three of these variables simultaneously, through basic statistical inquiry and through case studies, to determine whether one or all help us to understand why terrorism occurs. We chose to focus on Asia and Africa because we believe that myopia has developed, especially in terms of Western governmental counterterrorism efforts, which produce a single-minded focus on the Middle East. We believe that it is foolhardy, and even dangerous, to ignore terrorism that has developed in Asia and Africa. In the early years of the United States, the U.S. government's greatest threat emanated from the Barbary Coast pirates of northern Africa who, supported by Islamic Sultans, felt that Christians were less than human and, therefore, fair game for robbery, torture, and enslavement (Oren, 2007). Further, few people know or remember that Osama bin Laden built the Al-Qaeda organization and committed several major terrorist attacks while headquartered in Sudan. We believe that the future of terror will emanate more from Asia, especially South Asia, and Africa than the Middle East. For these reasons we have focused our study specifically on these regions.

Our study is twofold. In the first part of the book, we examine twenty-nine years of terrorism data from the Memorial Institute for the Prevention of Terrorism–Terrorism Knowledge Base (MIPT-TKB), examining the effects of democracy, civilization, poverty, and regime instability on both domestic and international terrorism. Many studies ignore domestic terrorism, and much of this oversight is due to the fact that domestic terrorism data have been unavailable until recently, but we believe that impetuses for international terror groups might be profoundly different than the driving forces behind domestic terrorism. As a result, we have attempted to examine international and domestic terrorism separately. In the second part of our book, we examine specific cases by region in Asia and Africa looking specifically at the history of the state, the reasons behind terrorism in our state cases, and focusing on the roles that democracy, civilizational aspects, poverty, and instability play. We feel that instability is an important fourth cause of terrorism that may, in fact, be the key cause fomenting terrorism around the world. It is also a factor that might be linked to regime change, especially to democracy, poverty, and civilizational differences within and between states, so instability is also intertwined with the three most often researched causes of terrorism.

This book is intended to provide an analysis of terrorism that will be useful for students studying the subject as well as policymakers crafting counterterrorism strategies. Our findings contradict the current argument that forcing democracy on the world system will result in the end of terrorism. What we find most often in our study is that anything that produces great instability in society can provide a strong foundation for a sustained terror movement. It does not matter whether this is a cultural difference, a transition to democracy or away from it, or poverty aimed at a specific out-group in society; all of these factors can provide the catalyst needed for terrorism. Further, both military, hard-line tactics and government concessions can reduce or eliminate the terrorist threat. In fact, both Malaysia and Singapore, which have had the most success in Southeast Asia keeping terrorism from impacting their people and government, have used a combination of carrots and sticks.

The remainder of the book is divided into the following chapters. Chapter 2 is a theoretical examination of the definition of terrorism, which concludes with our definition of terrorism; this definition was used to guide our selection of cases. Chapter 3 contains a review of the literature on the Democratic Peace, Clash of Civilization, and the poverty–terrorism nexus as it relates to how this current research was designed and conducted. Chapter 4 provides a brief description of the methodology employed in our research. Chapter 5 presents our statistical findings and analysis regarding international terrorism in Asia and Africa, while Chapter 6 contains our statistical findings and analysis regarding domestic terrorism in the same countries. Chapters 7 and 8 include examinations of state cases in Southeast Asia and East Asia, respectively. Chapters 9 and 10 then examine the cases in South and Central Asia. Chapters 11 and 12 contain an examination of cases in North Africa as well as Sub-Saharan Africa. It is in the final chapter, Chapter 13, that we provide our conclusions and proscriptions for students studying terrorism, the general public, and policymakers.

References

Alexander, Yonah. (2002). "Introduction." In *Combating Terrorism: Strategies of Ten Countries*. Alexander Yonah, editor. Ann Arbor, Mich.: University of Michigan Press: 1–20.

Benjamin, Daniel, and Steven Simon. (2002). *The Age of Sacred Terror*. New York: Random House.

Bueno de Mesquita, Ethan. (2005). "The Quality of Terror." *American Journal of Political Science*. Volume 49, Number 3, July: 515–30.

Curl, Joseph. (20 January 2005). "Bush to Embrace a Bold Agenda." *The Washington Times*: A1.

Eubank, William and Leonard Weinberg. (1998). "Terrorism and Democracy: What Recent Events Disclose." *Terrorism and Political Violence*. Volume 10, Number 1: 108–18.

Everyman, Joe. (1998). "Terrorism and Democratic States: Soft Targets or Accessible Systems?" *International Interactions*. Volume 24, Number 2: 151–70.

Haleem, Irm. (2005). "Pakistan, Afghanistan, and Central Asia: Recruiting Grounds for Terrorism?" In *Democratic Development and Political Terrorism*. William Crotty, editor. Boston: Northeastern University Press: 121–46.

Li, Quan, and Drew Schaub. (2004). "Economic Globalization and Transnational Terrorist Incidents: A Pooled Time Series Analysis." *Journal of Conflict Resolution*. Volume 48, Number 2: 230–58.

Lippman, Thomas W. (9 August 1998). "Terrorists Will Not Prevail." *The Washington Post*: A25.

Morgan, Matthew J. (2004). "The Origins of New Terrorism." *Parameters*. Spring: 29–43.

Olcott, Martha Brill, and Bakhityar Bahajanov. (2003). "The Terrorist Notebooks." *Foreign Policy*. March/April: 30–40.

Oren, Michael B. (2007). *Power, Faith, and Fantasy: America in the Middle East 1775 to the Present*. New York: W. W. Norton & Company.

Voeten, Erik. (2000). "Clashes in the Assembly." *International Organization*. Volume 54, Number 2: 185–215.

Weinberger, Jonathan. (Winter/Spring 2003). "Defining Terror." *Seton Hall Journal of Diplomacy and International Relations.* Volume 4, Number 1: 63–81.

Wright, Robin, and Glenn Kessler. (9 February 2004). "Bush Aims for 'Greater Mideast' Plan: Democracy Initiative to Be Aired at G-8 Talks." *The Washington Post*: A1.

CHAPTER 2

Defining Terrorism

The First Step in an Effective International Counterterrorism Strategy

BEFORE A STUDY REGARDING any aspect of terrorism can be conducted, an accurate and useful definition of terrorism must first be offered. Several researchers have, in the past, delved into research on terrorism without offering a very compelling definition of terrorism or by simply referring to another author's vague notion of the term. This seems reckless, considering that the definition of terrorism serves as a foundation for the study of terrorist acts. Further, terrorism is such an essentially contested concept in and out of academia, having no common or internationally agreed upon definition, that it becomes paramount to examine the arguments revolving around this term thoroughly. This point comes across clearly in Alex Schmid and A. J. Jongman's seminal work on political terrorism. In this 2005 revision of an earlier work, Schmid and Jongman attempt to find a common definition of terrorism. Unfortunately, after exhaustively examining the research, Schmid and Jongman discover an amazing plethora of vastly differing definitions. This underscores even more how important it is to find a universally acceptable definition of terrorism.

Earlier it was stated that terrorism must be accurately and usefully defined. But what does this mean? For the purposes of this chapter, accuracy includes addressing all the pertinent aspects of a potential definition of terrorism which, as Yonah Alexander so aptly puts it, include: (1) illegality of the threat, (2) definition of perpetrators, (3) targets, (4) objectives and intended outcomes, and (5) methods (Alexander, 2002:3). "Usefulness" is meant in a strictly utilitarian sense. A useful definition of terrorism would lack unfair pejoratives (i.e., a term that is used by a state to mischaracterize any opposition action it finds distasteful) or ideological bent.

Such a definition would be universally applicable and readily usable in international legal convention. Finally, a useful definition of terrorism "must be readily distinguishable from other forms of violence especially other forms of political violence" (Richardson, 1998: 52). It is important that an internationally accepted definition of terrorism is created in order, as Martin A. Kalis puts it, that an atmosphere where international cooperation can flourish is produced and it is also necessary as a foundation for an effective international counterterrorism strategy (2001).

But not all scholars and analysts agree that even defining 'terrorism' is a good idea. For example, John Whitbeck wrote in editorial in the *Beirut Daily Star* that terrorism was fundamentally a political "epithet and term of abuse" and that it was without "intrinsic meaning" (2001: 1B). He ultimately concluded that "perhaps the only honest and globally workable definition of terrorism is an explicitly subjective one—violence which I don't support" (ibid.). These types of assertions are unhelpful in the extreme, for if one follows Whitbeck's proscriptions nothing can be done from an international standpoint to fight terrorism or construct an international counterterrorism strategy, as terrorism really does not exist. Yet even extreme views can resonate, although not quite as loudly, in academic thinking.

There is a great deal of concern that terrorism has taken on a negative connotation that is somehow unfair. Jonathan Weinberger argues that "Terror and acts of terror can easily be seen as positive (and hence not terrorism) or negative (and hence terrorism)" (2003: 66). This, too, is unacceptable. It is as if we cannot discuss terrorism as a negative event for fear of hurting terrorists' and governments' that sponsor terrorism collective feelings. As Joseph Goldberg so appropriately points out, just because we view an act in a negative way, this does not "invalidate the term as a descriptive of a political phenomenon" (1991: 79). Goldberg goes on to note that "the study of political phenomena, because of their very nature, requires we use concepts and words that do express value judgments. Whether the term is terrorism, treason, tyranny, despotism, or perjury, the political scientist as well as citizen recognizes the negative connotation in each of them" (ibid.).

Brief History of the Term "Terrorism"

The historical root of the word "terrorism" is often attributed to the French revolution (see, for example, Alexander, 2002: 4; Maskaliunaite,

2002: 40; Guelke, 1998: 44). There is nearly universal agreement that in the eighteenth century this term was used to describe terror from above or ter-ror that emanated from the state, describing the guillotining of the aristoc-racy by the revolutionaries who had recently taken France by force and es-tablished themselves as the legitimate governmental power (Guelke, 1998: 44). What is interesting is that both Alexander and Maskaliunaite go on to point out that the concept enjoys roots that may be a little deeper in the form of two well-known terrorist campaigns. The first was mounted for sev-enty years in the first century by the Zealot Sicarii, which was a Jewish op-position movement aimed at the Romans occupying Judea (Alexander, 2002: 4). The Zealot Sicarii often used unorthodox tactics such as random murders in the midst of large crowds (Maskaliunaite, 2002: 40) and torching the public archives or poisoning public wells in Jerusalem (Weinberger, 2003: 64). For two hundred years, between the eleventh and thirteenth cen-turies, the Hashashin (assassins) attacked crusaders with unorthodox sui-cide or martyrdom missions (Alexander, 2002: 4). These well-documented acts of terrorism share nothing with the guillotining of the aristocracy per-petrated during the French revolution. This brings us to our first major de-bate over defining terrorism: Can states perpetrate acts of terror? In some respects it depends on whether or not one accepts that the definition of terrorism emanates accurately from the French Revolution or if what the revolutionaries did when they took power is more accurately categorized under international law as something other than terrorism (perhaps geno-cide). We will leave this debate regarding who can perpetrate terrorist acts for later and concentrate now on the issue of illegality.

Terrorism as an Illegal Act

It might seem safe to assume that there is universal agreement that terror-ism is an illegal act and that there would be well-established international law concerning the crime of terrorism and appropriate punishment. But nothing could be further from the truth. It has been said in several arti-cles, opinion editorials, and books on terrorism that "one man's terrorist is another man's freedom fighter." If this is accepted as true, then the debate can end right here for, as Peter Sproat so aptly puts it, this is an "academic dead end" (Sproat, 1997: 125). This is exactly the problem. There must be a clear legal and definitional distinction between the two or the defini-tional waters become so muddied that the problem of terrorism cannot be properly addressed. The key is that guerilla warfare has a very adequate definition. So terrorism must be, in part, something completely distinct from guerilla warfare and insurgency movements.

Why is terrorism illegal? The crux of the argument revolves around targets and perpetrators. In guerilla warfare or an insurgency, the attacker is attempting to expel an invader or an illegitimate government through violent coercion. The actions of guerillas and insurgents are directed at military targets or some other legitimately recognized governmental agents (such as police officers). When a person or group attacks civilians, then this group or person is engaging in a different type of violence that is more accurately dubbed terrorism. Why is attacking civilians illegal? The answer is because there is very well-developed international law that not only prohibits the arbitrary or wanton killing of civilians during times of war but also includes treaties—like the 1949 Geneva Conventions—that deal with the humane treatment of prisoners of war. There are also prohibitions against states committing mass executions of civilians (Resolution on Human Rights, United Nations, 1968), torture (Convention Against Torture and Other Cruel, Inhuman or Degrading Treatment or Punishment, 1987), and ethnocide and genocides (The Convention on the Prevention and Punishment of the Crime of Genocide, 1951) against civilians under their rule. In short, there is a well-established international legal history that prohibits the killing of civilians except in war, and during war there are strict prohibitions against the wanton killing of civilians (i.e., collateral damage to civilian populations is unavoidable during a bombing campaign, but even this collateral damage is to be kept to a minimum). Soldiers in modern warfare are prohibited from firing on unarmed combatants. In fact, soldiers cannot fire on surrendering enemy troops. The topic of targets is later discussed in more detail. But suffice it to say that the distinction between civilian versus military targets is one of the key ingredients that makes it impossible for one man's terrorist to be another man's freedom fighter.

International Law and Terrorism

Yonah Alexander argues that it "was not until the late 1960s that terrorism became a constant fixture of international life" (2002: 4). He argues that it was the rapid technological development of communications and travel that allowed groups to more freely engage in international and domestic terrorism (ibid.). International law bears out this assertion, as we do not see our first major international treaty on the subject of terrorism until 1963, and it was not until early 1970 that a spate of international treaties appeared. The reader should not conclude that international law on terrorism took off from there, for there are only thirteen international treaties addressing differing and very specific aspects of terrorist acts. The most recent is a United Nations (UN) Convention for the Suppression of Acts of Nuclear Terrorism, adopted unanimously by the United Nations General Assembly (UNGA) on 13 April 2005. This is the only international treaty that has been developed, passed, and entered into force since the 9/11 bombings.

Despite the dearth of international legal conventions on terrorism, all thirteen address the illegality of terrorist acts. In fact, modern international law is itself marked by the attempt to prohibit the use of violent force. The United Nations was originally formed to prohibit aggressive use of force by states. Article 2 paragraph 4 and Article 34 are the most instructive in the modern international predilection against aggressive state violence. Article 2 paragraph 4 prohibits war and also the threat or perpetration of violence of any kind against another state (acts of self-defense excluded), while Article 39 vests the United Nations Security Council (UNSC) with the legal monopoly on the use of force and as the sole international body that shall determine when a state has illegally used force.

Leaving for a moment the question of whether or not states can commit acts of terrorism, it must be noted that the thirteen international treaties on terrorism expand this notion of prohibiting violent acts. All thirteen treaties prohibit specific acts of terrorism or what we will call pre-terrorist activity.[1] Further, all thirteen seem to have been passed either following a major terrorist incident or following a series of terrorist incidents, and all but the UNGA International Convention for the Suppression of Acts of Nuclear Terrorism (Nuclear Terrorism Convention) bear a direct relationship in content to the particular act or acts that preceded them.

The thirteen treaties on terrorism are easily accessible from the UN's "Treaty Collection" page, so we do not go into detail regarding each convention. However, some treaties deserve mentioning, as well as the event or events that preceded them. Airline hijacking has the lion's share of international legal conventions, with four separate treaties dealing with this issue.[2] Three of these treaties occurred between the decades of the 1970s and 1980s. The reason for this stems from the increased amount of airline hijackings and bombings in the 1970s and the degree to which these hijackings and bombings were increasingly resulting in casualties, culminating with the most devastating bombing incident involving a plane, Pan Am Flight 103, which was destroyed over Lockerbie, Scotland, by a bomb on board, resulting in 270 deaths (Johnston and Shenon, 1998). All of these treaties have something in common. They all deal with individuals or sub-national groups committing acts of violence against civilians. This is an important theme that is repeated in all thirteen international treaties.

Two international treaties deal with the taking of hostages.[3] Both treaties prohibit the actual or threatened kidnapping, seizure, or killing of civilians, including official governmental personal. States are compelled to both monitor and punish offenses as well as to take the parties involved in the kidnapping of civilians into custody and extradite to trial where necessary. On 5 September 1972 at the Munich Olympics eleven Israeli athletes were taken hostage and eventually killed by their eight Palestinian captors (Gross, 1994). The eight gunmen were members of the Black September terrorist movement and demanded, among other things, that several hundred Palestinian prisoners be released (ibid.). While the initial response to this incident was lukewarm, as the United States and Israel could not convince the UNGA to pass a resolution condemning the kidnapping and murders of these athletes, it did serve to wake up the collective international consciousness regarding terrorism and helped to serve as a foundation for these two treaties.

The hijacking of the luxury cruise ship *Achille Lauro* in 1985 by men who claimed to represent the Palestinian Liberation Front (PLF) was a key example of the expansion of hijacking incidents from air to sea vessels. Led by Abu Abbas, who planned the mission, the *Achille Lauro* was hijacked and eventually turned over to officials peacefully, but not before one elderly American Jew aboard was murdered and thrown unceremoniously overboard (Cowell, 1988: A3). Abbas himself compared the killing of the elderly man as no more of an event than an automobile accident. Yasser Arafat attempted to distance himself and the Palestine Liberation Organization (PLO) from this statement by condemning it as an embarrassment (ibid.). Despite the fact that this hijacking resulted in only one death, it occurred at a time when international anxiety over terrorism was running high. By 1985, the Red Brigade in Europe had conducted several noteworthy airline hijackings, several Arab terrorist groups had succeeded in hijacking Israeli and other international flights, 241 marines had been killed in Beirut, Lebanon, by a lone suicide bomber, and Anwar Sadat had been assassinated by a group that was displeased over the Camp David Peace Accords. It is not surprising that the *Achille Lauro* incident struck a chord with the international community and was, in large part, responsible for the passage of the 1988 Convention for the Suppression of Unlawful Acts against the Safety of Maritime Navigation. This expanded the scope of what was internationally recognized as terrorism, but it did not expand the scope overly much.

Three modern treaties are indicative of a new wave in international legal history regarding terrorism. They all deal with new and distinct acts of terrorism, and one goes a long way toward being a treaty that is applicable toward a broad range of terrorist threats. They are also unique in their strength and condemnation of terrorism. One author cogently notes that the first ten treaties did not even use the term "terrorism" in their title and they were very narrowly defined, with some question revolving around their enforcement power as well (Peterson, 2004: 184). Two of the three treaties were far reaching indeed, while the third is very forceful in its condemnation of terrorism but, as we shall argue, is highly problematic.

The first two modern treaties we discuss here were a direct reaction to the first World Trade Center (WTC) bombing. The mastermind behind the 1993 WTC bombing, Sheikh Omar Ahmad Abdel Rahman, had also hoped to follow this bombing with the destruction of the United Nations and several key tunnels leading to New York City (Weiser, 2001: 27). The bombing itself resulted in six dead and over one thousand wounded (Reuters, 1995) but this result was considered a horrible failure by Sheikh Rahman and many of the actual participants in the bombing (Benjamin and Simon, 2002: 15). One key participant, Ramzi Yousef, had wished to kill 250,000 Americans in a series of bombings over what he thought would be a long campaign of terror. For Ramzi this number equated to the number of people the American government killed in the nuclear bombings during World War II of Hiroshima and Nagasaki (ibid.: 9).

These attacks shook the United States and the world. They resulted in one of the strongest and most far-reaching international conventions the International Convention for the Suppression of Terrorist Bombings of 1997. Article 2 Section 1 of this treaty explains:

> Any person commits an offence within the meaning of this Convention if that person unlawfully and intentionally delivers, places, discharges or detonates and explosive or other lethal device in, into or against a place of public use, a State of government facility, a public transportation system or an infrastructure facility:
>
> a) With the intent to cause death or serious bodily injury; or
>
> b) With the intent to cause extensive destruction of such a place, facility or system, where such destruction results in or is likely to result in major economic loss.

This is a fascinating piece of law for a number of reasons. First, it encompasses a host of acts. The phrase "explosive or other lethal device" allows for the inclusion of gas attacks similar to the ones conducted in the Tokyo subway system. The perpetrator is in violation of the law whether or not the device actually explodes. Most interesting is the assertion that an act of terrorism can occur when civilians are not targeted if the intent is to cause a "major economic loss."

Surprisingly, as broad as this definition was, it was insufficient to cast a net large enough to include the mastermind of the 1993 WTC bombings, Sheikh Rahman. A second broad treaty was enacted in 1999, the International Convention for the Suppression of the Financing of Terrorism. Under Article 2 of this treaty, a person is engaging in terrorist activities if he or she "directly or indirectly, unlawfully and willfully, provides or collects funds with the intention that they should be used" to carry out acts intended to "cause serious bodily injury to a civilian." Again the recurring emphasis emerges on the theme that terrorists are terrorists in part because their targets are civilian in nature. This treaty is an acknowledgment that terrorists do not operate in a vacuum, that they need outside support, and that any willing accomplice at any stage is as guilty as the terrorists who actually perpetrate the crime. This treaty helped to secure the arrest and conviction of Sheikh Rahman.

The most recent treaty on international terrorism is a direct — but odd — response to the 11 September 2001 attacks. The first treaty on terrorism after 9/11 is more anticipatory than any other pervious treaty. The Nuclear Terrorism Convention, approved in 2005, is an attempt to thwart a feared future nuclear terrorist attack. Article 2 Section 1 of this treaty prohibits the unlawful possession of radioactive materials and devices with the intent to cause "death or serious bodily injury" or "to cause substantial damage to property or the environment." This same article prohibits the damaging of any nuclear facility with the same intents in mind. Article 2 Section 2 makes it unlawful to even threaten these acts. Article 2 Section 4 makes any accomplice at any stage to either of these two events liable as well. The treaty also makes it clear that states are obliged to cooperate in investigations of lost or stolen nuclear materials and that suspects are to be extradited for trial when appropriate. Not surprisingly, this treaty was hailed by the United States as a great success and a basis for international cooperation in the war on terror (Edwards, 2005: A17). But this treaty bears more resemblance to the piecemeal attempts to address terrorism found in the 1970s and 1980s than to the far broader attempts to address terrorism found in the 1997 and 1999 conventions. Unfortunately, in none of these conventions is a broad definition of terrorism to be found. No all-encompassing treaty exists, like the Convention for the Prevention of Genocide, which deals in a broad way with terrorism. It is as if there are thirteen separate protocols floating out in international legal space without a core treaty to bind them together. Unfortunately, despite all of these conventions, we are still left without a satisfactory definition of terrorism.

State versus Non-State Actors

Despite this fact, the incomplete international legal foundation for defining terrorism serves as a good springboard into the five remaining aspects of a definition of terrorism. While there are some detractors, a majority of scholars and foreign policymakers accept that terrorism is unlawful. Now we turn our attention toward the possible perpetrators of terrorism. There are two main possible perpetrators: (1) state and (2) non-state actors. State actors refer to states or governments, while non-state actors can include clandestine subnational or supranational organizations[4] or even lone individuals. The debate mainly revolves around whether or not states can commit acts of terrorism.

It should be stated from the outset that very few scholars make the assertion that state actors can commit acts of terrorism. Further, none of the thirteen international treaties on terrorism designate state actors as possible perpetrators of terrorism. Generally, there is a rich international legal tradition which defines only non-state actors as potential perpetrators of terrorism.

Some authors assert that definitions that exclude state entities as potential terrorist actors are definitions which suffer from "myopia" (Selden and So, 2004: 5). This is a particularly important assertion for editors Mark Selden and Alvin So, as their recent book focuses exclusively on examining state terrorist incidents. These authors conclude that because legitimate states control sometimes amazing military force projection capabilities, it therefore follows that states could use this force to terrorize domestic or international populations (ibid.). Seldon and So assert that the atomic attacks against Nagasaki and Hiroshima were quintessential examples of state terrorism, as the aims of these attacks were to "terrorize the population through mass slaughter" and force surrender from the Japanese government (2004: 10). The problem here is the same one that occurs when authors talk about the Reign of Terror during the French revolution. Many actions can cause terror. Genocide can cause extreme terror. Hurricanes, tsunamis, and floods can also cause terror. But all that causes terror is not terrorism. Can one argue that the Nagasaki and Hiroshima bombings were a war crime? The answer is, yes. But these actions cannot be labeled terrorist.

The problem with labeling these actions as "terrorism" becomes a little clearer as Seldon and So attempt to define state terrorism themselves. Seldon and So claim that, "In *state terrorism,* a state systematically directs violence against the civilian population of its own or another state." So when the Hutu-dominated military in Rwanda attacked the Tutsi population, which resulted in millions being murdered, that was not genocide; that was terrorism. When the United States secretly mined the Nicaraguan harbor during the reign of the communist FSLN in the 1980s, that was not a clear violation of well-established international law on human rights; that too was terrorism. One could list myriad cases of state human rights abuses, some of which have been brought to trial and resulted in convictions for the perpetrators of these crimes. The point is that attempting to argue that state terrorism exists results in exactly the legal and theoretical quagmire related earlier. There is already a great deal of established international legal precedence regarding state abuses of power. It only serves to confuse the issue of both terrorism and concepts such as genocide when authors label an act of state violence against civilians as terrorist.

Peter Alan Sproat, a proponent of states being included as terrorist actors, actually hits this core problem himself when he acknowledges that actions that are considered to be war crimes, genocide, or similar human rights violations cannot be determined to be terrorist in nature (1997: 126). To label these acts as terrorist, as apparently Seldon and So wish to do, would lead to a theoretical impasse whereby one scholar's genocide is another's terrorist act. Ironically, Sproat himself falls into this definitional trap when he uses the purges perpetrated by Stalin in the former Soviet Union as an example of terrorism (1997: 119). Most authors and most international organizations would label the purges as a massive human rights abuse or genocide and not a terrorist act.[5]

Targets of Terrorism

There is a consensus in the thirteen international treaties on terrorism that the targets of terrorism are civilians. But there is some debate revolving around even this contention, and there is a need to clarify how civilians can be targeted.

We have already argued that one of the key features in international law and academic argument that makes terrorism illegal is the fact that terrorist acts target civilians. Some regional organizations, like the Organization of Islamic Conference (OIC), and some scholars (see Byford, 2002; Jabara, 2002; Weinberger, 2003) attempt to argue against this assertion through various just war lines of argumentation.

In a communiqué the OIC did condemn the 11 September 2001 World Trade Center (WTC) attacks as "brutal" and running counter to Islamic teachings (OIC, 2001: Section 1). However, the OIC was quick to point out that it rejected "any linkage between terrorism and rights of Islamic and Arab peoples, including the Palestinian and Lebanese peoples, rights to self-determination, self-defense, sovereignty, resistance against Israeli and foreign occupation" (Section 6). In short, the OIC believed that certain terrorist acts were wrong and ought to be punished, but others were legitimate and should not be punished.

This sentiment is echoed by Jonathan Weinberger, who argues that terrorists have to attack civilian targets for they cannot be expected to attack well-armed militaries who would win handily in a face to face combat situation (2003: 74). Abdeen Jabara postulates that for many people in developing nations "a scrupulously honorable struggle is an unaffordable luxury" (2002: 5). Further, Jabara claims that "fighters with a halfway decent cause may be forgiven much. Fighters with a noble objective and no alternatives may perhaps be forgiven everything" (ibid.). For these authors, terrorism is defined by motivation and ability of the attacker and not those that the terrorist targets. Grenville Byford asserts that "civilians are not always mere bystanders and are crucial to any war effort" (2002: 36). He also contends that "The United States, furthermore, is a democracy; its citizens help decide how its military power is used. Are they truly innocent?" (ibid.).

There is a hidden danger with this line of argumentation that neither the OIC nor the authors just cited have realized. By arguing so vehemently that civilians are legitimate targets, the potential then exists for major powers to accept this contention and determine that insurgents and terrorists in Iraq, for example, draw great support from the local civilian population. As Byford argued, civilians are not innocent. Following this argument to its natural conclusion, major powers could feel justified in killing local citizens in an attempt to quell support for terrorist cells, in torturing suspects, in arbitrarily detaining suspects, and so on. Further, we can never agree on what terrorism is if we insist that motives and abilities are what differentiate terror from legitimate resistance.

Contrary to these authors' assertions, Lawrence Freedman warns that defining terrorist acts as warlike "dignifies them and gives the perpetrators an unnecessarily heroic status" (2002: 44). Bruce Hoffman states that we ought not to be confused by the honors bestowed on terrorists either. Hoffman says, "The fact that Yasser Arafat received the Nobel Peace Prize ought not to rationalize his murderous terrorist activities" (1997). In other words, people can change but the terrorist acts of the past must be recognized for what they are.

In short, it is incumbent for any definition of terrorism that the targets be clearly defined as civilian. If the targets are governmental or military in any way, then the action is insurgency or rebellion. The civilian nature of the targets of terrorism is what gives the act its illegality and, therefore, serves as the lodestar around which all international conventions and international counterterrorism strategies can navigate. To deny this fact flies in the face of modern just-war doctrines, established in treaties like the Geneva Conventions, which place an emphasis on protecting civilian life and dignity even in a time of war.

One final point of clarification must be made regarding civilian targets. International law recognizes that damaging people and damaging property are both attacks on civilian targets. However, until recently, the property damage clause was understood to mean that through the course of a violent attack, where civilians become casualties, property is often destroyed. More recently, however, some authors have begun to assert that terrorism can take a nonviolent or low-violence form through such acts as disrupting the electrical grid in a wide swath of a target state or disrupting Internet banking systems (Laqueur, 1996: 35). Such acts that may not cause human casualty are still aimed at disrupting civilian life by causing economic discomfort, panic, and possibly lowering civilian confidence in the economic or governmental system, and, we feel, should be labeled terrorist.

Objectives and Intended Outcomes

There are intended outcomes of the particular terrorist attack as well as sometimes both short- and long-term objectives. The intended outcome is psychologically disproportionate to the physical damage caused by the attack (Cox, 2005: 257). But expectations of intended outcomes may be shifting slightly, as John Deutch notes that a new trend in expectations may be to achieve "more bang for the buck" through the use of weapons of mass destruction that are nuclear, chemical, and biological in nature

(1997: 11). This trend appeared to be accelerating in the 1990s as the number of international terrorist incidents dropped while the number of casualties caused by terrorist attacks hit an all-time high of three thousand dead[6] (Hoffman, 1997: 13). But even if a terrorist organization does successfully orchestrate a strike that produces tens of thousands of casualties, the goal is still to produce terror and panic in a much larger target audience.

Terrorists are by their very nature outmatched by their opponents. Terrorists are dealing in asymmetric warfare and have neither the capabilities nor funding to meet their adversary head-to-head on an open battlefield. Therefore, a terrorist can never hope to attack in such a way as to defeat the opponent militarily. So why is there an increasing emphasis on casualty rate? One author argues there is a belief by terrorists that the lethality of the attack itself will best help the organization advance its goals (Nacos, 2003: 1).

The immediate intended outcome for a terrorist or terrorist organization is to produce an event, or series of events, that causes immediate psychological terror. But the long-term objective is to sway an audience. The goal is to sway an audience far beyond the immediate victims and their families (Kalis, 2001). The goal is to change policies nationally or internationally that the terrorist group has identified as important. This often means that the terrorist is interested in terrorizing the public in hopes that the government or military of a particular nation attacked will change its policies. Therefore, disruption and chaos caused by terrorism are every bit as important as the actual damage caused by the attack. An attack that causes havoc with the air traffic control system or the nation's power production facilities can be every bit as effective as a major bombing event in which hundreds are killed (Deutch, 1997: 12).

Further, if the goal is to create prolonged terror in order to change or shift a state's policy, then a premium must be placed on repeated attacks. For example, the 2005 attacks on the London underground railway system, which produced hundreds of casualties, could be followed by nonlethal attacks on the electronic grid supplying the underground subway. The effect would largely be the same. Economic disruption would occur in the form of interrupted public transportation for London workers and tourists. Psychological terror could be produced by both events, as both events lead to mistrust in the reliability, safety, and national control of the system. Finally, if enough people become sufficiently terrorized and inconvenienced by these events, they could place pressure on the government to change its foreign policy in Iraq, which was the stated goal of the attackers.

Methods of Attacks

The methods terrorists use have been largely covered throughout the course of this chapter; hence a brief summary is provided here. The methods terrorists use can range from nonlethal cyberterrorist attacks to theoretical nuclear, chemical, and biological attacks. It should be noted that the notion that terrorist attacks can be nonlethal in nature is not a new one. Several successful hijacking incidents in which the perpetrators escaped immediately after the event involved no loss of life. The *Achille Lauro* cruise ship hijacking incident produced only one death.

Most modern terrorist attacks involve some sort of unconventional use of force (suicide bombings, rocket propelled grenades, etc.) aimed at civilians and civilian gathering places. Cyberterrorism is a very recent threat and major nuclear, biological, and chemical attacks have yet to materialize. New methods will likely be developed, but all methods past, present, and future can be linked to a current definition of terrorism if motivation is taken into account. There has been much discussion regarding religious versus political motivation behind terrorist attacks. This discussion is largely unnecessary when one is attempting to develop a universally applicable definition of terrorism. There are only two general aspects of motivation that relate to methods that are important to this discussion: (1) Is the intent to target civilians or disrupt civilian life? (2) Is the intended outcome of this event or series of events to influence a larger audience to change a particular policy stance? If the answer is yes to both questions, then the method employed by the individual or group falls under the general rubric of terrorism.

Terrorism: Accurately and Usefully Defined

Considering all of the preceding, we can now produce a definition of terrorism that will, hopefully, be accurate and universally applicable. The components of the definition should mirror the components addressed in this chapter and satisfactorily address all the concerns raised. Bearing this in mind, our definition of terrorism is:

> Any premeditated violent act perpetrated against civilian noncombatants by subnational or international groups, clandestine agents, or individuals sympathetic to larger terrorist groups and movements, with the intent to influence a target audience larger than the intended victims toward or against a particular policy action.

Note that the motivation for terrorists is to perpetrate an act that influences policy in the target state. Whether it is politically or religiously motivated beyond that is immaterial. States are left out as actors, for reasons already stated, but terrorist groups can be either subnational, like Jema'ah Islamiyah in Indonesia, or supranational, like Al-Qaeda, which is suspected of both operating in multiple countries and having various headquarters in multiple countries. Individuals, too, can perpetrate terrorist acts, regardless of whether or not they are officially connected in any way to larger terrorist organizations.

While we are sympathetic to the argument that cyberterrorism is a real and important form of terrorism deserving more attention by scholars and politicians, we specifically left cyberterrorism out of our definition as we are only examining violent terrorist attacks in our study. Further, we feel that cyberterrorism is deserving of a separate definition as it is truly a separate category of terrorism.

One immediate criticism that must be addressed is what is left out of this definition. We anticipate that scholars will be quick to point out that both the bombing and subsequent killing of numerous U.S. marines in Beirut, Lebanon, in 1983 and the *U.S.S. Cole* bombing in 2000 that killed dozens of U.S. sailors would not fit under this definition of terrorism. They might further conclude that this weakens our definition and highlights how impossible a task it is to produce a truly comprehensive definition of terrorism. We agree that both the Beirut and *U.S.S. Cole* bombings do not fit our definition of terrorism. However, we see this as strength, not a weakness. In order for a useful definition of terrorism to work, it must draw a bright, shining line between terrorist acts and other forms of violence. When actors perpetrate violent acts against military forces, no matter how heinous or unconventional the act, these acts must be classified as something other than terrorism. The acts we have just described most likely fall under the definition of insurgency or guerilla warfare. This should not be interpreted as minimizing the pain these acts caused.

One of the major benefits of this definition of terrorism is not only that a coherent international counterterrorism strategy can be modeled around it, but that politicians can be held accountable when they mislabel as terrorist violence they do not condone. Military spokespeople have done a great job in labeling attacks perpetrated against them in the current occupation of Iraq as insurgent or guerilla actions. Politicians tend to lump all attacks against U.S. and Iraqi citizens, soldiers, and law enforcement agents as "terrorist" because it suits their political needs. It seems that it is often assumed by opponents of a universal definition of terrorism that an agreed-upon definition will be a one-way street favoring the rich and powerful states and leaders. We believe that is untrue. Once terrorism is defined, "violence which I do not approve of" will no longer be an acceptable justification for labeling an action as terrorist.

The data set we used for our statistical analysis in this book comes from the Memorial Institute for the Prevention of Terrorism. The scholars that worked on the MIPT-TKB data set used a definition that differed from the one just given. The difference is not great but it is important to how we coded data. The key difference is that the researchers defined terrorism more broadly to allow for attacks from terrorist groups on military and police personnel to count as terror attacks. We, respectfully, do not believe these events should be counted as terrorism and we believe that these events fall more neatly under the general rubric of insurgent activities. We have systematically excluded these events from our examination, leaving only events that correlate directly with our definition of terrorism.

Notes

1. Pre-terrorist activity applies most directly to the recently passed UNGA International Convention for the Suppression of Acts of Nuclear Terrorism, which makes it quite clear that it refers to any person or groups of people attempting to illegally obtain materials that can be used in the manufacturing of nuclear weapons with the intent to use them in a terrorist attack.

2. These include: the Convention on Offenses and Certain Other Acts Committed on Board Aircraft, Tokyo, 14 September 1963; the Convention for the Suppression of Unlawful Seizure of Aircraft, the Hague, 16 September 1970; the Convention for the Suppression of Unlawful Acts against the Safety of Civil Aviation, Montreal, 23 September 1971; and Protocol on the Suppression of Unlawful Acts of Violence at Airports Serving International Civil Aviation, supplementary to the Convention for the Suppression of Unlawful Acts against the Safety of Civilian Aviation, Montreal, 24 February 1988.

3. These include: the Convention on the Prevention and Punishment of Crimes against Internationally Protected Persons, Including Diplomatic Agents, New York, 14 December 1973; and the International Convention against the Taking of Hostages, New York, 17 December 1979.

4. For example, Al-Qaeda is probably more properly labeled as supranational because various cells continuously operate throughout several major states in the world.

5. The Stalinist Purges fall squarely under the United Nations' definition of genocide, which is defined as any act with the "intent to destroy, in

whole or in part, a national, ethnical, racial or religious group" (Article 2 of the United Nations General Assembly Resolution 260 [9 December 1948] *Convention for the Prevention and Punishment of the Crime of Genocide*).

6. It should be noted that this record set by terrorists had been eclipsed by the middle of the first decade in the twenty-first century.

References

Alexander, Yonah. (2002). "Introduction." In *Combating Terrorism: Strategies of Ten Countries.* Alexander Yonah, editor. Ann Arbor, Mich.: University of Michigan Press: 1–20.

Benjamin, Daniel, and Steven Simon. (2002). *The Age of Sacred Terror.* New York: Random House.

Byford, Greenville. (July/August 2002). "The Wrong War." *Foreign Affairs.* Volume 81, Issue 4: 34–43.

Cowell, Alan. (14 November 1988). "Hijacker Defends Achille Lauro Killing." *The New York Times.* A3.

Cox, Dan G. (2005). "Political Terrorism and Democratic and Economic Development in Indonesia." In *Democratic Development and Political Terrorism: The Global Perspective.* William Crotty, editor. Boston: Northeastern University Press: 255–68.

Deutch, John. (Fall 1997). "Think Again: Terrorism." *Foreign Policy.* Number 108: 10–21.

Edwards, Steven. (14 April 2005). "UN Members Agree on 'Terrorist' Definition: Washington Hails Agreement. According to Accord, Anyone with Nuclear Material Obtained Illegally is a Terrorist." *The Montreal Gazette.* A17.

Freedman, Lawrence. (2002). "The Coming War on Terrorism." In *Superterrorism: Policy Responses (Political Quarterly Special Issues).* Lawrence Freedman, editor. Oxford: Blackwell Publishing: 40–56.

Goldberg, Joseph E. (Spring 1991). "Understanding the Dimensions of Terrorism." *Perspectives in Political Science.* Volume 20, Issue 2: 78–88.

Gross, George. (21 August 1994). "That Tragic Time in Munich." *The Toronto Sun.* SP8.

Guelke, Adrian. (Fall 1998). "Wars of Fear." *Harvard International Review.* Volume 20, Issue 4: 44–47.

Hoffman, Bruce. (Spring 1997). "Terrorism." *World Policy Journal.* Volume 14, Issue 1: 97–104.

Hoffman, Ted (July/August 1997). "New Targets for the '90s Terrorist." *International Security Review.* Issue 99: 13–15.

Jabara, Abdeen. (Spring/Summer 2002). "Introduction." *Arab Studies Quarterly.* Volume 24, Issues 2 & 3: 1–10.

Johnston, David and Philip Shenon. (9 August 1998). "The World: A Score-card on Terrorist Attacks." *The New York Times*. Section 4, page 5.

Kalis, Martin A. (Summer/Autumn 2001). "A New Approach to International Terrorism." *International Affairs Review*. Volume 10, Number 2: 80–95.

Laqueur, Walter. (September/October 1996). "Postmodern Terrorism." *Foreign Affairs*. Volume 75, Issue 5: 24–36.

Maskaliunaite, Asta. (2002). "Defining Terrorism in the Political and Academic Discourse." *Baltic Defense Review*. Volume 2, Number 8: 36–50.

Nacos, Bridgette L. (January/February 2003). "The Terrorist Calculus Behind 9–11: A Model for Future Terrorism?" *Studies in Conflict and Terrorism*. Volume 26, Number 1: 1–16.

Organization of Islamic Conference. (10 October 2001). "Final Communiqué of the Ninth Extraordinary Session of the Islamic Conference of Foreign Ministers. Doha, Qatar.

Peterson, M. J. (2004). "Using the General Assembly." In *Terrorism After September 11th*. Jane Boulden and Thomas G. Weiss, editors. Bloomington, Ind.: Indiana University Press: 173–97.

Reuters. (31 January 1995). "Fiery Cleric Planned 'War,' Bomb Conspiracy Trial Told." *The Toronto Star*. A2.

Richardson, Louise. (Fall 1998). "Global Rebels." *Harvard International Review*. Volume 20, Issue 4: 52–56.

Seldon, Mark, and Alvin Y. So. (2004). "Introduction: War and State Terrorism." In *War and State Terrorism: The United States, Japan & the Asia-Pacific in the Long Twentieth Century*. Mark Seldon and Alvin Y. So, editors. Lanham, Md: Rowman and Littlefield: 1–18.

Schmid, Alex P., and A. J. Jongman. (2005). *Political Terrorism: A New Guide to Actors, Authors, Concepts, Data Bases, Theories, and Literature*. New Brunswick, N.J.: Transaction Publications.

Sproat, Peter Alan. (Winter 1997) "Can the State Commit Acts of Terrorism?: An Opinion and Some Qualitative Replies to a Questionnaire." *Terrorism and Political Violence*. Volume 9, Number 4: 117–50.

Weinberger, Jonathan. (Winter/Spring 2003). "Defining Terror." *Seton Hall Journal of Diplomacy and International Relations*. Volume 4, Number 1: 63–81.

Weiser, Benjamin. (4 February 2001). "Going on Trial: United States Accusations of a Global Plot; In Embassy Bombings Case, The Specter of a Mastermind." *The New York Times*. 27.

Whitbeck, John V. (12 July 2001). "Terrorism: The Word Itself is Dangerous." *Beirut Daily Star*. 1B.

CHAPTER 3

A Clash of Civilizations, the Democratic Peace, the Poverty–Terrorism Nexus, or Regime Instability

O NE OF THE MAIN FOCUSES of this book is to explain terrorism in Africa and Asia. To this end, we examine four factors that may inhibit or encourage terrorist activity. We will examine the effect that differences in civilization, democratization levels, poverty, and instability have on both international and domestic terrorism levels. The Clash of Civilizations Thesis and the Democratic Peace Thesis are both well-established theories in political science. The poverty–terrorism nexus is a more recent theory in political science. Instability has been used quite often in studies of conflict as both a control and an explanatory variable.

Clash of Civilizations

Samuel Huntington's 1993 article in *Foreign Affairs*, "The Clash of Civilizations?," and his subsequent book *The Clash of Civilizations and the Remaking of World Order* (1996) serve as the seminal works on the civilization thesis. These works are not without controversy, and many scholars have found the arguments contained within to be xenophobic. The main gist of the Huntington argument is that the post–Cold War world will be increasingly defined by a clash of divergent and incompatible civilizations. For Huntington, relationships between states will not be predominantly defined by realist notions of power relations or liberalist adherence to international institutions and international law. Instead, conflict and cooperation between states will increasingly be defined by cultural similarities and differences. Huntington identifies eight major "civilizations" and argues that international and domestic fault lines, where conflict becomes likely if not inevitable, emerge when disparate civilizations bump up against one another.

Huntington further argues that globalization is simultaneously separating people from national identities, thus causing them to identify with more amorphous and far broader notions of civilization, while also placing disparate civilizations into closer proximity through rapid and easy transportation and communication outlets (1993: 26). Huntington also notes that religious revival provides a new basis for identity that "transcends national boundaries and unites civilizations" (1993: 26). Finally, Huntington notes that conflict between Arab Islamic civilization and Western/Christian civilization is one of the "great antagonistic interaction[s]" (1993: 33). Why did Al-Qaeda perpetrate the World Trade Center bombings and Pentagon bombings on 11 September 2001? For Huntington it was because ease of global transportation and communication made it possible for the Islamic civilization to strike out against the Western/Christian civilization.

Huntington is no longer the lone voice envisioning a serious clash between Islamic and Christian culture. From the "Terrorist Notebooks" — notes kept by members of an Uzbekistani Islamic, fundamentalist, terrorist group — we find a connection between the clashes of civilizations, Islam versus Christianity, being used as a justification to rise up against secular governmental rule. In one of the recovered notebooks it was written, "To make a declaration of the fact that unbelievers and the government are oppressors; that they are connected with Russians, Americans and Jews to whose music they are dancing; and they don't think about their people" (Olcott and Babajanov, 2003: 36). In the Uzbekistani terrorist mind, any government that is not predominated by Islamic teachings and/or that traffics with Western/Judeo-Christian states is illegitimate.

Daniel Benjamin and Steven Simon relate that a document procured at an Al-Qaeda terrorist training camp speaks about a continued clash of civilization between the Islamic and Western/Christian world. The "letter of introduction" to the training camp reads, "The Jihad today is an appointed duty and every Muslim has no legal excuse. It is a sin to abandon the jihad, for if one inch of Muslim land is occupied, it is the duty of the Muslims to save that inch" (2002: 8). What is most disturbing about this Al-Qaeda directive is that Osama bin Laden has stated, on several occasions, a state that is considered need not be all or even predominantly Islamic. Any state with a "significant" Muslim population must be liberated. What percentage must be Muslim has never been defined by Al-Qaeda.

The fault line between Islam and Christianity is also apparent in United Nations General Assembly (UNGA) voting patterns. Islamic states voted in line with Western states during the Cold War. But Erik

Voeten found that "Islamic countries were, in the 1990s, relatively further removed from the 'West' than during the Cold War era," which he attributed to "increasing civilizational conflict between the Western and Islamic countries" (2000: 212).

Polls indicate that the divide between civilizations also exists at the domestic level. In June 2003, only 1 percent of Jordanians and people living within the Palestinian authority had a favorable opinion of the United States (Pew Research Center, 2003). Moreover, Osama bin Laden was "among the top three leaders most often trusted to 'do the right thing'" by survey respondents in Indonesia, Jordan, Morocco, Pakistan, and the Palestinian authority (Pew Research Center, 2003).

But Islamic terrorism is and the Islamic/Christian clash of civilizations is only one of many potential fault lines in the world today. Matthew Morgan notes that while "Islamic radicalism is the most notorious form of the new culture of terrorism . . . it is far from the only variety" (2004: 30). Indeed, modern religious terrorism seems to bolster the Clash of Civilizations Thesis. For example, Jewish extremist Bouch Goldstein's suicide attack on a Palestinian Mosque, which resulted in twenty-nine deaths, and the Buddhist cult Aum Shinrikyo's sarin gas attack on a Tokyo subway provide prominent examples of non-Islamic religious radicalism (Ranstorp, 1996).

The disputed Kashmir region in northeastern India offers further credibility to the assertion of multiple fault lines. In the Kashmiri case, Kashmir seems to serve as a fault line between the Islamic and Hindu civilizations. One author believes that Kashmir is a pawn in a greater conflict of civilizations. Jonah Blank notes that most Kashmiris would vote for a multireligious state independent of both Pakistan and India (1999: 41). This claim is juxtaposed against the reality that all four of the main rebel groups are backed and work closely with the Pakistani government (Blank, 1999: 42). Pakistan seems to be using the separatist movement, which it is fueling, to incite violence with its Hindu neighbor.

Similarly, David Makovsky argues that building a fence between Israel and the Palestinian West Bank is an admission that a diplomatic solution between these two civilizations has failed. He notes that "with little trust between the two sides and a history of bitterness and bloodshed, a negotiated partition is out of reach" (2004: 50). Makovsky examines four proposed fence lines in his article, noting in his conclusion that polling shows Israeli citizens prefer a plan that leads to a homogeneous, Jewish, democratic state, as "Zionists have [historically] chosen demographics over geography whenever the two have clashed" (2004: 64).

Stephen Saideman examined elected executives and their support for secessionist movements in neighboring states. He found that national leaders were likely to support secessionist movements abroad when the group of people attempting to secede was of the same ethnicity as one of the leader's major domestic political groups. This was found to be true even if such support was likely to spark a secessionist movement from a different ethnic group in that leader's nation. As Saideman puts it, "Ethnic ties influence foreign policymaking, because support for ethnic kin abroad can be a litmus test for a politician's sincerity on ethnic issues at home" (1997: 727).

So there appears to be a clash of civilizations occurring in the post-Cold War period, but does this clash relate to terrorism? Bruce Hoffman would answer in the affirmative. He notes that there has been an unprecedented expansion in religious terrorists over the past three decades (Hoffman, 1993). While religious clashes of civilization can occur between any two or more different civilizations, Magnus Ranstorp argues that Muslim terrorists may be the hardest to deal with because religion and politics are not separated under fundamental Islamic thought (1990). Much attention is paid by Western scholars to the Wahhabist fundamental Islamic movement, but the Deobandis offshoot, which occurs mainly in Asia, is often underemphasized. One example of how this newer form of Islamic extremism might be spurring on violence and terrorism comes from Afghanistan. Amed Rashid observes that Afghanistan used to be tolerant, but once the Taliban took over it used its own Deobandis interpretation of Islam to justify killing even other Muslims who it perceived to be too progressive or Western (1999: 23).

Islamic extremism obviously played a role in the Al-Qaeda attacks on U.S. targets on 11 September 2001, but the extent of Western animosity and the pervasiveness with which it has penetrated large swaths of the Islamic world are alarming. Daniel Benjamin and Steven Simon argue that the Al-Qaeda attack "was an act of consummate religious devotion. Those who committed it were deeply pious. They expressed their motives in indisputably religious terms and they saw themselves carrying out the will of God" (2002: 39–40). Benjamin and Simon write that "within Arab Muslim countries, especially those that are vital to regional stability and U.S. interests, the radicals may have lost the war against the state but they have won the theological debate" (2002: 172).

Not all scholars agree that terrorism is mainly, or even partially, influenced by ethnic or religious differences. Robert Pape's book *Dying to Win* is an examination of suicide terrorism. His study leads him to believe that the main motivating factor for suicide terrorists is foreign occupation, not a clash of civilizations. He writes that "modern suicide terrorism is best understood as an extreme strategy for national liberation against democracies with troops that pose an imminent threat to control the territory the terrorists view as their homeland" (2005: 23). It should be noted that Pape's sample size is small, as he confines his examination narrowly to what he defines as protracted "suicide campaigns." Further, he cannot entirely discount the influence of civilization on suicide terrorism, as he found that when the perceived foreign occupier and the terrorists are of different religious backgrounds, religion tends to "inflame nationalist sentiments in ways that encourage mass support for martyrdom and suicide terrorism" (2005: 88, italics removed). Also, religious animosity produces a zero-sum conflict in the minds of the terrorists, allowing no room for compromise, and it allows for total demonization of the perceived aggressors (2005: 89–90).

Other scholars believe, as we show later in this chapter, that poverty is the main motivation for terrorist activity. But Amilcar Barreto warns that political extremism is not best explained by "love or profit." Instead, he believes factors such as "hatred for the out group, or resentment toward real or perceived injustices" will provide better guides for explaining terrorist groups and their activities" (Baretto: 2005: 24).

Whether clashes between civilizations best, or even partially, explain terrorism in Asia and Africa remains to be seen. But past research indicates the very strong possibility that religious and ethnic differences fuel terrorist extremism and can encourage terrorist martyrdom.

Democratic Peace

The extensive literature on the Democratic Peace is also shrouded in controversy. We have said this, although most statistical analyses of the Democratic Peace have provided strong evidence for the assertion that democracies do not war with one another. Compelling statistical evidence from the University of Michigan *Correlates of War* project supports the claim that no two democracies have warred with one another since 1812. When scholars have attempted to explain why this is so, no clear answer has been provided. Further, scholars have found that while democracies do not fight one another, they are no less war-prone than nondemocratic regimes.

Still, the fact remains that no two democracies have warred with one another since 1812. This has led scholars to examine whether or not the democratic peace extends to other violent acts such as coups and terrorism. There are coherent theoretical arguments for and against democracies being less or more prone to terrorist attacks.

On an internal, domestic level the democratic norm of free, fair, and regularly scheduled elections is argued by democracy proponents to allow citizens with complaints an opportunity to peacefully gain policy changes. This, according to democratic proponents, lessens the resort to violence or terrorism as a means of gaining change, as the risks involved with violent behavior outweigh the risks involved with electoral behavior (Schmid, 1992; Ross, 1993). William Crotty links democracy to a lessening of social and economic inequalities that he sees as important antecedents to terrorism. "The point is that inclusive, representative democratic systems offer outlets to identify and address social and economic inequalities effectively enough to make terrorism as a political act moot and when engaged in, largely ineffective" (Crotty, 2005: 9).

These assertions are countered by arguments that the open nature of democratic states makes them particularly susceptible to terrorist attacks. Susan Ogden argues that democratic states are "unable or unwilling to undertake strong counter terrorist actions" (2005: 244). Ogden notes that democratic states tend to err on the side of preserving civil rights over ensuring security. Lawrence Hamilton and James Hamilton compare democratic regimes' and non-democratic regimes' responses to terrorist attacks and found that non-democracies' ability to act forcefully, quickly, and decisively enabled them to more effectively inhibit terrorist activity than their democratic components (1983: 52). Quan Li argues that democratic nations can "provide relatively more freedom of speech, movement, and association, permitting parochial interests to get organized reducing the costs of conducting terrorist activities" (2005: 278). Finally, recent elections in the Palestinian authority, which produced a Hamas ruling coalition, and the recent resurgence of Hezbollah, both militarily and politically, under the fledgling democracy in Lebanon show that democracy does not ensure that extremist movements will die simply because free and fair elections are in place. In fact, in both cases, extremist movements seem to have successfully used the democratic political process to peacefully seize political power and influence.

In an international sense, one could use the Democratic Peace research to speculate that spreading democracy will lessen the likelihood of international terror events. Many scholars have theorized and the empirical proof demonstrates that democracies do not war with one another (Chan, 1984; Maoz and Russet, 1993). The compelling empirical proof that comes from the University of Michigan's *Correlates of War* data set is the closest thing to a scientific proof that political science has yet produced. However, despite this seemingly unassailable finding, democracies are not more pacific than nondemocracies and no single component of democratic states has been found that adequately explains this compelling finding.

Finally, the few statistical studies examining the effect of democracy on terrorism do not support the assertion that democracy will inhibit either domestic or international terrorism. William Eubank and Leonard Weinberg find that terrorist groups are most often found operating in democratic societies as opposed to authoritarian ones (1994). New democracies and, in fact, any regime in transition seem particularly susceptible to terrorist attack (Everyman, 1998; Eubank and Weinberg, 1998). Quan Li and Drew Schaub use the ITERATE data set on transnational terrorism and use democracy as a control variable. Unfortunately for democracy proponents, their study finds democracies far more prone to international terrorism (2004). In a more recent article, Quan Li breaks out specific potential democratic effects on terrorism, such as the level of political participation and the degree of checks and balances, and he examines proportional versus winner-take-all systems of democracy. He finds that proportional democracies actually inhibit terrorism, while too many checks and balances tend to frustrate out-groups and lead more to resort to terrorism (2005: 294). Hence the results for democracy appear mixed in the most recent study of transnational terrorism, depending on what aspect of democracy is examined.

The contradictory theoretical assertions regarding the effect of democracy on terrorism are compelling. It makes logical sense that the openness in speech and participation present in democracy would largely obviate the need for groups to resort to terrorism. However, an equally compelling argument is that the openness of democratic regimes and respect for civil rights and civil liberties will create an atmosphere conducive to the formation and operation of terrorist organizations. The empirical evidence that has focused solely on international terrorism is somewhat mixed, but the preponderance of evidence suggests that democracy does not inhibit, and most likely encourages, international terrorism.

Poverty and Terrorism

Fewer studies focus specifically on the potential connection between poverty and terrorism. Several, but not all, of the examinations of democracy and terrorism use some sort of economic control variables, but few empirical analyses aimed specifically at examining this connection exist. It had been assumed theoretically by several researchers that poverty greatly encouraged terrorist activity, but recent research has begun to refute that claim. Domestically, economic deprivation was assumed to create a fertile ground of unemployed, underemployed, and generally angry impoverished citizens from which to draw adherents and suicide bombers. Also, if economic deprivation was far-reaching within a state, then the unstable environment this deprivation would produce should also draw and encourage terrorist responses.

Many interesting and probing studies link economic deprivation with other forms of violence such a coups d'état, civil war, and revolution. It is most likely the empirical evidence from these studies that encouraged theoretical speculation would hold true for another form of political violence: terrorism. Gary King and Christopher Murray note that numerous past studies have linked insecurity with severe economic deprivation using macro level measurements of income (2001–2002: 593–94). They argue that examinations of poverty and violence going forward should not focus solely on one indicator, income, and they suggest other economic benchmarks like relative deprivation and educational attainment (2001–2002: 599, 601). James Fearon and David Laitin examine forty-five civil wars between 1945 and 1999 and find that impoverished governments are more likely to experience insurgencies due to their inability to organize effective military resistance against the insurgents (2003: 88). Phillip Nel finds that income inequality does create instability within Sub-Saharan African states and that this can be causally linked with violent instability (2003: 633). Both macroeconomic deprivation and deprivation between classes seem to correlate well with domestic violence.

In regard to terrorism specifically, arguments have been made that economic inequality and the poverty level of a state are closely linked to terrorist outbursts. Benjamin and Simon argue that in the Middle East the "deligitimation of regimes and the emergence of religious violence are unquestionably linked to the failure of leaders to cope with massive region-wide socioeconomic problems" (2002: 175). However, Robert Pape reaches a far different conclusion, noting that members in suicide terrorist organizations came from low, middle, and upper classes in society (2005). Irm Haleem posits that this finding does not necessarily obviate the connection between poverty and terrorism. Haleem is one of the first scholars to define a poverty–terrorism nexus. Haleem explains that the key to "understanding the poverty–terrorism nexus is that while extremist groups recruit from impoverished masses, their leadership — not unlike revolutionary leadership — is often derived from the privileged middle and upper class" (2005: 129). Ethan Bueno de Mesquita finds empirical proof that economic deprivation is linked to terrorist recruitment. He finds that once one takes into consideration screening in terrorist recruitment, past literature finding no link between class and recruiting or terrorists melts away (2005: 526–27). As a result, the presence of middle- and upper-class individuals in a terrorist organization does not automatically provide evidence contrary to the poverty–terrorism nexus thesis.

In a study of diasporas and war, Yossi Shain and Aharon Barth find an interesting link between poverty and clashing civilizations. Diasporas are "a people with a common origin who reside, more or less on a permanent basis, outside the borders of their ethnic or religious homeland" (2003: 452). In economically weak states, diasporic influencers either are able to demand concessions from the government or are comfortable attempting to force concessions through violence (2003: 464).

Regime Instability

In a very real way the three previous concerns deal with regime instability and, as we argued in the introduction, we feel that democratization levels, differences in civilization, and poverty are all inextricably tied to the main instability theme, which is the focus of this current research. As other authors have argued, democracy is linked to stability, but the transition period to democratic governance is asserted by several prominent scholars to be one of the most unstable and tenuous periods a state can experience. Poverty has also been linked to political instability and violence. For example, Philip Nel asserts that income inequality, as measured by GINI coefficients, creates political instability (2003: 625). Finally, state proximity to different civilizations or the presence of conflicting civilizations domestically has been argued, most forcefully by Sam Huntington, to create political instability and violence.

Although we have said this, regime interruptions, which can by caused by myriad factors, are rarely examined as the sole independent variable when explaining political violence. Further, this is not often used as a significant control variable. This is not the first study to link regime or governmental interruptions with political stability. In fact, Alberto Alesina, et al. defined political instability as the propensity for a regime or government to collapse, in their study of political instability and economic growth (1992).

There are few studies that pay serious attention to the potentially destabilizing and violence-inducing effects of regime interruptions, such as civil wars, revolutions, and coups d'état. There are no studies that we know of that attempt to examine the correlation between these types of governmental disruptions and terrorism. But that does not mean there is no plausible link between regime instability and political violence. For example, Havard Hegre, et al. argue, "When authoritarianism collapses and is followed by ineffectual efforts to establish democracy, the interim period of relative anarchy is ripe for ethnonational or ideological leaders who want to organize rebellion" (2001: 34). In their own very rigorous statistical analysis, Hegre, et al. find clear evidence for the notion that regimes in flux, especially those transitioning from authoritarian to democratic, are the most likely to experience political violence in the form of civil war (2001: 42). Other authors' studies find evidence that any political change is linked to a greatly increased chance of civil war (Sahin and Linz, 1995; Tarrow, 1994).

In an ancillary way, James Fearon and David Laitin's work adds to the finding that regime instability is linked with political violence. In their study of the effect of ethnicity on insurgency and civil war, they find that weakness of the central government, not ethnic rivalries, is a greater determinant of insurgency and civil war (2003: 75). Linking this to the previously cited research on political instability and political violence that finds governments to be weakest during regime change, especially change from autocracy to democracy, Fearon and Laitin's findings can be interpreted as lending further evidence linking regime change with political violence within a state. But it should be noted that political violence and terrorism are not the same thing, hence this finding might not occur when one examines terrorism specifically.

Whether or not all political violence is the same remains to be seen. It could be the case that terrorism is a unique form of political violence that arises from actual or perceived oppression. If this is true, then strong and even stable regimes might draw more terrorism. Further, terrorism may be civil war or insurgency by the few. Where one finds active and widespread civil war or genocide, one might not find much or any terrorism.

Conclusion

These four theoretical debates over democratization, civilization, poverty, and regime instability guided and helped to shape every stage of our research. Unfortunately, there are no clear theoretical assertions in the literature that lend confidence that any one, or all, of these factors will inhibit or encourage terrorism. Because study on the subject of terrorism is still relatively new, explorations linking these theoretical concerns to terrorism are sparse or nonexistent.

The assertion that different civilizations will clash violently is not new. Further, there is at least some evidence to support this assertion in Bosnia, and, one could argue, with the recent and growing fundamental Islamic terrorism aimed at Western civilization. But support for this assertion is not universal and counterexamples do exist. This theory is one of the most contended in international relations and a consensus has yet to emerge.

The openness of democracy has been argued by several scholars to offer so many avenues of political participation that terrorists, and those who would support terrorist activity, are dissuaded by peaceful means available to change governmental policy. Other authors contend that it is the very openness and respect for civil liberties over security that allow terrorist cells and organizations an ease of operation that is not present in oppressive autocracies. Work on the Democratic Peace suggests that democracies do not war with one another, and hence one could assume that democracies would not encourage terrorism against one another. Yet the recent election of the terrorist organization Hamas in the Palestinian authority indicates that democracies do not always produce friendly or even antiterrorist regimes.

Poverty has been linked to all sorts of political violence. Yet again, there is contradictory evidence. Poverty has been linked to regime instability, but many impoverished states are very stable and some, like Malawi, are stable democracies. There is a contention in the literature that poverty allows terrorists ease of recruitment, but even this assertion, which was once taken at face value, has fallen into deep contention.

Finally, regime interruptions are often linked in an ancillary fashion to political violence, but the evidence is sparse and not without detractors. Further, no study exists, as far as we can find, that attempts to examine regime instability and terrorism. The theoretical debates alone provide a pressing interest in examining all four of these factors and their potential effects on terrorism.

References

Alesina, Alberto, Sule Ozler, Nouriel Roubini, and Phillip Swagel. (1992). "Political Instability and Economic Growth." NBER Working Paper Number 4173. Washington, D.C.: National Bureau of Economic Research.

Barreto, Amilcar Antonio. (2005). "Toward a Theoretical Explanation of Political Extremism." In *Democratic Development and Political Terrorism.* William Crotty, editor. Boston: Northeastern University Press: 3–16.

Benjamin, Daniel, and Steven Simon (2002). *The Age of Sacred Terror.* New York: Random House.

Blank, Jonah. (1999). "Kashmir Fundamentalism Takes Root." *Foreign Affairs.* Volume 78, Number 6: 22–35.

Bueno de Mesquita, Ethan. (2005). "The Quality of Terror." *American Journal of Political Science.* Volume 49, Number 3, July: 515–30.

Chan, Steven. (1984). "Mirror, Mirror on the Wall . . . Are the Freer Countries More Pacific?" *Journal of Conflict Resolution.* Volume 28: 617–48.

Crotty, William. (2005). "Democratization and Political Terrorism." In *Democratic Development and Political Terrorism.* William Crotty, editor. Boston: Northeastern University Press: 18–31.

Eubank, William, and Leonard Weinberg. (1994). "Does Democracy Encourage Terrorism?" *Terrorism and Political Violence.* Volume 6, Number 4: 417–43.

Eubank, William, and Leonard Weinberg. (1998). "Terrorism and Democracy: What Recent Events Disclose." *Terrorism and Political Violence.* Volume 10, Number 1: 108–18.

Everyman, Joe. (1998). "Terrorism and Democratic States: Soft Targets or Accessible Systems?" *International Interactions.* Volume 24, Number 2: 151–70.

Fearon, James D., and David D. Laitin. (2003). "Ethnicity, Insurgency, and Civil War." *The American Political Science Review.* Volume 97, Number 1, February: 75–90.

Haleem, Irm. (2005). "Pakistan, Afghanistan, and Central Asia: Recruiting Grounds for Terrorism?" In *Democratic Development and Political Terrorism.* William Crotty, editor. Boston: Northeastern University Press: 121–46.

Hamilton, Lawrence C., and James D. Hamilton. (1983). "Dynamics of Terrorism." *International Studies Quarterly.* Volume 27, Number 1, March: 39–54.

Hegre, Havard, Tanja Ellingsen, Scott Gates, and Nils Petter Gelditsch. (2001). "Toward a Democratic Civil Peace? Democracy, Political Change, and Civil War, 1916–1992." *The American Political Science Review.* Volume 95, Number 1, March: 33–48.

Hoffman, Bruce. (1993). "Future Trends in Terrorist Targeting and Tactics." *Special Warfare.* Issue 6, Number 3, July: 30–35.

Huntington, Samuel P. (1993). "The Clash of Civilizations?" *Foreign Affairs.* Volume 72, Number 3: 22–49.

Huntington, Samuel P. (1996). *The Clash of Civilizations and the Remaking of World Order.* New York: Simon and Schuster.

King, Gary, and Christopher J. L. Murray. (2001–2002). "Rethinking Human Security." *Political Science Quarterly.* Volume 116, Number 4, Winter: 585–610.

Li, Quan. (2005). "Does Democracy Promote or Reduce Transnational Terrorist Incidents?" *Journal of Conflict Resolution.* Volume 49, Number 2, April: 278–97.

Li, Quan, and Drew Schaub. (2004). "Economic Globalization and Transnational Terrorist Incidents: A Pooled Time Series Analysis." *Journal of Conflict Resolution.* Volume 48, Number 2: 230–58.

Makovsky, David. (2004). "How to Build a Fence." *Foreign Affairs.* Volume 83, Number 2: 50–64.

Maoz, Zeev, and Bruce Russett. (September 1993). "Normative and Structural Courses of Democratic Peace, 1946–1986." *American Political Science Review.* Volume 87, Number 3: 624–38.

Morgan, Matthew J. (2004). "The Origins of the New Terrorism." *Parameters.* Spring: 29–43.

Nel, Philip. (2003). "Income Inequality, Economic Growth, and Political Instability in Sub-Saharan Africa." *Journal of Modern African Studies.* Volume 41, Issue 4: 611–39.

Ogden, Suzanne. (2005). "Inoculation Against Terrorism in China: What's in the Dosage?" In *Democratic Development and Political Terrorism.* William Crotty, editor. Boston: Northeastern University Press: 227–54.

Olcott, Martha Brill and Bakhityar Babajanov. (2003). "The Terrorist Notebooks." *Foreign Policy.* March/April: 30–40.

Pape, Robert A. (2005). *Dying to Win: The Logic of Suicide Terrorism.* New York: Random House.

Pew Research Center for the People and the Press, The. (2003). "Views of a Changing World: June 2003." Volume 2 of *Pew Global Attitudes Project.* Washington, D.C.: Pew Research Center for the People and the Press.

Ranstorp, Magnus. (1996). "Terrorism in the Name of Religion." *Journal of International Affairs.* Volume 50, Number 1: 41–62.

Rashid, Amed. (1999). "The Taliban: Exporting Extremism." *Foreign Affairs.* Volume 78, Number 6, November/December: 22–35.

Ross, Jeffrey Ian. (1993). "Structural Causes of Oppositional Political Terrorism: Towards a Causal Model." *Journal of Peace Research.* Volume 30, Number 3: 317–29.

Sahin, Yossi, and Juan J. Linz. (1995). *Between States: Interim Governments and Democratic Transitions.* Cambridge: Cambridge University Press.

Saideman, Stephen M. (1997). "Explaining the International Relations of Secessionist Conflicts: Vulnerability Versus Ethnic Ties." *International Organization*. Volume 51, Number 4, Autumn: 721–53.

Schmid, Alex P. (1992). "Terrorism and Democracy." *Terrorism and Political Violence*. Volume 4, Number 4: 14–25.

Shain, Yossi, and Aharon Barth. (2003). "Diasporas and International Relations Theory." *International Organization*. Volume 57, Number 3, Summer: 449–79.

Tarrow, Sidney. (1994). *Power in Movement: Social Movements, Collective Action and Politics*. Cambridge: Cambridge University Press.

Voeten, Erik. (2000). "Clashes in the Assembly." *International Organization*. Volume 54, Number 2: 185–215.

CHAPTER 4

Methods Used to Investigate the Causes of Terrorism in Asia and Africa

THE MAIN PURPOSE DRIVING OUR RESEARCH is to examine four factors—civilization, democracy, poverty, and regime stability—and their potential impact on international and domestic terrorism. As we have previously stated, we believe such an inclusive examination of terrorism is novel. Further, no study that we have come across examines domestic terrorism in multiple states. There is a small but growing research body that examines the impact of democracy on terrorism, but we feel research on terrorism is still in its embryonic stages.

The book is divided into two distinct research sections. The first section is a quantitative examination of the four factors of civilization, democracy, poverty, and regime stability and their effect on both international and domestic terrorism. Except for regime interruptions, multiple variables were used to measure civilization, democracy, and poverty.

The second section is broken down into distinct chapters that examine regional case studies. Our selection of relevant case studies was largely driven by our statistical findings. States experiencing high levels of domestic and/or international terrorism were automatically included as cases for examination. Similarly, some of the states experiencing low or no terrorism were used to compare and contrast with states experiencing high levels of terrorism. The examination of our regional cases is also conducted through the lenses of civilizational, democratic, poverty, and regime instability factors.

We decided early on in this project to present our statistical findings as graphical, bivariate scatter plots using the SPSS statistical program. There are several reasons for our decision. First, while the Memorial Institute for the Prevention of Terrorism–Terrorism Knowledge Base (MIPT-TKB) contains twenty-nine years of data that we can use in our current study on international terrorism, there are currently only six years of data available on domestic terrorism. Because we wanted to compare findings on international and domestic terrorism, and because six years of domestic terrorism data do not allow for enough degrees of freedom for an advanced regression technique, we decided that a graphical, frequency representation of our results was the best course of action.

Second, this is a first effort at such a wide examination of international and domestic terrorism, and we wanted to make the results accessible to scholars, students, and policymakers. We place special emphasis in our goal of producing a work that will benefit policymakers.

Third, graphical representations of cases allow for greater and easier interpretation of our results. Outliers are easier to pick up, and trends that might exist graphically, but that are harder to discern statistically, can be more readily examined and expounded upon. It is our hope that this book will provide a basis for further and more detailed inquiries.

Having said this, our techniques do allow for a certain degree of statistical sophistication. SPSS allows us to add a constant to the binomial equation and generate a rough r-squared statistic. This allows some interpretation of the strength of the relationship. In a general sense, an r-squared of .05 indicates that roughly 5 percent of the variance in the dependent variable, which will be either international or domestic terrorism, is explained by the independent variable, some measure of civilization, democracy, poverty, or regime instability.

SPSS also allows us to generate a fit line. This gives us a graphical representation of the directionality of our relationship. By "directionality" we are referring to the positive or negative nature of the correlation. If the slope of the line is upward, then the relationship is positive. If the slope of the line is downward, then the relationship is negative. A positive relationship means that when more of whatever you are measuring, like democracy, is present in society, then there is a greater frequency of terrorism. A negative relationship means that when there is more of whatever you are measuring, such as democracy, there is a lower frequency of terrorism. Unfortunately, we were unable to generate a significance level, but higher r-squared statistics generally correlate with higher significance in the relationship.

In order to generate points on our scatter plots, averages for most statistics were used. For the international variables, averages were generated over the twenty-nine years of data, and for the domestic data the average spanned the six years of available data. There is some missing data in our data set. Some missing data comes from simple missing data points in our data sets. The GINI coefficient data, for example, is produced sporadically in states, if it is produced at all. Other data are missing because of major geopolitical landscape shifts. Kazakhstan, for example, did not exist as a separate state until after the fall and dissolution of the Soviet Union. In all cases of missing data, we decided to exclude the missing data years from our averages such that the averages produced represent only years where data are available. If a state had no data for a particular variable, the state was excluded from that particular analysis.

We must note that we excluded extremely small states, ones with populations less than one million, from our study and states, like North Korea, for which there is no reliable data. Except for these few minor exclusions, we have attempted to represent all of the states in Asia and Africa in our examination. The final number of included states for study was seventy-five.

Measuring Terrorism

Terrorism is not easy to measure. The definition alone can cause serious contention, as "one man's terrorist is another man's freedom fighter." We have outlined the definitional debate in Chapter 2, and we have arrived upon a definition that we use for our study. To reiterate, terrorism is:

> Any premeditated violent act perpetrated against civilian non-combatants by subnational or international groups, clandestine agents, or individuals sympathetic to larger terrorist groups and movements, with the intent to influence an audience toward or against a particular policy action.

Therefore, we do not measure any action by any group that targets military personal or installations. Unfortunately, the MIPT-TKB is more inclusive in its characterization of terrorist events. For example, in Uganda several attacks by the Lord's Resistance Army insurgency movement against the Ugandan military were counted as terrorist attacks by the MIPT-TKB coders. We do not agree that such attacks should be coded as terrorism. We would characterize such actions as insurgency. However, this does not mean that any action taken by the Lord's Resistance Army fails to count as terrorism. There are several attacks by this group on civilians and civilian businesses. These attacks, with the intent to change the government, are properly characterized as terrorism. For each of the seventy-five states in our study, we went through each case year by year and excluded attacks on the military or the police force. This left us with only cases of terrorism as defined as violence by nongovernmental, nonmilitary groups against noncombatants or civilians.

Operationalization of the Variables
Used in the Statistical Analysis

Three of the four main factors we feel will have an impact on international and domestic terrorism — civilization, democracy, and poverty — can be measured in a number of different ways. While one research project could not and, most likely, should not use all of the possible measures for a particular variable, we did decide, based on past studies and theoretical literature, to use several relevant measures for each of the aforementioned factors.

Democracy has long been used in numerous studies of political violence and war as an explanatory variable. Both William Crotty and Quan Li (Crotty, 2005: 9; Li, 2005: 278) identify the inclusiveness and multiplicity of outlets in a democratic system as being key factors in inhibiting terrorist activity. Therefore, we included the Polity IV competitiveness of participation variable as a separate measure of democracy in order to test this theoretical assertion.

In a much more straightforward measurement of democracy, we use the Polity IV democracy score (which ranges from 0 to 10) not only in an attempt to directly measure democratization levels but also in an effort to replicate past research on democracy and political violence.

We did want to use this measure in two ways, though. First, we wanted to measure movement toward democracy. In other words, do states that have more democracy in their governing process, whether they would be considered fully functioning democracies or not, fare better than those with little or no democracy? We expected a strong negative correlation between democracy and terrorism. In other words, as states became more democratic, we expected that the number of terror incidents would recede.

In case there was a democratic tipping point, we used a common cutoff point for democracy (a score of 6 or higher on the 0 to 10 scale) and dichotomized our sample. Those states with an average democracy score below 6 were coded undemocratic and those with 6 or above were coded democratic. This is a common technique used in the literature examining democracy's effect on political violence. The theoretical argument is that more democracy is only better after a certain democratic threshold is reached. The difference between a 1 and a 2 or 3 on the scale is not great enough to merit consideration by treating the 3 as significantly more democratic than the 2 or 1. Obviously, the threshold level of 6 is somewhat arbitrary but it is the most common cutoff point that past scholarship has used.

Poverty is another contentious variable that has produced mixed results when examining its effect on political violence and, more importantly, terrorism (Fearon and Laitin, 2003; King and Murray, 2001–2002; Pape, 2005; Benjamin and Simon, 2002). Some past studies have found evidence of a link between poverty and terrorist activity and recruitment, while others have justly pointed out (Pape, 2005) that not even all suicide terrorists are uneducated and impoverished. We decided to use two measurements of poverty, gross domestic product (GDP) per capita purchasing power parity (GDPpcPPP) and the GINI coefficient measure for income inequality.

GDPpcPPP is an excellent measure of the comparative wealth between states. It is arguably the most often used measure of wealth of a state in the social sciences, and it is popularly used for good reason. Straight GDP statistics for states do not take into consideration the size of the state or the population. GDPpcPPP is a per capita measure, so the result is a comparable average yearly income. This statistic also controls for myriad other factors such that the resultant number is a purchasing power parity comparison, meaning that one dollar in China is equivalent to one dollar in Namibia. The inherent controls in this measure make it uniquely suited for accurately measuring wealth, on a per capita basis, for states.

One deficiency of GDPpcPPP is that it is a poor measure of income inequality within society. Because it is an average statistic, it can be artificially inflated by extremely high income levels that may only represent a small fraction of the total population. Further, small but still sizable minorities within a population may uniformly experience extreme poverty, while 70 to 90 percent of the population does not. France is often noted for its high GDPpcPPP, while it is widely acknowledged that the 15 percent minority population comprised of Muslims from North Africa does not share in this national income wealth.

In order to ensure we did not miss this economic phenomenon, we decided to also use GINI coefficient data as a measure of poverty. GINI coefficient data are survey data that measure income inequality between citizens in a state. The data are generally thought to be a good measure of comparable income inequality but are not as widely used as GDPpcPPP because they are so sporadically taken and many states have no data whatsoever.

Despite the deficiencies of our two measures of poverty, we believe they are the best measures of a state's wealth and income inequality. These two measures allowed us to examine the correlation between macro-level economic prosperity and internal income inequality that may be present.

We are very interested in examining the effects that clashing civilizations have on terrorism. We are interested in how internal civilization differences affect both international and domestic terrorism. Because we are measuring internal civilization differences, we assume that the effect will be stronger for domestic terrorism, as internal differences would logically more readily lead to internal violence. However, globalization has made the world a much smaller place, hence external civilizations can reasonably be expected to support international terror campaigns against opposing civilization in at least some cases.

Samuel Huntington (1993) placed great emphasis on religious, ethnic, and linguistic differences in his examination of clashing civilizations. We believe that religious and ethnic differences are the most important potential schisms between which political violence will occur. We used the *CIA World Factbook* to obtain our statistics on religions and ethnicities present within society. We are interested in major religions and ethnicities within society but understand that terrorism is often the political violence tool of an adversary facing superior military opposition; we do not want to miss potential clashes between great majorities and fairly small minorities. We had to draw the line somewhere, so we arbitrarily included all ethnic and religious minorities present within a state that comprised 10 percent or more of the total population for a state.

Huntington felt that religion, especially clashes between Christianity and Islam, would produce prodigious amounts of political violence. We agree that religion is worthy of examination but we expand upon his thesis a little by including all differences in ethnicity and not just those linked to historical megacivilizations, like his predicted clash between Confucian and Japanese civilizations. In Africa in particular, it seems that pronounced hatreds between tribes or ethnicities can extend hundreds if not thousands of years and produce all manner of political violence including genocide. In fact, the way the Hutu and Tutsi have dehumanized one another in Rwanda and Burundi has allowed these two ethnicities to produce the second worst genocide on historical record. Because these two ethnicities do not fall within one of Samuel Huntington's eight major civilizations, one could exclude them from a study of clashing civilizations. But we think that would be a mistake. We are not offering this insight as a criticism leveled against Huntington's Clash of Civilizations Thesis. Instead, we see this as a logical extension of his work.

Africa poses some problems for coding a handful of states, because tribes, ethnicities, and religions have been severed along ill-conceived colonial borders drawn by European colonizers, and because certain areas of Africa contain a multitude of ethnicities in some cases. A few African states were excluded from this portion of the study because they contained no ethnicities or religions that comprised greater than 10 percent of the total population. These states are often referred to in the literature as "fragmented" and these "fragmented" states often contained twenty, fifty, or in one case, almost one hundred and fifty different ethnicities. It might be interesting, in future research, to examine these "fragmented" states separately to see whether they experience more or less political violence.

The last major factor we examine is regime instability. Regime instability has been used as the main independent variable in only a very few studies of political violence (see Hegre, et al., 2001, for example) and because there is a dearth of studies examining political terrorism, it has been used infrequently as a control variable as well. Yet it makes logical sense that revolutionaries, insurgents, and other violent actors seeking to resist or overthrow a government might well resort to terrorism. Past research has also shown that nothing invites violence like a power vacuum. Therefore, we felt it necessary to examine regime instability as a possible impetus to terrorism.

Regime instability is measured simply using the Polity IV data set. Polity IV codes each regime interruption separately as a revolution, insurgency, or coup d'état. We are not interested in the differences in regime interruption, although future researchers might find this an interesting avenue of exploration; we are interested in the instability that regime interruptions cause. Therefore, we coded all interruptions the same.

Further, we are not interested in the duration of the interruption but in the frequency of interruptions over time. Therefore, a one-year revolution is coded the same as a two-year revolution. Our thinking is that frequent interruptions are a better measure of overall regime instability than length of interruptions. The instability measure we produce, we believe, will correlate well with increased international and domestic terrorism.

Conclusion

This study is very broad, encompassing both a statistical examination and detailed case studies. The choice of which cases to establish in detail was largely driven by our statistical findings. Throughout both the statistical and case study examinations, we focused our attention on four main factors we felt might impact both international and domestic terrorism: (1) democracy, (2) poverty, (3) civilization differences, and (4) regime stability. No other study of terrorism has examined all four of these factors simultaneously or in as great a detail as our current research does. Further, we believe this is the first attempt to examine domestic terrorism. We understand that the data are sparser for domestic terrorism but we believe that is worthy of research, and one of the most striking findings from our examination is that six years of domestic terrorism for Asia and Africa have produced far more terrorist events than twenty-nine years of international terrorism. The myopic obsession researchers have with studying international terrorism may be largely unwarranted, as domestic terrorism may pose a greater threat to international stability than international terrorism does. This does not mean study of international terrorism should be abandoned. It simply means that there is a great deal more that needs to be done before we can fully understand the complexities and dangers that terrorism poses.

References

Benjamin, Daniel, and Steven Simon. (2002). *The Age of Sacred Terror*. New York: Random House.

Crotty, William. (2005). "Democratization and Political Terrorism." In *Democratic Development and Political Terrorism*. William Crotty, editor. Boston: Northeastern University Press: 18–31.

Fearon, James D., and David D. Laitin. (2003). "Ethnicity, Insurgency, and Civil War." *The American Political Science Review*. Volume 97, Number 1, February: 75–90.

Hegre, Havard, Tanja Ellingsen, Scott Gates, and Nils Petter Gleditsch. (March 2001). "Toward a Democratic Civil Peace? Democracy, Political Change and Civil War, 1816–1992." *American Political Science Review*. Volume 95, Number 1: 16–33.

Huntington, Samuel P. (1993). "The Clash of Civilizations?" *Foreign Affairs*. Volume 72, Number 3: 22–49.

King, Gary and Christopher J. L. Murray. (2001–2002). "Rethinking Human Security." *Political Science Quarterly*. Volume 116, Number 4, Winter: 585–610.

Li, Quan. (2005). "Does Democracy Promote or Reduce Transnational Terrorist Incidents?" *Journal of Conflict Resolution*. Volume 49, Number 2, April: 278–97.

Pape, Robert A. (2005). *Dying to Win: The Logic of Suicide Terrorism*. New York: Random House.

Analyzing International
Terrorism in Asia and Africa

A MAJOR GOAL OF THIS BOOK is to examine four major factors (democracy, economics, civilization, and regime stability) in order to determine whether one of more of these factors inhibits or enables the development of terrorism. We use both statistical analysis and case studies to accomplish this goal. This chapter is the statistical examination portion of our study of international terrorism, while Chapter 5 is a statistical examination of domestic terrorism.

As laid out in the preceding chapter, we are examining twenty-nine years of international terrorist incidents for the Asian and African states included in our study. The results are largely depicted in this and the subsequent chapter through scatter plots generated by the SPSS statistical program. We decided to use the twenty-nine-year average for a given variable in order to examine and compare all the states in our study simultaneously.

Each point in any of the scatter plots represents one state in our study. There is some overlap, as some states scored exactly the same for a given variable. Because we used SPSS to generate our scatter plots, we were able to add a constant, a fit line, and produce a rudimentary *r*-squared statistic. This allowed us to depict the direction and the strength of the correlation between any two variables we were examining.

The total number of states in our study is seventy-five. A very few states were excluded because their populations were below one million or, in the case of North Korea, no reliable information was available. However, this represents almost every Asian and African state and should provide sound insight into terrorism in these two regions. Lower numbers of cases reported for some tables resulted from missing data for that particular variable. When some data were missing for a particular state, the missing data years were dropped and only the years with valid data were used to compute the average for that particular state.

Democracy and Terrorism

Some notable scholars have argued that democracies are more susceptible to terrorist attacks. This is due to the openness of democratic regimes. Citizens and legal aliens are allowed to travel and assemble freely not only within democratic states but between democratic and nondemocratic states, allowing for ease in planning, training, and carrying out terrorist attacks. Also, democratic states are less likely to violate civil rights and, therefore, less likely to intrude into a citizen's private affairs. This is argued to give terrorists an advantage in planning and carrying out attacks.

In opposition to this view are scholars who believe that democracies offer so many different avenues of peaceful political activism, such as public protest, voting, party competition, interest-group activism, and so on, that groups with a grievance will not have to resort to violence or terrorism. Further, the vast literature on the democratic peace indicates that democracies do not wage war with one another. While no definitive cause has been found for this statistical fact, some authors have speculated that democratic citizens are more reluctant to support prolonged military action in general and unwilling to support war against other democracies. If democratic citizens are generally more pacific, then they might be less likely to become terrorists and/or to support terrorism.

Figure 1 is a scatter plot of a state's average competitiveness of participation score by the state's average number of international terrorist events. The competitiveness of participation score from the Polity IV data set ranges from 0 to 5, with 0 representing no competitiveness or avenues of political expression for the average citizen and 5 representing the highest competitiveness and political access. The Polity IV variable code book defines this variable as the "extent to which non-elites are able to access institutional structures for political expression." This makes this variable ideal for measuring the potential dilutionary effect democracy has on terrorism.

Figure 1 shows no appreciable correlation between competitiveness or participation and international terrorist events. The r-squared value is 0, giving us confidence that there is no correlation between these variables, despite a slight uptrend in the fit line. If there is no correlation between international and domestic terror groups and their actions, then this finding is

Figure 1 ■ The average number of international terrorist incidents by the average Polity IV Competitiveness of Participation score from 1975 to 2003 for Asian and African states.

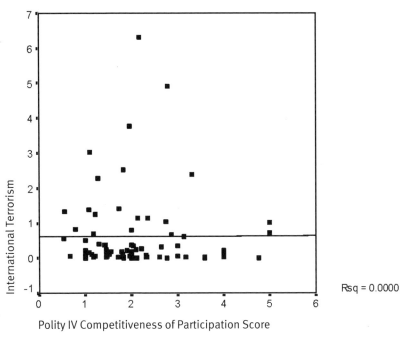

Polity IV Competitiveness of Participation Score

N = 75

Source: Monty G. Marshall and Keith Jaggers. (2002). Polity IV data set. [Computer file; version p4v2002] College Park, Md.: Center for International Development and Conflict Management, University of Maryland, and the National Memorial Institute for the Prevention of Terrorism: Terrorism Knowledge Base data set (updated September 28, 2006).

not all that surprising. However, if domestic groups often work in concert and sympathy with larger international terror organizations, then this finding is the first nail in the democracy proponents' coffin.

Figure 2 is a scatter plot of the average Polity IV democracy score and the average international terrorist event score. With this figure we are examining the potential correlation between international terrorist events and the level of democratization. A hard examination between established democracies and nondemocracies is contained in Figure 3.

Figure 2 is an attempt to capture whether or not more democracy is better than less in preventing international terrorism. This allows us to examine the democratization process and include regimes in the process of

Figure 2 ■ The average international terrorist incidents by the average Polity IV Democracy score from 1975 to 2003 for Asian and African states.

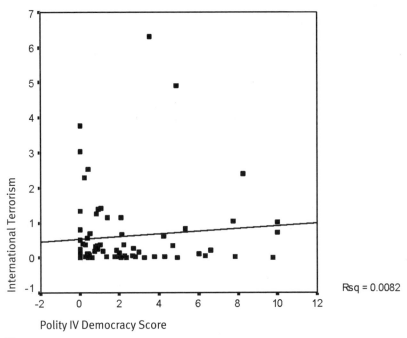

N = 75

Source: Monty G. Marshall and Keith Jaggers. (2002). Polity IV data set. [Computer file; version p4v2002] College Park, Md.: Center for International Development and Conflict Management, University of Maryland, and the National Memorial Institute for the Prevention of Terrorism: Terrorism Knowledge Base data set (updated September 28, 2006).

democratization over the twenty-nine year period of study that might not meet the threshold to be considered a fully functioning democratic regime.

There are several notable articles in which the author(s) argue that that the period of change between nondemocracy and democracy is actually the most dangerous and tumultuous time for any state. This argument, coupled with the facts that international terrorist events emanate outside the target state and that democratic societies are more open, led to compelling reasons to believe democracies will be more susceptible to international terrorism.

We were, therefore, unsurprised to find a weak correlation in Figure 2 between international terrorist events and increasing levels of democracy. The results are not consistent over both Figures 2 and 3, but because there are only nine states that qualify as democratic in Figure 3, those results may not be overly reliable. Having said this, it must be noted that the results in Figure 3 do not provide contrary evidence as Figure 3 finds no correlation between democracy and international terrorism rates.

Figure 2 indicates that there is no correlation between democracy and terrorism. This means that forcing democracy on the international system might not prevent the spread of international terrorism, and because of the openness of democratic societies such a foreign policy course might actually increase the likelihood of international terrorism.

In Figure 3 we dichotomized the democracy variable. We use a Polity IV democracy cutoff score of 6, which is a commonly used delineation point. States with an average democracy score over the twenty-nine-year

Figure 3 ■ The average number of international terrorist incidents by the dichotomized Polity IV Democracy score from 1975 to 2003 for Asian and African states.

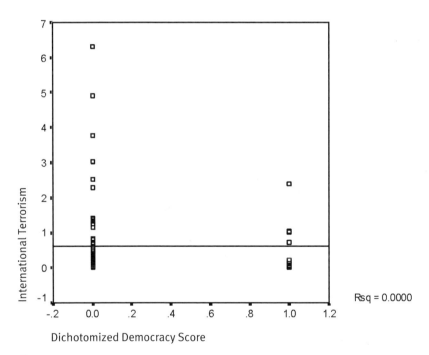

N = 75

Source: Monty G. Marshall and Keith Jaggers. (2002.) Polity IV data set. [Computer file; version p4v2002] College Park, Md.: Center for International Development and Conflict Management, University of Maryland, and the National Memorial Institute for the Prevention of Terrorism: Terrorism Knowledge Base data set (updated September 28, 2006).

Table 1 ■ Democratic States and International Terrorism Rates

State	Average Polity IV Democracy score	Average number of international terrorist incidents per year
1) Australia	10.00	.75
2) Japan	10.00	1.55
3) Mauritius	9.75	.00
4) India	8.24	2.38
5) Botswana	7.83	.03
6) South Africa	7.74	1.03
7) Sri Lanka	6.31	.07
8) Namibia	6.00	.10

Source: Monty G. Marshall and Keith Jaggers. (2002.) Polity IV data set. [Computer file; version p4v2002] College Park, Md.: Center for International Development and Conflict Management, University of Maryland, and The National Memorial Institute for the Prevention of Terrorism: Terrorism Knowledge Base data set (updated September 28, 2006).

time period of 6 or above were coded as democratic, while states with scores below 6 were deemed undemocratic.

Figure 3 shows no correlation between democracy and international terrorism. This result shows that democratic and nondemocratic regimes are equally likely to experience international terrorism.

Tables 1 and 2 show the prominent examples of democratic and nondemocratic states that were produced using an average Polity IV democracy score of 6 as the dividing line between democracy and nondemocracy.

One of the glaring facts that should be immediately evident in Table 1 is that there are only eight of seventy-five states that meet the criteria for being classified as democratic. Despite this small sample size for democracies, four states average almost one or more international terror incidents a year. The four hardest hit by terrorism are extremely surprising cases. Japan and Australia are arguably the most surprising. Japan is averaging 1.00 international terrorist attack a year and Australia posts a 0.72 average. Australia and Japan represent two of the richest, most stable and democratic states in the study, yet they both experience an alarmingly high rate of international terrorism. The reasons behind this are explored at greater length in later chapters.

India and South Africa are a little less surprising as high terrorist incident cases. Despite India and South Africa having average democracy scores of 8.24 and 7.74, respectively, both are considered nations in transition, economically and politically. Further, India has a hostile neighbor to the north in Pakistan, and groups within Pakistan, especially groups supporting Pakistani control of the Kashmir region, are not averse to cross-border terrorist attacks. It should be noted that the enmity flows both ways and Pakistan, a nondemocratic state, averages 6.48 international terrorist attacks a year.

South Africa does not have a consistent, proximate state rival per se, but several bordering states have acted in sympathy with anti-apartheid groups. Terrorist attacks have not ended with the end of apartheid but they have become far less frequent and sporadic, with no international terrorist attacks since 2000.

Table 2 shows the nineteen most undemocratic states in our study. All nineteen have an average democracy score of zero. It is interesting

Table 2 ■ Undemocratic States and International Terrorism Rates

State	Average Polity IV Democracy score	Average number of international terrorist incidents per year
1) Afghanistan	0	3.14
2) Bhutan	0	.00
3) China	0	.21
4) Democratic Republic of Congo	0	.07
5) Republic of Congo	0	.07
6) Egypt	0	3.75
7) Eritrea	0	.09
8) Gabon	0	.03
9) Laos	0	.21
10) Libya	0	.52
11) Mauritania	0	.24
12) Morocco	0	.79
13) Myanmar	0	.00
14) Rwanda	0	.17
15) Somalia	0	2.07
16) Swaziland	0	.07
17) Turkmenistan	0	.00
18) Uzbekistan	0	.08
19) Vietnam	0	.03

Source: Monty G. Marshall and Keith Jaggers. (2002.) Polity IV data set. [Computer file; version p4v2002] College Park, Md.: Center for International Development and Conflict Management, University of Maryland, and The National Memorial Institute for the Prevention of Terrorism: Terrorism Knowledge Base data set (updated September 28, 2006).

that the nine democracies in this study boasted three states with average international terrorist incident scores above 1.00 and the nineteen most undemocratic states also had only three averaging over 1.00 incident per year.

Egypt and Somalia, with 3.75 and 1.34 terrorist incidents per year, respectively, are discussed in greater detail in later chapters. Afghanistan is dealt with in greater detail later as well, but an interesting discovery in the statistics regarding Afghanistan deserves some attention here.

While Afghanistan posts a 3.03 yearly incident average, most of that high average is driven by the last two years in our study — 2002 and 2003. Slightly over 50 percent of all the international terror strikes in Afghanistan took place in the two years following the U.S. invasion and occupation. The power vacuum, chaos, and instability caused by the invasion and occupation appear highly correlated with the dramatic increase in international terrorism in Afghanistan. Unfortunately, in the next chapter it is shown that the consequences of forcible take over and occupation are even worse when it comes to domestic terrorism.

Poverty and International Terrorism

The Democratic Peace Thesis, specifically, and the democracy argument, in general, did not fare too well in terms of international terrorism. We now turn our attention to economic factors and the poverty–terrorism nexus. Figure 4, Tables 3 and 4, and Figures 5 and 6 examine the potential effects poverty has on international terrorism. It is thought that more impoverished states will provide a greater base of potential terrorists and that they might create greater hatred of the government or in-group and thus be more likely to engage in terrorism as a recourse to address their grievances. We felt from the onset that this would apply more forcefully to domestic rather than international terrorism, as the grievances and income inequalities would be generated domestically against a specific state's citizens.

In fact, when hypothesizing concerning international terrorism, we believe that the effect on the international level should be just the opposite. Logically, if impoverished, disenfranchised citizens resort to terrorism more frequently in poor states, then when international terrorist groups from impoverished and historically exploited states attack, they should be more likely to lash out against richer nations that they feel may have unfairly exploited their group or state.

Figure 4 is an examination of the average gross domestic product (GDP) per capita purchasing power parity (referred to henceforth as

Figure 4  The average number of international terrorist incidents by the average GDPpcPPP from 1975 to 2003 for Asian and African states.

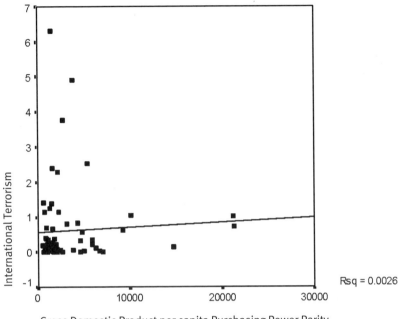

N = 69

Source: The World Development Indicators (2005/CDROM), The International Bank for Reconstruction and Development/The World Bank, and the National Memorial Institute for the Prevention of Terrorism: Terrorism Knowledge Base (updated September 28, 2006).

GDPpcPPP) per year by the average yearly international terrorism incident rate. GDPpcPPP was chosen as the major indicator of state wealth because it allows us to control for variances in economy size, exchange rate fluctuations, and so on and provides us with a one-to-one comparable wealth ratio.

Figure 4 shows no correlation between terrorism and wealth of a state. Despite this statistical finding, when one breaks the states into categories ranging from wealthy to extremely poor, it does appear that international terrorism is somewhat correlated with the wealth of a state but not in the way we expected.

The top twenty and bottom twenty states by average GDPpcPPP produce starker contrast to this initial finding. The twenty wealthiest nations are depicted in Table 3. Six of the twenty nations, Japan, South Africa,

Table 3 ■ Twenty Wealthiest States and International Terrorism Rates

State	Average GDPpcPPP	Average number of international terrorist incidents per year
1) Australia	$21,236	.75
2) Japan	$21,190	1.55
3) Singapore	$14,723	.14
4) South Africa	$10,137	1.03
5) South Korea	$9,249	1.24
6) Mauritius	$7,047	.00
7) Gabon	$6,697	.03
8) Namibia	$6,266	.10
9) Malaysia	$5,923	.35
10) Algeria	$5,402	2.55
11) Botswana	$4,969	.03
12) Tunisia	$4,801	.55
13) Kazakhstan	$4,600	.00
14) Turkmenistan	$4,585	.00
15) Thailand	$4,353	.83
16) Philippines	$3,863	5.45
17) Swaziland	$3,784	.07
18) Morocco	$3,165	.79
19) Egypt	$2,787	3.75
20) Sri Lanka	$2,405	.07

Source: The World Development Indicators (2005/CDROM), The International Bank for Reconstruction and Development/The World Bank, and the National Memorial Institute for the Prevention of Terrorism: Terrorism Knowledge Base (updated September 28, 2006).

South Korea, Algeria, the Philippines, and Egypt, have high international terrorism rates averaging over 1.00 event per year. Three more states, Australia, Thailand, and Morocco, have high rates averaging just less than 1.00 event a year. This means that almost 50 percent of the wealthiest nations in our study are experiencing serious international terrorism. It is interesting to note that Australia, Japan, and South Korea are all also currently considered stable democracies, with South Africa, Thailand, and the Philippines considered to be rising, transitional democracies.

Table 4 lists the opposite end of the spectrum. Only two states, Mozambique and Ethiopia, average over 1.00 international terrorist incident a year. Further, only two more states, Uganda and Sierra Leone, have average terrorist incidents approaching 1.00. Most of the poorest states experience little or no terrorism.

Figure 4 and Tables 3 and 4 support our hypothesis that wealthier states will be targeted more often by international terrorists. While we cannot say conclusively why this is, we speculate that terrorist organizations may often emanate from Third World states, and, as shown later, possibly come from states and groups with different religious and ethnic backgrounds than the richer states that they are attacking. It is also possible that these organizations have an historical complaint, that is, past colonialism, or a current economic gripe.

While we had very specific expectations for GDPpcPPP, we did not expect to find a correlation between income inequality and terrorism. We do expect income inequality to be a catalyst for domestic terrorism, as income inequality within a state could logically be argued to create domestic animosity. We do not expect it to be a major factor in fomenting

Table 4 ■ Twenty Poorest States and International Terrorism Rates

State	Average GDPpcPPP	Average number of international terrorist incidents per year
1) Nepal	$1040	.17
2) Kenya	$1037	.35
3) Uganda	$1010	.93
4) Zambia	$999	.21
5) Niger	$939	.03
6) Madagascar	$932	.00
7) Burkina-Faso	$905	.00
8) Chad	$904	.38
9) Republic of Congo	$903	.07
10) Benin	$877	.03
11) Nigeria	$867	.38
12) Guinea-Bissau	$844	.03
13) Sierra-Leone	$841	.69
14) Eritrea	$816	.09
15) Burundi	$757	.45
16) Mali	$733	.07
17) Mozambique	$699	1.21
18) Ethiopia	$633	1.59
19) Malawi	$555	.00
20) Tanzania	$514	.20

Source: The World Development Indicators (2005/CDROM), The International Bank for Reconstruction and Development/The World Bank, and the National Memorial Institute for the Prevention of Terrorism: Terrorism Knowledge Base (updated September 28, 2006).

Figure 5 ■ The average number of international terrorist incidents by the average GINI coefficent from 1975 to 2003 for Asian and African states.

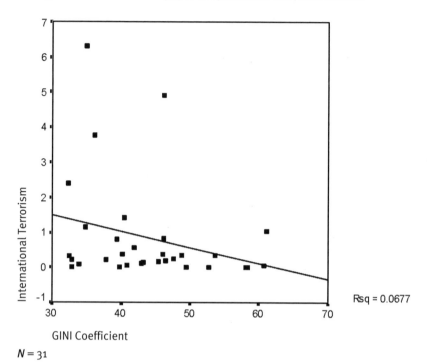

Rsq = 0.0677

N = 31

Source: United Nations University: World Income Inequality Database (June 2005), version 2.0, and the National Memorial Institute for the Prevention of Terrorism: Terrorism Knowledge Base (updated September 28, 2006).

international terrorism, as international terrorists would have to be moved to intervene in a state for largely altruistic reasons.

Figure 5 produces some surprising results. In this scatter plot we use the average yearly GINI coefficient, a survey measure of income inequality against yearly international terrorism rates. The fit line shows a deep downward-trending slope indicating that states with less inequality experience more international terrorism. As income inequality increases, international terrorism declines. The *r*-squared test is fairly robust for a bivariate test at .068. However, there are several reasons we do not have a great deal of confidence in this finding. First, we do not have a theory or even a theoretical supposition driving this finding. Second, because GINI coefficient data are sparse, our *N* dropped significantly to thirty-one cases (or less than half of our possible cases). We strongly believe this correlation is spurious. We debated whether to even include this test for international terrorism and finally decided to include it for the sake of continuity, as we do expect income inequality to play a large role in domestic terrorism.

Clash of Civilizations and Terrorism

In Figures 6, 7 and 8 we examine the Clash of Civilizations Thesis. This is accomplished by a simple examination of the number of religions and ethnicities present within a nation. We assumed, from the outset, that as the number of civilizations collided within a state, both the international and domestic terrorism incidents would increase. We expected this finding to be more pronounced for domestic terrorism and that there was a strong possibility that more homogeneous states would suffer more international terrorism as divergent, hostile cultures from outside a particular state might attack more readily. For example, when two different cultures share a border, we expected to find high levels of interstate terrorism, possibly emanating from both states.

Figure 6 is an examination of the possible correlation between international terrorism and the number of major religions present in a society. Religions were only included in our calculation if the membership in that religion was 10 percent of the total population or higher. We believe this is a fair, but arbitrary, delineation point, given that we are interested in examining clashing civilizations. While smaller proportions of religious or ethnic factions can and do perpetrate terrorism and other violent acts against governments and civilians, we determined that any group under 10 percent of the total population does not constitute a major civilization cross-pressure on the state.

Figure 6 is fascinating as a partial confirmation of our expectations. As predicted, international terrorism strikes more frequently in states that are dominated by one major religion. This may indicate some strong support for the Clash of Civilizations Thesis if we find many of our international terrorism case studies to be occurring between groups and states with different religious orientations. What is most fascinating about this chart is the fact that the Clash of Civilizations Thesis seems to drop off precipitously in states that have more than two major religions. Samuel Huntington postulates forcefully that competing civilizations will come into violent conflict when these civilizations share borders. Whether or not this is true at the international level is debatable, but internally, it appears that the greater the diversity of religion within a society, the better.

Figure 6 ■ The average number of international terrorist incidents by the number of religions from 1975 to 2003 for Asian and African states.

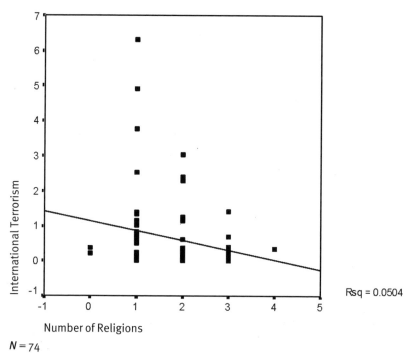

$N = 74$

Source: CIA World Factbook Online (2005) and the National Memorial Institute for the Prevention of Terrorism: Terrorism Knowledge Base (updated September 28, 2006).

This might be due to the fact that it becomes more difficult for one religion to seize power and abuse the human or economic rights of the outgroup. In other words, when power is distributed such that no single group can exploit its political or economic position in society, a more consociational and conciliatory outcome might be produced; this atmosphere of compromise could inhibit terrorism within that society. With an *r*-squared value of .050, this trend toward religious diversity leading to less international terrorism is fairly strong.

Figure 7 is an examination of the possible correlation between international terrorism and the number of major ethnicities within a society. Again, the cutoff point for what we considered to be a major ethnicity was 10 percent of the total population.

We again expected that divergent civilizations would clash and produce more terrorism. In Figure 7, we find another downward sloping correlation between ethnicity and international terrorism. The correlation is not as strong as the one found between religion and international terrorism, and this is largely due to the fact that the worst possible scenario for a state is one that contains two significant, competing ethnicities. Ethnically homogeneous states again fare poorly, but they are slightly better off than states supporting two ethnicities. This may mean that there is an international-level clash of civilizations that can be tapped into by the domestic clash of civilizations. By this we mean that competing ethnicities might appeal to similarly ethnic or religiously oriented international terror groups to conduct terror campaigns against the opposing ethnicity. It is very interesting to find that as the number of ethnicities increases past two major groups in society, international terrorism drops dramatically.

Figure 8 is an examination of international terrorism by a factor of religion and ethnicity. We simply took the religion and ethnicity scores and

Figure 7 ■ The average number of international terrorist incidents by the number of ethnicities from 1975 to 2003 for Asian and African states.

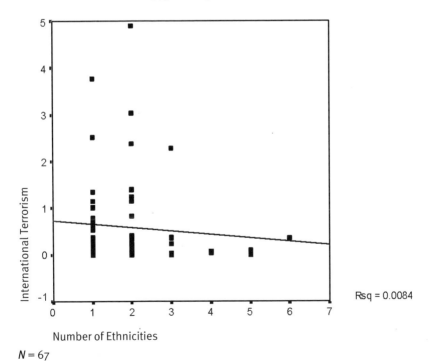

$N = 67$

Source: CIA World Factbook Online and the National Memorial Institute for the Prevention of Terrorism: Terrorism Knowledge Base (updated September 28, 2006).

Figure 8 ■ The average number of international terrorist incidents by the interaction score between the number of religions and the number of ethnicities from 1975 to 2003 for Asian and African states.

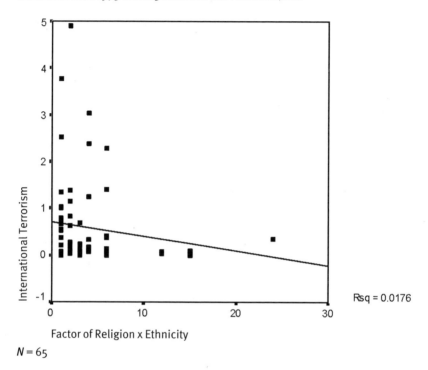

N = 65

Source: CIA World Factbook Online (2005) and the National Memorial Institute for the Prevention of Terrorism: Terrorism Knowledge Base (updated September 28, 2006).

multiplied them to give us a new measure of the interactive force of religion and ethnicity on terrorism. The results were very consistent with the previous two tables. There is a clear and significant downtrend in terrorism as a society becomes more diversified. Again, when a state contains few dominant religions and ethnicities, terrorism is higher than when there is greater ethnic and religious diversity in society.

We now turn to our last major investigation regarding international terrorism levels: instability. We use a gauge of regime interruption from the Polity IV data set. The Polity IV measure "durable" codes regime changes as zeros in the data set. Each year of interruption (i.e., revolution, coup d'état, anarchy, etc.) receives a zero in the data set. However, we are more concerned with the number of interruptions rather than the duration of interruption. We feel that a state suffering three separate regime interruptions, for example, is far more unstable than a state that experienced one three-year period of regime change. Therefore, we coded the number of regime interruptions and not the duration, in order to more accurately measure regime instability.

Figure 9 represents the results of this examination of regime instability by international terrorism. The chart results conform to our expectations that instability and terrorism go hand in hand. As regime instability increases, so do international terrorist events. With an *r*-squared value of .047, this is one of the strongest findings in this section, and the implication of this finding is that stabilizing states and preventing internal political chaos should be top priorities in preventing the spread of international terrorism.

Figure 9 ■ The average number of international terrorist incidents by the number of regime interruptions from 1975 to 2003 for Asian and African states.

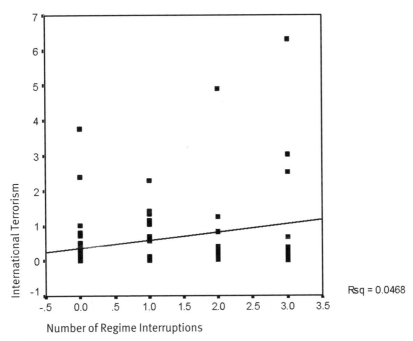

N = 75

Source: Monty G. Marshall and Keith Jaggers. (2002.) Polity IV data set. [Computer file; version p4v2002] College Park, Md.: Center for International Development and Conflict Management, University of Maryland, and the National Memorial Institute for the Prevention of Terrorism: Terrorism Knowledge Base data set (updated September 28, 2006).

Conclusion

The statistical findings were mixed for the four factors we examined. We were surprised to find that democracy not only fails to lead to less international terrorism, it may actually increase the likelihood of international terrorist events. Neither competitiveness of participation nor level of democratization provided any shield against international terrorist events. It appears that the openness of democratic societies creates an opening that international terrorists exploit. While we were hopeful that the findings would be the opposite, our findings do conform to the statistical research completed thus far on democracy and international terrorism.

Economic factors conformed a little more to our expectations but not to the assertions postulated by poverty–terrorism nexus proponents. We find a weak correlation between the overall wealth of a nation, as measured by GDPpcPPP, and international terrorism. International terrorism rates increased slightly but noticeably as states became wealthier. A poverty–terrorism nexus proponent believes that impoverished nations not only potentially provide more fertile ground for recruitment, due to high unemployment rates, but that the overall instability created by economic hardship creates an environment ripe for terrorism. We are sympathetic to these arguments but believed from the onset that there might be a larger First World versus Third World mindset that would lead to higher terrorism rates in First World states. The findings bear out our hypothesis to a lesser degree.

Unfortunately, this economic assertion is not confirmed by the data on GINI coefficients. We did not expect a correlation between income inequality and international terrorism. Again, while a poverty–terrorism nexus proponent argues that terrorism will increase with poverty and income inequality levels, we felt that international terrorists would be largely unmoved by the income inequality present within a state. While an international terror group might look at the world broadly in terms of First/Third or industrialized/developing terms, we did not believe that international terrorists would act like global "Robin Hoods" looking to right internal economic injustice. Therefore, we were slightly surprised to see that as income inequality went up, so did international terror rates. However, we believe this finding to be largely spurious due not only to the fact that no theory exists to explain this phenomenon, but also as a result of our sample size being severely limited by data unavailability.

The factor of civilization, as measured by religions and ethnicities present in society, produced some strong results. Though this was not a complete vindication of the Clash of Civilizations Thesis, it was a strong partial victory. Our findings lead to the conclusion that if a society has one or two dominant religions and/or ethnicities, international terror rates increase precipitously. This largely conforms to Huntington's assertion that different civilizations cannot coexist peacefully with one another.

Having said this, we must note that there is an interesting diversity effect present in our findings. While one or two major religions or ethnicities in a society produce more violence and terrorism, once you get past two, international terrorist events drop dramatically. When collaboration is forced upon divergent religion/ethnicities/civilizations, through the fact that no one group can capture and retain enough power to exploit the other two or more divergent groups in society, then terrorism (and probably violence) as a means of political expression becomes largely unviable.

The last fact we examined was regime stability. Not surprisingly, we found that unstable regimes were far more likely to experience international terrorism than stable regimes. This was one of our strongest findings and conformed to our expectations.

These findings, in total, paint quite a clear picture of what factors need to be avoided in order to mitigate international terrorism. Some can be addressed fairly straightforwardly, while others seem to be systemic at the international level. The worst-case scenario is a state that has two or fewer religions and/or ethnicities, is part of the First World or perhaps closely allied or linked with a First World state, and is in regime change, particularly if this regime change leads to an unstable democracy. Also, states that do not have the international religious/ethnic composition that predisposes them to international terror events will be susceptible if they border another distinct civilization. We next examine our cases with these findings in mind in an effort to determine whether these assertions hold up under closer scrutiny.

CHAPTER 6

Analyzing Domestic Terrorism
in Asia and Africa

THIS CHAPTER EXAMINES the same four factors (democracy, economics, civilization, and regime stability) in relation to domestic terrorism in Asia and Africa. Domestic terrorism is often overlooked in the embryonic lexicon of research on terrorism. This is largely due to the current U.S. foreign policy emphasis on international terrorism after the 11 September 2001 Al-Qaeda terrorist attacks and the fact that international terrorism data are more readily available over longer time periods. It is true that the domestic terrorism data are limited. The only source for comprehensive domestic terrorism statistics is the MIPT-TKB, and the data contained at this institute only provide us with six years (1998 to 2003) for use in our study, as the Polity IV data end in 2003. This is unfortunate, as the MIPT-TKB provides domestic data through September 2007. Despite these limitations, we believe that it is important to address domestic terrorism.

Democracy and Domestic Terrorism

We begin this chapter in the same fashion as the last, with an examination of democracy and terrorism. Despite the arguments presented by proponents of democracy that the ability of citizens to settle grievances peacefully through the democratic system will prevent citizens and groups from resorting to terrorism, we still believe that the openness of democratic society will make democracies more prone to terrorist attack.

Figure 10 presents the average Polity IV competitiveness of participation score by the average number of domestic terrorist incidents. The relationship is not very strong (*r*-squared value of .015), but this correlation did not exist for international terrorism. This finding, while weak, stabs at the heart

Figure 10 ■ The average number of domestic terrorist incidents by the average Polity IV Competitiveness of Participation score from 1975 to 2003 for Asian and African states.

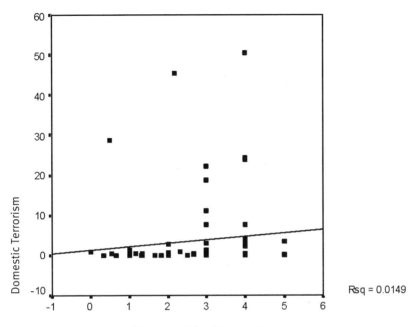

Polity IV Competitiveness of Participation Score

N = 75

Source: Monty G. Marshall and Keith Jaggers. (2002.) Polity IV data set. [Computer file; version p4v2002] College Park, Md.: Center for International Development and Conflict Management, University of Maryland, and the National Memorial Institute for the Prevention of Terrorism: Terrorism Knowledge Base data set (updated September 28, 2006).

of the pro-democracy contingent, as the more a society offers competitiveness of participation, the greater the likelihood of domestic terrorism.

Figure 11 examines the level of democratization against domestic terrorism. The findings for democracy are now consistent for both international and domestic terrorism, although the correlation is much stronger for domestic terrorism (*r*-squared value of .037). It appears that the openness of democracy allows too great an opportunity for domestic groups with a grievance to attempt to change governmental policies through terrorism. Further, the instability and tenuous hold of provisional, fledgling democratic government may offer more opportunities for domestic terrorists to exploit.

Figure 11 ■ The average number of domestic terrorist incidents by the Average Polity IV Democracy score from 1975 to 2003 for Asian and African states.

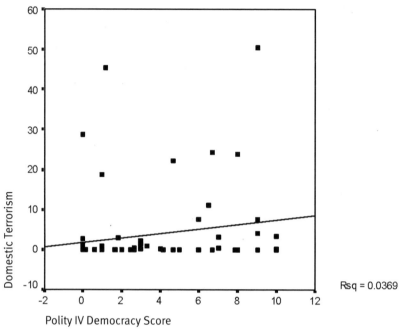

$N = 75$

Source: Monty G. Marshall and Keith Jaggers. (2002.) Polity IV data set. [Computer file; version p4v2002] College Park, Md.: Center for International Development and Conflict Management, University of Maryland, and the National Memorial Institute for the Prevention of Terrorism: Terrorism Knowledge Base (updated September 28, 2006).

Finally, democracies do not have the draconian methods available that nondemocratic governments have, and the historical respect for privacy and civil rights all blends into an opportunity that domestic terror groups seem to be exploiting.

When we dichotomize democracy, we find further confirmation that democracies are more susceptible to domestic terror attacks. Because we only have six years of data to draw from, we were able to obtain twenty-one democratic states that met the average Polity IV democracy score of 6 or greater. With this greater sample size, we find that democracies defined in this way experience a significantly higher rate of domestic terrorism.

The upward trending fit line is significant (*r*-squared value of .037) in Figure 12, and Tables 5 and 6 confirm, to a much greater degree, that democracies are far more prone to domestic terror events. Table 5 is a listing of all of the states that met the average Polity IV democracy score of 6. There are far more data points in this table than were present in the international terrorism table and this gives us a little more confidence in interpreting our findings in Figure 12.

Of the twenty democracies, eight, almost half, average one or more domestic terrorist attacks a year. These eight states, Japan, India, South Africa, Thailand, the Philippines, Indonesia, Sri Lanka, and Bangladesh, generally average far more than one domestic terror event a year. India averages over 180 terror events a year, followed by the Philippines at almost 24 and Sri Lanka at almost 12. This is an exceedingly high amount of terror

Figure 12 ■ The average domestic terrorist incidents by the dichotomized democracy score from 1975 to 2003 for Asian and African states.

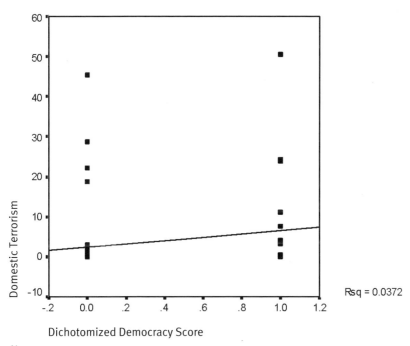

$N = 75$

Source: Monty G. Marshall and Keith Jaggers. (2002.) Polity IV data set. [Computer file; version p4v2002] College Park, Md.: Center for International Development and Conflict Management, University of Maryland, and the National Memorial Institute for the Prevention of Terrorism: Terrorism Knowledge Base data set (updated September 28, 2006).

Table 5 ■ Democratic States and Domestic Terrorism Rates

State	Average Polity IV Democracy score	Average number of domestic terrorist incidents per year
1) Australia	10	.17
2) Japan	10	3.33
3) Mauritius	10	.00
4) Mongolia	10	.00
5) India	9	182.83
6) South Africa	9	4.17
7) Taiwan	9	.00
8) Thailand	9	7.50
9) Korea, South	8	.00
10) Philippines	8	23.83
11) Botswana	7.83	.00
12) Madagascar	7.00	.33
13) Indonesia	6.67	25.00
14) Malawi	6.67	.00
15) Sri Lanka	6.50	11.83
16) Bangladesh	6.00	7.67
17) Benin	6.00	.00
18) Mali	6.00	.00
19) Mozambique	6.00	.00
20) Namibia	6.00	.00

Source: Monty G. Marshall and Keith Jaggers. (2002). Polity IV data set. [Computer file; version p4v2002] College Park, Md.: Center for International Development and Conflict Management, University of Maryland, and The National Memorial Institute for the Prevention of Terrorism: Terrorism Knowledge Base data set (updated September 28, 2006).

attacks, and all of these occurred in democratic states. These cases are explored in greater detail later, and baffling cases, such as Japan, have gone largely unnoticed by scholars studying terrorism and are surely deserving of some examination.

As striking as the democracies are for their penchant for domestic terrorism, the twenty-two most undemocratic nations are striking in their lack of domestic terrorism (Table 6). These cases again represent only the states averaging 0.00 for the Polity IV democracy score. Only three states, Afghanistan, China, and Uganda, average over one domestic terror event a year. Most of the twenty-two undemocratic states experience little to no terrorism. In fact, eleven, half of the cases, experienced no domestic terrorism between 1998 and 2003. Further, of the three cases, one, Afghanistan, is clearly anomalous.

Despite Afghanistan posting a six-year domestic terrorism average of 28.67, it is not an overstatement to claim that Afghanistan had very little experience with domestic terrorism prior to the U.S. invasion and occupation. In fact, of the 172 domestic terrorism incidents, 169 occurred in 2002 and 2003 after U.S. occupation. Therefore, one can argue that the worst case of domestic terrorism found in the twenty-two most undemocratic

Table 6 ■ Undemocratic States and Domestic Terrorism Rates

State	Average Polity IV Democracy score	Average number of domestic terrorist incidents per year
1) Afghanistan	0	28.67
2) Azerbaijan	0	.83
3) Bhutan	0	.00
4) China	0	1.33
4) Democratic Republic of Congo	0	.00
5) Republic of Congo	0	.00
6) Egypt	0	.33
7) Eritrea	0	.00
8) Gabon	0	.00
9) Laos	0	.17
10) Libya	0	.00
11) Mauritania	0	.00
12) Morocco	0	.17
13) Myanmar	0	.00
14) Rwanda	0	.00
15) Somalia	0	.33
16) Sudan	0	.33
17) Swaziland	0	.33
18) Turkmenistan	0	.16
19) Uganda	0	2.67
20) Uzbekistan	0	.00
21) Vietnam	0	.17
22) Zimbabwe	0	.00

Source: Monty G. Marshall and Keith Jaggers. (2002.) Polity IV data set. [Computer file; version p4v2002] College Park, Md.: Center for International Development and Conflict Management, University of Maryland, and The National Memorial Institute for the Prevention of Terrorism: Terrorism Knowledge Base data set (updated September 28, 2006).

states is an anomaly. Invasion and occupation of one state by another is such a rare event that this domestic terrorism finding can be perceived as unnatural.

The findings regarding democracy and domestic terrorism are unambiguous. It did not matter whether we measured democracy by the competitiveness of participation, by the level of democratization, or by a hard and fast dichotomized delineation of democracy and nondemocracy, democracies were far more prone to domestic terror attacks. This finding largely conforms to our findings regarding international terrorism. It is very damning for democracy proponents that there is not a single finding in this study that supports the assertion that the open, democratic political process, respect for privacy, and emphasis on civil rights lessen the desire to commit terrorist acts. These findings further corroborate previous statistical studies that consistently find democracy to be no deterrent against international terrorism. It appears that one price citizens of an open, democratic society pay is an increased risk of terror attack.

Poverty and Domestic Terrorism

We now turn our attention to economic variables and their effects on domestic terrorism. In Figure 13, Tables 7 and 8, and Figure 14, we examine different measures of economic attainment against domestic terrorism. We fully expect poverty to be strongly correlated with an increase in domestic terrorism. We believe that poverty will more directly correlate with domestic terrorism because the disaffected, impoverished individuals and groups within society are far closer to their governmental and business oppressors. As is shown next, this assertion does not hold up under statistical scrutiny.

Figure 13 is an examination of the average GDPpcPPP against the average domestic terrorism rate. There is statistically no correlation between wealth and domestic terrorism. This was surprising, as we thought terrorism would drop off precipitously as the middle class expanded within society and the overall wealth generated by a society increased. An argument could be made that Figure 13 does show some correlation between wealth and a drop in terrorism but that there are few states wealthy enough to have a global or, in this case, a regional impact. It does appear, from this figure, that once a state reaches a very high GDPpcPPP level, domestic terrorism abates. It appears that somewhere around the $8,000 to $10,000 mark domestic terrorism drops off. Unfortunately, of all the

Figure 13 ■ The average number of domestic terrorist incidents by the average GDPpcPPP from 1975 to 2003 for Asian and African states.

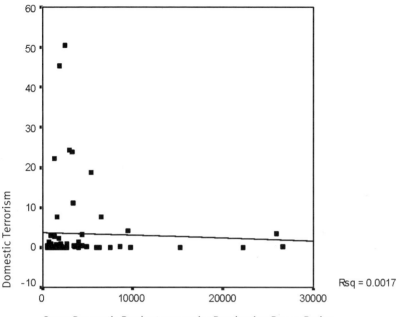

Gross Domestic Product per capita Purchasing Power Parity

$N = 69$

Source: *The World Development Indicators* (2005/CDROM), The International Bank for Reconstruction and Development/The World Bank, and the National Memorial Institute for the Prevention of Terrorism: Terrorism Knowledge Base (updated September 28, 2006).

Asian and African cases we have, we only have seven state cases that meet this lofty level of wealth.

States boasting respectable levels of economic development may still be so transitional that the instability present in this transition foments domestic terror. For example, Thailand, with a GDPpcPPP of $6,484, experiences over seven domestic terror attacks a year. This may have less to do with the growing wealth in Thailand and more to do with Thailand's transition to a capitalist and democratic society. Thailand has a history of military coups and has recently suffered a military takeover. While the military generally calls for democratic elections quickly, the fact that the check against rampant political corruption is military intervention indicates a very transitional and tenuous democratic system is in place. It becomes more apparent from

Table 7 ■ Twenty Wealthiest States and Domestic Terrorism Rates

State	Average GDPpcPPP	Average number of domestic terrorist incidents per year
1) Australia	$26,602	.17
2) Japan	$25,904	3.33
3) Singapore	$22,216	.00
4) Korea, South	$15,295	.00
5) Mauritius	$9,849	.00
6) South Africa	$9,542	4.17
7) Malaysia	$8,605	.17
8) Botswana	$7,534	.00
9) Thailand	$6,484	7.50
10) Tunisia	$6,291	.00
11) Gabon	$6,168	.00
12) Namibia	$6,040	.00
13) Algeria	$5,447	18.83
14) Kazakhstan	$4,920	.17
15) Swaziland	$4,404	.33
16) China	$3,992	1.33
17) Turkmenistan	$3,987	.16
18) Burundi	$3,983	.00
19) Morocco	$3,602	.17
20) Egypt	$3,534	.33

Source: The World Development Indicators (2005/CDROM), The International Bank for Reconstruction and Development/The World Bank, and the National Memorial Institute for the Prevention of Terrorism: Terrorism Knowledge Base (updated September 28, 2006).

this example, and Figure 13, that the type of economic stability necessary to dissuade local terrorists is attained by only a handful of states.

Tables 7 and 8 shed further light on the fact that increasing levels of wealth do not translate well to lower terrorism levels. In Table 7 we list the twenty wealthiest states as measured by GDPpcPPP. Of the twenty wealthiest states, five, Japan, South Africa, Thailand, Algeria, and China, have average yearly domestic terrorism rates greater than 1.00. Japan is again a strange case. Japan has the third-largest economy in the world, as measured by national GDP rates, and an extremely high GDPpcPPP, yet Japan averages 3.33 domestic terrorist attacks per year.

Table 8 is a listing of the twenty poorest states. These states fare far better in terms of domestic terrorism. Only three states, Uganda, Tajikistan, and Ethiopia, average over one domestic terrorist event a year. Eleven of the poorest states in our study experienced no domestic terrorism. This further solidifies the finding that there is little to no correlation between wealth and domestic terrorism.

Perhaps the overall wealth of a state has little or no effect in suppressing domestic terrorism, but income inequality might be more strongly correlated with increased terrorism rates. Figure 14 is a comparison of the GINI coefficient by domestic terrorism. The results from Figure 14 are very surprising and cannot be as easily dismissed as similar results were dismissed for international terrorism. The correlation is fairly strong (r-squared value of .038). The problem is that the correlation indicates that as income inequality increases, domestic terrorism rates go down somewhat. This does

Table 8 ■ Twenty Poorest States and Domestic Terrorism Rates

State	AverageGDPpcPPP	Average number of domestic terrorist incidents per year
1) Uganda	$1,275	2.67
2) Rwanda	$1,162	.00
3) Central African Republic	$1,126	.00
4) Burkina-Faso	$1,040	.00
5) Kenya	$1,004	.17
6) Benin	$988	.00
7) Mozambique	$938	.00
8) Chad	$937	.17
9) Republic of Congo	$903	.00
10) Nigeria	$887	.83
11) Mali	$866	.00
12) Tajikistan	$856	3.00
13) Eritrea	$816	.00
14) Zambia	$793	.17
15) Madagascar	$791	.33
16) Niger	$780	.00
17) Ethiopia	$671	1.33
18) Malawi	$580	.00
19) Tanzania	$533	.33
20) Sierra-Leone	$483	.00

Source: The World Development Indicators (2005/CDROM), The International Bank for Reconstruction and Development/The World Bank, and the National Memorial Institute for the Prevention of Terrorism: Terrorism Knowledge Base (updated September 28, 2006).

Figure 14 ■ The average number of domestic terrorist incidents by the average GINI coefficient from 1975 to 2003 for Asian and African states.

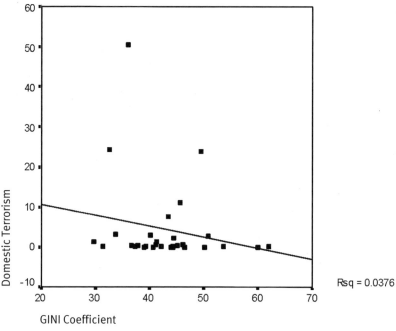

$N = 31$

Source: United Nations University: World Income Inequality Database (June 2005), version 2.0, and the National Memorial Institute for the Prevention of Terrorism: Terrorism Knowledge Base (updated September 28, 2006).

not make a great deal of sense theoretically, but it is consistent with the income inequality finding discovered in our examination of international terrorism. However, why this correlation exists is somewhat of a mystery.

The poverty–terrorism nexus argument has suffered a serious blow in our examination of domestic terrorism. We generally find very little to no correlation between poverty and increased levels of domestic terrorism, with one caveat. It does appear, although our N is small, that extremely wealthy, well-established, and stable capitalist systems experience much lower rates of domestic terrorism. In terms of income inequality, we find an inverse relationship. As income inequality increases, domestic terrorism decreases. This is a difficult finding to explain, but at least it can be said that increasing levels of income inequality do not seem to provide fertile ground for domestic terrorism to grow.

The Clash of Civilizations and Domestic Terrorism

Figures 15 through 17 deal with our examination of the Clash of Civilizations Thesis. We fully expect there to be a relationship between clashing civilizations and increasing terrorism rates at least equally strong as what we found in our study of international terrorism.

Figure 15 is an examination of the number of religions present in a society and the average domestic terrorism rate. Again there appears to be little correlation between the two variables. However, when one examines the chart more closely, it becomes apparent that domestic terrorism clusters around societies with one or two dominant religions. There is a similar diversity effect present in our figure that was also present in our examination of religion and international terrorism. It

Figure 15 ■ The average number of domestic terrorist incidents by the number of religions from 1975 to 2003 for Asian and African states.

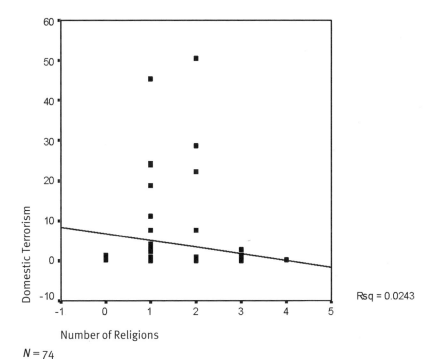

N = 74

Source: CIA World Factbook Online (2005) and the National Memorial Institute for the Prevention of Terrorism: Terrorism Knowledge Base (updated September 28, 2006).

Figure 16 ■ The average number of domestic terrorist incidents by the number of ethnicities from 1975 to 2003 for Asian and African states.

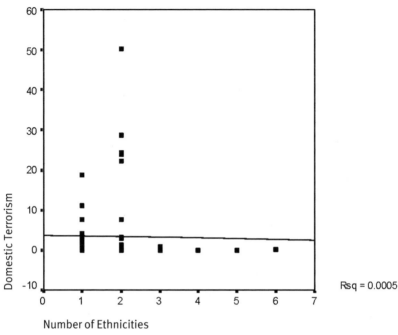

N = 66

Source: CIA World Factbook Online (2005) and the National Memorial Institute for the Prevention of Terrorism: Terrorism Knowledge Base (updated September 28, 2006).

appears that terrorism decreases once there are three or more major religions within a state.

We expected that two major religions would produce a Clash of Civilizations effect, but we are somewhat surprised to see that one major religion in society produces almost the same effect. There are several reasons that may explain this finding. First, societies with one dominant religion may be abusing the political and economic rights of very small religious minorities within society that feel their only recourse is to lash out with terrorism. Another possibility is that there may be a shared religion in a society with two or more dominant ethnic groups and that this religious bond is not enough to stop ethnic conflict manifesting in terrorism. Whatever the case, it does appear that there is at least some evidence for the Clash of Civilizations Thesis present here.

Figure 16 is an examination of the number of ethnicities present in a state and the average domestic terrorism rate. While the *r*-squared statistic indicates no correlation, this is actually our best piece of evidence yet for the modified Clash of Civilizations Thesis. While having one dominant ethnicity within society can produce appreciable levels of domestic terrorism, it appears from our findings that having two major ethnicities within society is most greatly correlated with increasing levels of domestic terrorist activity. We still find a diversity benefit starting with three or more major ethnicities within a society, but states with two major ethnicities are most prone to domestic terrorism.

Figure 17 is an examination of the interactive effect of religion and ethnicity on domestic terrorism rates. We create a factor of religion and ethnicity

Figure 17 ■ The average number of domestic terrorist incidents by the interaction score between the number of religions and number of ethnicities from 1975 to 2003 for Asian and African states.

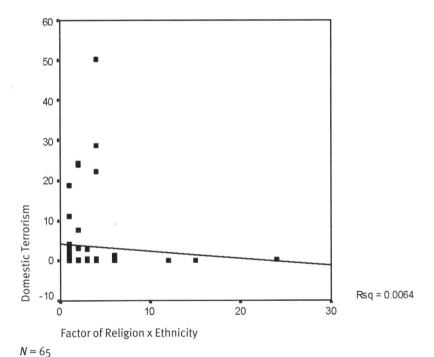

N = 65

Source: *CIA World Factbook Online* (2005) and the National Memorial Institute for the Prevention of Terrorism: Terrorism Knowledge Base (updated September 28, 2006).

and create a scatter plot against the average domestic terrorist rate. Our findings are consistent with the previous two figures, and we find that societies with a handful of major religions and ethnicities experience the greatest frequency of domestic terrorism. There is still a diversity benefit present in this figure, and it seems that the Clash of Civilizations effect drops noticeably as the society becomes more diverse.

Regime Instability and Domestic Terrorism

Terrorism does seem to rise slightly with less stable regimes. Regimes experiencing one or two interruptions in governance have a slightly higher terrorism rate than regimes that are stable through our entire three-decade period of study (Figure 18).

Figure 18 ■ The average number of domestic terrorist incidents by the number of regime interruptions from 1975 to 2003 for Asian and African states.

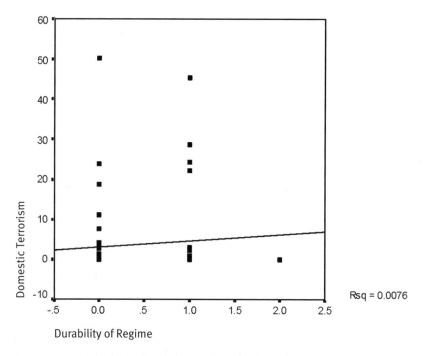

Source: Monty G. Marshall and Keith Jaggers. (2002.) Polity IV data set. [Computer file; version p4v2002] College Park, Md.: Center for International Development and Conflict Management, University of Maryland, and the National Memorial Institute for the Prevention of Terrorism: Terrorism Knowledge Base data set (updated September 28, 2006).

However, this relationship is surprisingly very small. We certainly cannot conclude that more stable regimes are significantly less likely to experience terrorism, and this finding fits in nicely with our finding that democracy is not proof against domestic terrorism either. It may be the case that stable democracies are as prone or even more prone to terrorism than unstable regimes or even less stable dictatorships.

Conclusion

It is disturbing, given the current U.S. foreign policy of forcing democracy on fundamental Islamic states, that democracy seems to promote domestic terrorism. We should expect now, and into the future of American occupation, that domestic terror will be present and will most likely increase over time. Further, stable democracies in the Western world should take heed that the openness of their societies may entice disgruntled domestic actors toward acts of terrorism. Democracy, so far, does not fare well as protection against terrorism.

There is no macro linkage between poverty and domestic terrorism. This finding is consistent across the analyses of both international and domestic terrorism. There may be some linkage found at the local or regional level in our case studies but, as it stands now, poverty does not induce terrorism. We should also note that wealth does not provide a disincentive to terrorism, as very wealthy states in our study suffered significant domestic terrorism.

One of the most interesting findings is the diversity dividend. While there does seem to be some civilizational motivation for terrorists, it appears that in societies with more than three ethnicities or religions, this civilizational rivalry melts away. Perhaps when one dominant ethnicity or religious group in society has only one rival that it can mistreat or target, the likelihood of terrorism goes up. When there are three or more rivals, perhaps conciliation and consensual policymaking become almost mandatory. We should also note that this finding held consistently across the study of both domestic and international terrorism.

A Brief Word Regarding Domestic and International Terrorism

We believed that it was appropriate to examine international and domestic terrorism simultaneously for all seventy-five cases as a cap to our individual statistical analyses of international and domestic terrorism. We generated one final table showing the total number of international and

Table 9 ■ Terrorist Incident Total by Type of Terrorism for All Asian and African States

State	1975–2003 International	1998–2003 Domestic
1) Afghanistan	91	72
2) Algeria	74	113
3) Angola	65	6
4) Australia	22	1
5) Azerbaijan	8	5
6) Bangladesh	8	46
7) Benin	1	0
8) Bhutan	0	0
9) Botswana	1	1
10) Burkina-Faso	0	0
11) Burundi	13	0
12) Cambodia	36	13
13) Cameroon	0	0
14) Central African Republic	1	0
15) Chad	0	1
16) China	6	8
17) Democratic Republic of Congo	2	0
18) Republic of Congo	2	0
19) Ivory Coast	3	0
20) Egypt	109	2
21) Eritrea	1	0
22) Ethiopia	46	8
23) Gabon	1	0
24) Gambia	0	0
25) Ghana	1	0
26) Guinea	1	0
27) Guinea-Bissau	1	0

domestic terrorist attacks for each state in our study. The results from Table 9 pose some far-reaching implications for U.S. and international efforts to combat terrorism worldwide.

First, it is amazing to see how many states have experienced terrorism. Only thirteen of the seventy-five Asian and African states have experienced no domestic or international terrorism during the time periods we examined. A number of nations have experienced dozens, even hundreds, of terrorist events over the years. While American citizens are justly upset

State	1975–2003 International	1998–2003 Domestic
28) India	79	1097
29) Indonesia	33	150
30) Japan	45	20
31) Kazakhstan	0	1
32) Kenya	10	1
33) South Korea	36	0
34) Kyrgyzstan	5	5
35) Laos	6	1
36) Lesotho	2	0
37) Liberia	0	0
38) Libya	15	0
39) Madagascar	0	2
40) Malawi	0	0
41) Malaysia	10	1
42) Mali	0	0
43) Mauritania	7	0
44) Mauritius	0	0
45) Mongolia	0	0
46) Morocco	23	1
47) Mozambique	0	0
48) Myanmar	0	0
49) Namibia	3	0
50) Nepal	5	135
51) Niger	0	0
52) Nigeria	11	5
53) Pakistan	188	273
54) The Philippines	158	143
55) Rwanda	5	0
56) Senegal	1	0
57) Sierra Leone	20	0

after the 11 September 2001 terror attacks, other nations have dealt with ongoing and devastating terror campaigns. Our blasé attitude toward terrorism prior to these attacks is the testament to the blind eye scholars and politicians had turned toward what must be considered a very real and persistent threat for many nations throughout the world.

It is not clear whether the U.S. foreign policymakers or the public at large are completely cognizant of the true scope of the terror threat. While U.S. policymakers and citizens are no longer blind to the dangers

Table 9 ■ *(continued)*

State	1975–2003 International	1998–2003 Domestic
58) Singapore	4	0
59) Somalia	60	3
60) South Africa	30	25
61) Sri Lanka	2	71
62) Sudan	36	2
63) Swaziland	2	2
64) Taiwan	1	0
65) Tajikistan	18	18
66) Tanzania	6	2
67) Thailand	24	48
68) Togo	3	0
69) Tunisia	16	0
70) Turkmenistan	0	1
71) Uganda	27	16
72) Uzbekistan	1	0
73) Vietnam	1	1
74) Zambia	6	1
75) Zimbabwe	0	0
TOTAL	1,377	1,626

of terrorism, an insidious myopia seems to be ever present. Table 9 indicates quite clearly that domestic terrorism may be a bigger threat to the states of the world than international terrorism. While Western governments and international institutions debate the proper course for dealing with international terror threats, and these threats do need to be dealt with, a burgeoning domestic terror threat goes largely unnoticed. The total number of international terror incidents for all seventy-five states in our study, over a twenty-nine-year period of examination, was 1,377. Contrast this with a total domestic terrorist incident rate for all seventy-five states of 1,626, noting that we only had six years of data for this statistic, and it becomes readily apparent that domestic terrorism is far more frequent than international terrorism.

While there is not a one-to-one correlation between domestic and international terrorism for all states in our study, it does appear that high international terrorism rates often go hand in hand with high domestic terrorism rates. In fact, we next show, through some of our case studies, that there is often an alarming degree of coordination between domestic terrorist groups and international ones. Focusing only on the international level or, worse still, focusing on one international terror group, like Al-Qaeda, is an oversight that will surely lead to ineffective and perhaps even counterproductive foreign policy to combat the terrorist threat.

CHAPTER 7

Terrorism, Transition, Economic Growth, and Instability in Southeast Asia

S OUTHEAST ASIAN STATES can best be described as states in transition. There is considerable economic transition from developing to developed. Once thought of as "Third World" states, most Southeast Asian nations boast strong or growing economies and rapidly advanced and diversified industries. Singapore, for example, has become the telecommunications hub for not only Southeast Asia but arguably China as well.

Politically, Southeast Asian nations are either transitioning to some form of democratic governance or have transitioned into a stable, semidemocratic form. Most notably, Malaysia and Singapore have the longest, most stable record of semidemocratic governance, while the Philippines, Thailand, and Indonesia all boast greater democratic freedom, but the fledgling nature of their democratic development produces instability in each of these states.

It is not surprising then that terrorism and insurgency are more common in the less-stable polities and economies. Layered on top of the instability are global terrorist forces that have infiltrated the region. One author estimated that the base of international terrorism has shifted from the former Soviet Union and the Middle East to Asia and Africa (Qadir, 2001: 304). More specific to Southeast Asia, it is estimated that one-fifth of Al-Qaeda's organizational strength had shifted to Asia by 2002 (Gunaratna, 2002). As discussed later, Al-Qaeda is one of the chief catalysts of Islamic fundamental terrorism in the region but it does not explain all, or perhaps even a majority, of the present terrorism.

We are not trying to leave the impression that Southeast Asia is riddled with terrorism and terrorist threats. In fact, in Australia, Brunei, Cambodia, Laos, Myanmar, Singapore, and Thailand there is little to no terrorism. But where it occurs regularly, in Indonesia, the Philippines, and Thailand, it seems to be a devastating and destabilizing force.

There is a vein of Muslim extremism that is associated with all of the terror campaigns in Southeast Asia. Arabinda Acharya notes that the substantial proliferation of fundamentalist "jihadi websites in recent months" is an indication of a growing Islamic radicalization in Southeast Asia (2006: 307). Recent polls seem to also support the assertion that Islamic fundamentalism is on the rise. For example, Osama Bin Laden received a very favorable rating by the majority of Indonesian respondents in 2002 (Gentzkow and Shapiro, 2004: 117). Further, almost 80 percent of Indonesians surveyed did not believe that Arabs committed the attacks of 11 September 2001 (Gentzkow and Shapiro, 2004: 120). A more recent poll by the Pew Research Center showed continuing unfavorable views of the United States in both Indonesia and Malaysia. Sixty-six percent of the Indonesians surveyed in this poll, and 69 percent of Malaysian respondents, had an unfavorable view of the United States in 2007 (Pew Global Attitudes Project, 2007).

But other observers correctly note that Islamic fundamentalism is not the only driving factor behind terrorism in Southeast Asia. Osman Bakar believes that Muslim extremist groups are motivated by a combination of insurgency or separatist motives and a desire to remove American or Western influences. However, he believes the latter are the primary motivations for terrorist groups (2005: 110). Maria Ressa contends that Islamic terrorism is, in large part, an attempt at insurgency in Southeast Asia. She argues that such committed terrorists are best fought through superior ideology rather than military tactics (2003).

Zachary Abuza offers some interesting insights toward explaining why Southeast Asia is such a fertile ground for terrorists. Abuza notes that while Southeast Asian societies and governments tend to be secular and tolerant, radical Islam is growing due to an increase in poverty, a failure of secular education to deliver to fundamental Islamic minorities, the spread of Wahabbism and Salafi Islam, and the emphasis on tourism in many Southeast Asian nations, which creates ease of movement for terrorists (2002: 428).

Whether it is democracy, economics, insurgency, or fundamental Islam driving terrorism is examined in this chapter. The rest of this chapter is divided into: an examination of Indonesia, the Philippines, and Thailand as examples of nations facing serious terrorist threats; Malaysia and Singapore as examples of nations that have, thus far, successfully dealt with serious terrorist threats; an examination of the global nature of terrorism in Southeast Asia; and an examination of the impact of democracy, economics, culture, and instability on terrorism in the region.

The Indonesian Experience with Terrorism

Indonesia has had problems since its formation as an independent state from Dutch colonization in 1945. One major problem is that Indonesia is a very ethnically and linguistically diverse state. Three hundred ethnic groups and 250 distinct languages are dispersed over the 3,000-island archipelago that comprises modern-day Indonesia (Brumberg, 2001: 395).

President Sukarno attempted to unite divergent ethnicities, cultures, and religions, including fundamental and secular Muslims, through a common ideology called "Panasila" or "The Five Principles." The Five Principles called for everyone to believe in a monolithic god but did not favor one religion or sect over another. There was an emphasis on consensual democratic decision making, social justice, and developing a common national identity (Brumberg, 2001: 396). Sukarno forced this vision on the Indonesian people, creating the foundation for groups to organize in violent opposition.

From the late 1960s through most of 1980, Suharto, Sukarno's successor, used an iron fist when dealing with fundamental Islamic groups and called for Sharia government. Suharto forced his dictatorial "New Order" governmental vision on Indonesia. Suharto "relied on authoritarian rule in pursuing political stability, economic growth, and the security of the state" (George, 1998: 697). Muslim political activists were discriminated against, persecuted, unfairly arrested, and prevented from participating in politics (Liddle, 1996: 614–15). Sukarno used authoritarianism in an attempt to build a coherent and cohesive national identity, but it seems as if Suharto became more preoccupied with crushing opposition.

There is some evidence that Suharto's repressive tactics, under his "New Order" regime, helped to spread Islamic fundamentalism and terrorism not only in Indonesia but throughout Southeast Asia. Indonesian extremists Abu Bakr Baasyir and Abdullah Sungkar, both key leaders of Jemaah Islamiyah (JI), fled repression under Suharto's "New Order" regime in 1985. The two fled to Malaysia and built a following among fundamentalist Malaysians and Indonesian émigrés (Tan, 2005: 74). These leaders strengthened their ties with the Mujahadeen in Afghanistan and JI actually became stronger, broader, and better organized. In fact, there was a "Group of 272" in Indonesia in the 1980s that represented 272 returning veterans from the Afghanistani Mujahadeen (Abuza, 2002: 431). These veterans from the war brought back jihad from Afghanistan and sought to impose it on Indonesian society.

Despite these developments, a significant percentage of Indonesian Muslims have adopted the secular, modernist, reformist approach to Islam called *ijtihad*. *Ijtihad* is an "individual interpretation of Qur'anic teachings" and this seemed to meld nicely with the Indonesian government's push for secularism (George, 1998: 696). Unfortunately, Arabinda Acharya (2006), Suzanne Brenner (1996), and Robert Hefner (1993) all point out that there is no unified Islamic community or thought in Indonesia. Therefore, despite the widespread adherence to *ijtihad*, large pockets of Islamic fundamentalism still exist.

Sukarno's authoritarian attempts at unifying the disparate Indonesian cultures and Suharto's repressive "New Order" regime create the stage upon which secession and terrorism play. Like terrorist movements in Thailand and the Philippines, there is a significant motivation for terrorism found in separatism. But one must be careful not to confuse purely guerilla or secessionist movements with terrorist campaigns that may have some secessionist motivations. Both the Free Aceh Movement or Gerakan Aceh Merdeka (GAM) and the Free Papua Movement (OPM) are separatist movements founded on well-justified claims of governmental mistreatment. GAM has been consistently lied to, has suffered unfair economic hardship, and has been the subject of violent military crackdowns stretching through the presidencies of Sukarno through Megawatti.

The ethnically distinct Papuan population on the western island of Irian Jaya has suffered genocidal attack by past governments. It is not surprising that OPM does not wish to negotiate with the Indonesian government.

GAM has also suffered violent governmental crackdowns, but this group has always sought reconciliation with the government in Jakarta. The population of Aceh shares a history of colonial struggle against the Dutch as well as an island with moderate Islamic Indonesians. Recently, the current President Susilo Bambang Yudhayono has tried a more conciliatory approach with the Aceh rebels. After the horrific tsunami hit the Aceh region on 26 December 2005, some felt the fight had been knocked out of GAM (Vatikiotis, 2006: 5). Instead of attempting to crush the beleaguered resistance movement, Yudhayono offered a generous peace agreement, showing that when dealing with groups with real grievances, governments gain more by negotiation than by taking a hard military line ("Fighting Rebellion," 2006: 38). The concessions Yudhayono offered were comprehensive and gracious. He agreed to allow Aceh-based political parties, a revenue-sharing scheme in which 70 percent of the profits from natural gas and other natural resources from the region went to Aceh and its people, and immediate amnesty to hundreds of imprisoned GAM rebels (Vatikiotis, 2006: 6).

In contrast to GAM and OPM are JI and Laskar Jihad. Both JI and Laskar Jihad have ties to Al-Qaeda and seem less willing to negotiate with the central government and more willing to use violent terrorism against Westerners, foreigners, and Christians.

Jemaah Islamiyah (JI) and Laskar Jihad

While JI was largely founded in Malaysia when Baasyir and Sungkar were in exile and undertook significant training exercises with militant groups in the Philippines and is still correctly deemed to be a regional terrorist organization, most of JI's terrorism occurs in Indonesia. JI was founded in the mid-1990s and has focused since on establishing a fundamentalist Islamic government in Indonesia (Shuja, 2006: 451). JI specifically wants to establish Sharia law based on strict Wahhabi practices. But while most of JI's terror operations have been carried out in Indonesia, leaders of JI have expressed a desire for a larger Islamic caliphate that would encompass Thailand, Malaysia, the Philippines, and Indonesia (ibid.).

JI was started by Abu Bakr Baaysir and Abdullah Sungkar as the leader of JI operations. These two were able to quickly recruit and indoctrinate young Indonesians and Malaysians who shared their Islamic orthodoxy (Shuja, 2006: 445). A link to Al-Qaeda was established early in the organization's history when Riduan Isamuddin, more commonly known as Hambali, joined JI. Hambali fought with the Mujahadeen in Afghanistan and was indoctrinated into the Wahhabi world view (ibid.). JI also quickly developed links with other like-minded groups in the region, including the Moro Islamic Liberation Front (MILF), Abu Sayyaf Group (ASG), and Kampulan Mujahadeen Malaysia (KMM) (Acharya, 2006: 307).

Terrorism is justified as a means by JI through a "belief that the physical and spiritual violence committed against Muslims inherent in the status quo is far greater than that caused by acts of terrorism designed to end this oppressive system" (Wright-Neville, 2004: 40). Westerners, foreigners, and non-Muslims are high on the JI target list (Shuja, 2006: 452). The Australian government has been a consistent specific target of JI's animus. JI admitted that it attacked the Australian embassy on 9 September 2004 because Australia continued to participate in the U.S.-led Iraq war despite JI's insistence that it pull out (Ramakrishna, 2005: 344). David Wright-Neville argues that the hatred and dehumanization of Westerners and foreigners leads to a terror campaign that has no remorse or compassion (2004: 40).

JI has launched a highly successful terror campaign in Indonesia aimed at the economic system, tourism, foreigners, and Western embassies. JI attacks of note include: the 12 October 2002 Bali nightclub bombing, which resulted in 202 dead, mostly foreign tourists; the October 2002 bombing of the U.S. Consulate in Denpassar, Bali; the dual bombings in April 2003 of the United Nations building and the Sukarno-Hatta International Airport in Jakarta; the July 2003 bombing of the Indonesian parliament compound in Jakarta; the 5 August 2003 bombing of the Jakarta Marriott Hotel; the Australian Embassy bombing of 9 September 2004; and the Bali restaurant bombing of 1 October 2005 (Collier, 2006: 29; Shuja, 2006: 452).

Ramakrishna notes that the 9 September 2004 attack on the Australian Embassy resulted in nine dead and 180 wounded but that most of the casualties were Muslims (2005: 344). Collier expounds on this theme, explaining that the 12 October 2002 Bali nightclub bombing, the 5 August 2003 Jakarta Marriott Hotel attack, and the Australian Embassy bombing all caused Muslim casualties. He argues that the taking of Muslim life by JI is what prompted a governmental crackdown that "eventually crippled JI's formal structures" (2006: 29).

The police and military crackdown has resulted in some notable disruption in JI. Recently, both Hambali and JI's spiritual leader, Abu Bakr Baasyir, have been arrested. Joint efforts with the governments of Singapore and Malaysia have resulted in JI cells there being almost completely destroyed (Acharya, 2006: 307). But this has not lessened the threat of JI and JI-sympathetic terrorism. In fact, one could argue the partially dismantled organization is even more dangerous after the military and police intervention. Collier correctly argues that JI was never a well-defined group and that internal tensions mounted as ultramilitants within the organization carelessly took the lives of fellow Indonesian Muslims (2006: 28–29). Since the group has splintered due to the success of the governmental crackdown, many JI factions exploited old Darul Islam (DI) ties. This allowed ultramilitants to act independently with no oversight. As Acharya puts it:

> Without any central command and control, but with very cohesive internal ties often based on marriage and family alliances, these factions now operate independently recruiting and training cadres including suicide volunteers from the old DI milieu for new missions. (2006: 307)

Hence old tensions within JI that have at least partially constrained ultramilitant factions in the past have disappeared, leaving these militants freer to pursue terrorist agendas.

Many writers might pass over Laskar Jihad or only note it in passing. But while this group is disbanded, the threat of Laskar Jihad still bubbles just below the surface in Indonesia. Laskar Jihad, or the "Holy War Warriors," was founded in 2000 by Jafar Uma Thalib. Thalib, like almost all of the terrorist leaders in Southern Asia, fought for the Mujahadeen in Afghanistan against the Soviets and was trained in radical Islam in the madrassahs of Pakistan. Just like JI, Laskar Jihad's stated goal was to install fundamental Islamic governance and Sharia law.

Laskar Jihad has been closely linked to Al-Qaeda and JI (Scarpello, 2007a). Laskar Jihad notoriously targeted Christians and actually was the first group suspected of the 2002 Bali nightclub bombings. Laskar Jihad was blamed for the Muslim-Christian war on the Maluku Islands and Central Sulawesi which ran from 1999–2001 and resulted in an estimated 15,000 fatalities (Scarpello, 2007b).

Laskar Jihad disbanded in 2002, shortly after the Bali nightclub bombings, but the group bears mentioning here as the still outspoken former leader, Thalib, continues to speak publicly in support of an Islamic theocracy. With close ties to JI and Al-Qaeda, Laskar Jihad could reconstitute in the not too distant future.

While a cursory examination of terrorism in Indonesia might leave the impression of stunning success on the part of the government through military and law-enforcement crackdowns, the threat in Indonesia still remains high. The success of the military and police should not be minimized, but with growing fundamental Islamic revivalism and some still unsettled secession disputes, Indonesia faces a tough road ahead.

Terrorism in the Philippines: Old and New Foes

The Philippines has become a state of intense interest in the U.S. global war on terror since the 11 September 2001 terrorism attacks. On 31 January 2002, joint military exercises between the Filipino and U.S. militaries were conducted. Shortly after, a joint military campaign was launched against the Abu Sayyaf Group (ASG) (Bakar, 2005:110).

There are several reasons behind the development of terrorism on the Southern Philippine island of Mindanao. First, there is an obvious clash of civilizations taking place between the Christian-dominated government and the Muslim majority (roughly 80 percent of the population) on Mindanao. But to view the conflict as strictly cultural in nature is only part of the story. This is also a conflict against perceived, long-term colonization. Many rebels cite the beginning of unfair colonization with the Spanish-American War, which spilled over into the Philippines in 1898, and with the Philippine-American War, which ensued the following year. But terrorist groups now view themselves as being held under unfair and unjustified colonial rule by the government in Manila.

Besides Islamic separatists in Mindanao and the Sulu Islands, the Philippine government has had a long-standing struggle with the New People's Army (NPA). The NPA is a communist revolutionary organization that has launched a number of terror attacks against civilians.

The Moro Islamic Liberation Front (MILF)

MILF originated from a split with the Moro National Liberation Front (MNLF). David Wright-Neville argues that the outward reason for this split resulted from disputes over strategy. Through the leadership of Hashim Salamat, MILF was formed. Salamat and his followers were unhappy with MNLF's reluctance to launch a full-scale insurgency against the Filipino government, so he and his followers decided on forming their own insurgency group (2004: 36). But Wright-Neville believes that linguistic and cultural differences also account for the split. Supporters of MILF tended to be Magindanaon speaking and located on the island of Mindanao, while adherents to MNLF came mainly from the Sulu archipelago and Tawi Tawi Islands and were Tausug[1] speaking (2004: 36).

Of the two groups, MILF and MNLF, MILF is far larger and poses a greater terrorist threat. MILF is estimated to field between 12,000 and 15,000 combatants (Abuza, 2002: 435). Although the name "Moro Islamic Liberation Front" intimates a religious undertone to the movement, and while the MNLF originated from clashes between Muslims and Christian émigrés to Mindanao in the 1960s, some scholars see MILF being driven more by a desire to secede rather than by religious hatred (Vitug and Gloria, 2000: 107). But several authors note that while parochial aspirations for secession may trump religious considerations, MILF has formed a strong link with Al-Qaeda and Al-Qaeda's global jihad (Abuza, 2002: 435; Banloi, 2002: 300; Castro, 2004: 200). American intelligence indicates that MILF was instrumental in sending over 1,500 Islamic militants from several Southeast Asian nations to training camps in Afghanistan (Castro,

2004: 200). Hashim Salamat is credited with personally sending 1,000 Filipino to Al-Qaeda training camps (Banloi, 2002: 300).

Despite the size of MILF, its links to Al-Qaeda, and its strong secessionist bent, it is not the most dangerous terrorist operation in the Philippines. Part of the reason for this stems from the disorganized upper-level leadership and severe internal splits in the MILF organization (Collier, 2006: 30). MILF is a large organization but it is not tightly organized. Besides these facts, MILF has also taken actions which indicate rationality and perhaps reasonableness. In August 2001, MILF signed a truce with the Philippine government (Shuja, 2006: 450). Some scholars and politicians were skeptical of the agreement initially and viewed it simply as a tactical maneuver by MILF, but the Malaysian government became involved as a neutral intermediary in 2003 and a fragile truce is still in place.

This does not mean that MILF poses no threat going forward. In fact, one could characterize the truce as only being partially fulfilled. The same organizational fractures that may have weakened MILF and forced it to the bargaining table also allow for enclaves within MILF to flout the spirit, if not the actual provisions, of the truce. Kit Collier reports that some enclaves presided over by independent rebel commanders continue to shelter foreign jihadis (2006: 30), which continues to destabilize the island of Mindanao and the peace process.

Abu Sayyaf Group (ASG)

Like MILF, ASG split from MNLF and formed in 1991. While much smaller than MILF, ASG is far more dangerous as a terrorist and criminal organization. ASG is responsible for a large part of the violent terror attacks reported in the MIPT-TKB. ASG numbered in the hundreds in the 1990s but swelled to over 1,000 after criminal activities drew profits and the United States invaded Iraq (Robles, 2007: 9).

Regardless of its size, ASG has been active in sowing chaos in the region. In the early 1990s, when the number of combatants was estimated to be in the mere hundreds, ASG "regularly bombed churches, shopping centres, and transportation hubs" (Shuja, 2006: 451). The motives behind these early attacks were calls for secession and a separate Islamic state. However, in 2000, ASG initiated a series of kidnapping-for-ransom schemes aimed at raising money for the group (Murphy, 2001). There were several major kidnappings in 2000 and 2001. These resulted in more than twenty people captured at major resorts. The targets were mainly Westerners and non-Filipino Asians (Shuja, 2006: 451).

Despite the shift to criminal activity, ASG still continues its terror campaign. In February 2004, ASG successfully attacked a ferry in Manila Bay and killed over one hundred Filipino civilians. Further, in March 2004, the Filipino government narrowly missed a Madrid-style train attack and fortunately arrested the potential planners of the attack and over thirty-six kilograms of explosives (Tan, 2005: 75).

Recently, ASG has suffered serious setbacks due to a U.S.-led counterterrorist campaign on Mindanao. Both U.S. troops and Filipino Special Forces have met with some success in quashing the ASG organization and capturing or killing key ASG leaders. In fact, on 16 January 2007 Abu Sulaiman, the principal leader of ASG, was killed in a fierce gun battle with Filipino troops on Jolo Island (Gomez, 2007: 7).

The New People's Army (NPA)

Most examinations of terrorism in the Philippines focus on the threats emanating from MILF and ASG. This is largely appropriate, as these two groups offer the most consistent and dangerous terrorist threat to the Filipino people and government.

However, there is a third major group operating in the Philippines that has offered a significant terrorist threat in the past and leveled a new terror campaign in recent times. That group is the NPA. According to the MIPT-TKB, the NPA conducted seventy-eight terrorist attacks against civilian targets between 1987 and 2006. This communist terrorist group conducted a good number of these attacks between 1987 and 1992, taking an almost ten-year hiatus before starting its terror campaign again in 2000. However, it is startling that the NPA has received little or no recent scholarly attention, as this group has carried out forty-two terrorist strikes between 2000 and 2006.

Perhaps one explanation for this omission has to do with the nature of the group itself. The NPA is a Maoist organization that formed in 1969 as the guerilla arm of the Communist Party of the Philippines (CPP). The communist nature of the organization may have caused some scholars and policymakers to ignore its continuing terrorist presence in the post-Cold War era. In fact, the U.S. State Department determined in 1997 that the NPA was so short on funds, and possibly in disarray due to a split from the CCP, that it posed no significant threat (*Patterns of Global Terrorism 1997*: U.S. State Department, 1998). Despite the split from the CCP, the NPA eventually found a way to fund itself through what it dubs "revolutionary taxes." These so-called taxes amount to nothing more than extortion, but this group has been successful enough at extortion to boast an estimated 11,000 armed combatants ("The Hornets Are Disturbed," 2002: 3).

The reaction to the increased violence and terrorism from the NPA has been quite harsh. In 2002, the U.S. government declared the NPA was a terrorist organization, given the civilian targets of some of their attacks ("The Hornets Are Disturbed," 2002: 31). The U.S. government began providing aid and weaponry to the Filipino government shortly after the declaration, and by 2006, President Gloria Macapagal-Arroyo had decided to wage war on the NPA, dedicating $19 million to an attempt to wipe out the insurgency ("Fighting Rebellion," 2006: 37). But this plan may be backfiring as President Arroyo continues her campaign, which includes "extrajudicial killings" or killing by the military without a trial. By August 2006, 729 members of the NPA had been killed "extrajudicially," and the public outcry from this prompted a second failed attempt to impeach President Arroyo (Cathcart, 2006: 14).

The terrorist groups in the Philippines pose a great challenge to the stability of a state that has been attempting to transition to a stable democratic/capitalist society for decades. Each group has some legitimate claim at secession, although the MILF/ASG claim for a Muslim state or home rule is more reasonable than the NPA call for a communist revolution. Each group is engaging in terrorism and criminality, which makes it harder to negotiate a peaceful settlement or to take truces seriously. These problems are magnified by the links of some of these groups to larger regional terror groups like JI and international terror organizations like Al-Qaeda.

An Explosion of Terrorism in Thailand

Thailand has experienced an explosion in domestic terrorism that, due to data constraints — namely Polity IV variables, which end in 2003 — was not captured in our data analysis. Despite this fact, we would be remiss if we did not address the recent development of Thai terrorism. The MIPT-TKB shows a huge expansion of terrorist attacks in Thailand. This is alarming because for three decades prior to 2004, Thailand would have been considered one of the states that had very little terrorist activity. In 2004, there were 169 terrorist attacks. In 2005, there were a staggering 363 acts of terrorism, of which 360 were perpetrated by domestic groups. In 2006, there were 352, with 344 being domestic in nature. The total of terror attacks in Thailand between 2004 and 2006 alone outstrips the total for any other Southeast Asian nation over a thirty-year time period. This is a significant and dangerous development in Southeast Asia.

Again, the common theme of separatism seems to be driving the current terror campaigns in Southern Thailand. This new, forceful claim for separatism by fundamentalist Islamic groups underscores how vulnerable many Southeast Asian nations are to extremist terrorism, even if they have experienced little or no terrorism in the past. The Thai separatist/terrorist groups are hard to define as they have only a very recent track record. Further, these groups operate largely in the dense, rural, jungle hinterland of the three southernmost provinces of Thailand, which border Malaysia ("Fighting Rebellion," 2006: 38). The attacks are growing more numerous and increasingly targeting civilian populations and centers. So successful and coordinated are these little-known fundamental Islamic groups that they were able to detonate fifty bomb attacks in one day on 15 June 2006 ("Fighting Rebellion," 2006: 38).

What is most difficult about combating many terrorist groups in Asia is best characterized by the Islamic separatist movement in Thailand. Different groups, or even factions within groups, can have competing agendas and goals. In Thailand, the boundaries are blurred between "rebels with a local cause, terrorists waging a global war and self-enriching criminals" ("Fighting Rebellion," 2006: 38). A self-enriching criminal might more readily accept amnesty facing tough military or police pressure and discontinue terrorism than a person or group that is part of a global jihad. Rebels might have more to gain from a negotiated peace that includes some local rule than either criminals or global jihadis. This means that the Thai government and other Southeast Asian governments facing similar situations have to be nimble and try a multitude of counterterrorism measures in order to achieve success with diverse terror groups that have differing end goals and motivations.

In February 2004, Prime Minister Thaksin Shinawatra won a second term in office by a landslide vote, but he still had to contend with a serious separatist/terrorist threat from the southern Thai provinces of Narathiwat, Pattani, and Yala (Vatikiotis, 2006: 7). Unfortunately, Thaksin decided on a course of tough military action that resulted in the government mishandling a protest outside a police station in southern Thailand and in the deaths of eighty-five Malay Muslims (ibid.). This and other acts by the government led to a nationwide public opinion backlash that may have emboldened the extremist groups toward greater terrorist action. Some authors argue that the Muslim separatist movement in southern Thailand is not so much anti-Western as it is anti-assimilation, fueled by bungling governmental policies (Gunaratna, Acharya, and Chua, 2005: 9).

Two groups have claimed responsibility for the bulk of the attacks, Pattani United Liberation Organization (PULO) and Barisan Revolusi Nasasional (BRN) or the National Revolutionary Front, but little is known about these groups. Part of the difficulty in identifying major groups and actors early in a separatist or secessionist movement lies in the fact that the call for secession or concessions by the government had been ignored by the government, scholars, and the media prior to the terror attacks. It was only after amazingly well-coordinated and devastating terror attacks, like the one in late October 2004 that comprised over 300 attacks on military and civilian targets (Vatikiotis, 2004: 8), that the Thai government and the rest of the world took note.

Here lies one of the great conundrums of counterterrorism. It is far easier to deal with legitimate, reasonable demands by groups that could potentially resort to terrorism prior to these groups and people becoming so aggrieved that they actually resort to violence. But politics revolves around allocating scarce resources with a short time horizon, in order that the politicians can keep and retain office. As a result, the type of forward thinking suggested here rarely occurs. Even if it did, the government would still be hard pressed to determine legitimate grievances from unreasonable demands. Finally, giving into every demand may only create unrealistic future expectations by groups and people. Despite this, analysts, policymakers, and scholars need to devote a significant amount of time and research toward studying out-group demands and claims in order to help governments and international organizations craft effective counterterrorism strategy and in the hopes that another Thai explosion does not occur elsewhere.

Effectively Dealing With Terrorism in Malaysia and Singapore

Terrorism in Malaysia and Singapore is largely nonexistent. However, both the Malaysian and Singaporean governments claim to have active, militant, Islamic extremist groups operating in their respective states. Both states have engaged in a multifaceted counterterrorism strategy that has, thus far, been successful.

JI originated in Malaysia and has been conducting a devastating terror campaign in Indonesia. However, JI has always had plans to expand its operations to other Southeast Asian nations such as Singapore. Even prior to the 11 September 2001 terror attack on the United States, both Malaysian and Singaporean governments have been cracking down on suspected terrorist and terror groups (Bakar, 2005: 110). In January 2002, the government of Singapore used its recently gained powers under the Internal Security Act to arrest and detain fifteen suspected terrorists (ibid.). Thirteen of the fifteen were alleged to be directly tied to JI. In Malaysia, both former Prime Minister Mahatir Mohammed and his successor, Abdullah Badawi, have been very forceful in their denouncement of terrorism as "un-Islamic" (Bakar, 2005: 112). While Prime Minister Badawi has promised a more liberal democracy to Malaysian citizens, he has also emphasized the need to remain firm in dealing with terrorists (Bakar, 2005: 122).

Overall, Singapore and Malaysia have had a successful track record in preventing terrorist attacks. Both states have used heavy-handed means to thwart or dismantle terrorist groups and their attempted attacks. Singapore treats terrorism as the number one and most immediate threat to their nation and economy (Acharya, 2006: 308). Successes for Malaysia and Singapore include the arrests of key JI commanders, including the chief operational officer, Hambali, and the spiritual leader, Abu Bakr Baasyir (Acharya, 2006: 307).

Despite these setbacks, intelligence reports indicate that JI continues to serve as a regional conduit for Al-Qaeda. While Singapore has successfully thwarted several planned attacks by JI, the infusion of Afghan combat experience and the militant teachings that Southeast Asians receive in the Madrassahs of Afghanistan and Pakistan have raised both the sophistication and deadliness of local terror groups in Singapore and the region (Desker, 2003: 495).

Both the Malaysian and the Singaporean governments do not rely solely on "sticks" when dealing with terrorists. While violent extremists have been effectively dealt with through what some might categorize as heavy-handed tactics, both Malaysia and Singapore have attempted to address some of the legitimate grievances of the larger Muslim communities. In 1970, the Malaysian government introduced the New Economic Policy (NEP), which offered scholarships to Malay Muslims in the hopes of broadening the Muslim middle class (Kadir, 2004: 209). Singapore introduced new institutions, but not an affirmative action policy, in an attempt to improve the economic position of the small Malay Muslim minority in their society (ibid.). Both of these policies attack the base of support for terrorism and make it more difficult for groups to find support or recruits.

Kampulan Mujahidin Malaysia (KMM)

There is an interesting radical Islamic group operating in Malaysia that has, thus far, perpetrated no terrorist attacks within Malaysia and can only be linked cursorily to terror attacks and organizations that operate outside of Malaysia. KMM is a radical group in Malaysia whose leaders openly state that rebellion is not out of the question when a corrupt government fails to carry out Sharia law (Tan, 2005: 75). A key leader in KMM, Abu Jibril, has been detained since 2001 for alleged terrorist activity (ibid.), but linking KMM directly to terrorist attacks is difficult. One KMM member is alleged to have hosted some of the 11 September 2001 Al-Qaeda suicide bombers, and KMM is accused of ferrying in food supplies to Laskar Jihad in Indonesia (Desker, 2003: 498). Despite these allegations, it is still difficult to label KMM a terrorist organization for the simple fact that no terror attacks have ever been directly linked to it.

The reader may wonder why we include KMM in our discussion of terrorism and terrorist organization in Southeast Asia. The answer is twofold. First, one of the defining characteristics of terrorism in Southeast Asia is the regional organization. There a great deal of incredibly sophisticated organization between groups. Most of this organization filters through larger umbrella groups like JI or Al-Qaeda and these groups will call on others, like KMM, for support and resupply. When engaging in counterterrorism, policymakers might find an easier time influencing support groups rather than butting heads directly with the terrorist organizations. Eroding the foundation might cause the roof to collapse.

The second reason relates to the recent Thai experience. As previously explained, terrorism in Thailand was almost nonexistent until 2004. In the years since, Thailand has moved into the top position in terms of the total number of terrorist attacks. KMM could be a terror group waiting to boil over, so it bears particularly close scrutiny going forward.

Overall, Malaysia and Singapore have achieved a great deal of success in combating potential terrorism in their nations through a combination of hard-line and conciliatory domestic initiatives. But the threat in these two states still exists, and Al-Qaeda and JI continue to have agendas that target both states. Vigilance is the key for these two governments as they continue their multifaceted counterterrorism efforts.

Democracy, Poverty, Civilization, and Instability

Why did Al-Qaeda turn to Southeast Asia? First, there is a connection with the Mujahadeen. It is estimated that between 1,000 and 1,500 Southeast Asian Muslims fought with the Mujahadeen against Soviet occupation (Abuza, 2002: 431). Also, fundamental Islamic groups have leveled most of their complaints against the domestic economic and governmental systems. Zachary Abuza notes that fundamental Islamic groups often have legitimate complaints regarding economic privation and a lack of religious freedom (2002: 433). These real grievances can be stoked by Al-Qaeda to translate into terrorist responses against secular governments. In short, Al-Qaeda would have a far more difficult time finding allies and comfort if there were not real problems underpinning many Southeast Asian governments and economies.

The way one views democratization in Southeast Asia depends on perspective. The Polity IV data set does not categorize any of the states in Southeast Asia as stable, established democracies. But even in the Polity IV data set one can see that in the past five or ten years there have been real democratic gains in Indonesia, Malaysia, Thailand, and Singapore. The Philippines, too, has been striving toward the goal of democracy for decades but the goal has yet to be realized.

Thailand is a special case that deserves a little more elaboration. While Thaksin Shinawatra won an astounding landslide for his second term, this term was cut short by a bloodless military coup in 2006. Thaksin was accused of mishandling the Muslim uprising in Southern Thailand and also accused of abusing his power through the over 3,000 alleged "extrajudicial" killings ordered during his war on drugs (McGirk, 2006: 2). This was Thailand's first coup d'état in fifteen years and it led some to immediately question Thailand's democracy and stability (Mydons and Fuller, 2006: A1). But Thailand is somewhat unique in its democratic development. While the coup in 2006 is an undeniable setback and probably indicative of instability, it may also be a sign for hope going forward. As Elliott Kulick and Dick Wilson argue, coups in Thailand may not be a sign of political decay (1994: 27–28). The Thai military learned in the 1970s that it had a vested interest in stopping corruption and promoting democratic capitalism because that system produced the most regular payments to military commanders and personnel. As a result, the Thai military has often intervened when Thailand has fallen off the democratic course or slipped into deep corruption. While Thailand has experienced great instability, one can be somewhat hopeful that the ship is righting itself.

It is interesting that Indonesia, a fledgling democratic experiment of less than a decade, the Philippines, a consistently unstable and struggling democratic experiment, and Thailand, a state that recently suffered a military takeover, are the three states experiencing the greatest amount of terrorism. Singapore and Malaysia, two very stable governments and economies, have any potential terrorism problem under control. We could add Vietnam, although obviously not democratic, to the list of stable governments with flourishing economies and no terrorism. Unfortunately for democracy proponents, this does not bode well for the argument that Western-style democracy is the panacea for terrorism.

Poverty, too, seems to correlate well with terrorism in Southeast Asia. Several authors have noted that poverty, especially privation aimed at Muslim or fundamental Muslim minorities, seems like a sure-fire recipe for separatist movements and the development of terrorism. In a continuation of this argument, Lawrence Reardon argues that economic dislocation caused by the 1997/1998 Asian financial crisis "put into question the legitimacy of the government's development strategies" (2005: 198). This allowed extremist groups to spring up when local schools failed to deliver to Muslim minorities or when governments, like the Suharto regime in Indonesia, exploited fundamental Muslim populations in resource rich areas.

There is a Clash of Civilizations element to the terrorism in Southeast Asia as well. Almost all of the terror groups in Southeast Asia are fundamental Islamic and all prefer Western, foreign, and non-Muslim targets. But the Clash of Civilizations Thesis only goes so far in explaining terrorism in Southeast Asia. Not every nation with a significant Muslim population is experiencing terrorism. Also, the largest Muslim nation in the world, Indonesia, is experiencing a great deal of terrorism and Muslims in Indonesia have been victims of JI. Further, many of these terrorist organizations are partially or even primarily motivated by separatism or secession and not a true hatred of cultures different from their own. Yet it cannot be denied that there is a heavy cultural component to the terrorism of Southeast Asia.

Unfortunately, in the end it appears that terrorism in Southeast Asia is too complex to be addressed by one single policy or initiative. There is no silver bullet, such as forcing democracy on the nations of Southeast Asia, that will address all of the underlying motivations for the disparate terror groups. It appears that states fare best when they are stable politically and economically, approach threats with a multifaceted counterterrorism strategy that includes "carrots and sticks," and are willing to concede when legitimate complaints are voiced. The best thing the U.S. and international organizations could do to help combat terrorism in Southeast Asia is to support legitimate military efforts against unreasonable terror groups and help unstable economies develop a foundation that produces a large and diverse middle class.

Note

1. David Wright-Neville reported that supporters of MNLF were "Taussig" speaking, but we agree with Kit Collier that the correct spelling is "Tausug."

References

Abuza, Zachary. (December 2002). "Tentacles of Terror: Al-Qaeda's Southeast Asian Network." *Contemporary Southeast Asia*. Volume 24, Number 3: 427–65.

Acharya, Arabinda. (2006). "India and Southeast Asia in the Age of Terror: Building Partnerships for Peace." *Contemporary Southeast Asia*. Volume 28, Number 2: 297–321.

Bakar, Osman. (April 2005). "The Impact of the American War on Terror in Malaysian Islam." *Islam and Christian-Muslim Relations*. Volume 16, Number 2: 107–27.

Banloi, Rommel C. (August 2002). "The Role of Philippine–American Relations in the Global Campaign Against Terrorism: Implications for Regional Security." *Contemporary Southeast Asia*. Volume 24, Number 2: 294–312.

Brenner, Suzanne. (1996). "Reconstructing Self and Society: Javanese Muslim Women and 'The Veil.'" *American Ethnologist*. Volume 23, Number 4: 673–97.

Brumberg, Daniel. (Autumn 2001). "Dissonant Politics in Iran and Indonesia." *Political Science Quarterly*. Volume 116, Number 3: 381–411.

Castro, Renato Cruz De. (2004). "Addressing International Terrorism in Southeast Asia: A Matter of Strategic or Functional Approach?" *Contemporary Southeast Asia*. Volume 26, Number 2: 193–217.

Cathcart, Brian. (28 August 2006). "The Killings Gather Pace." *New Statesman*. Volume 135, Issue 4807: 14.

Collier, Kit. (2006). "Terrorism: Evolving Regional Alliances and State Failure in Mindanao." In *Southeast Asian Affairs 2006*. Daljit Singh and Lorraine Carlos Salazar, Editors. Singapore: Institute of Southeast Asian Studies: 26–38.

Desker, Barry. (2003). "The Jemaah Islamiyah (JI) Phenomenon in Singapore." *Contemporary Southeast Asia*. Volume 25, Number 3: 489–507.

"Fighting Rebellion the Wrong Way." (1 July 2006). *Economist*. Volume 380, Issue 8484: 37–38.

Gentzkow, Matthew A., and Jesse M. Shapiro. (Summer 2004). "Media, Education and Anti-Americanism in the Muslim World." *Journal of Economic Perspectives*. Volume 18, Number 3: 117–33.

George, Kenneth M. (August 1998). "Designs on Indonesia's Muslim Communities." *Journal of Asian Studies*. Volume 57, Number 3: 693–713.

Gomez, Jim. (18 January 2007). "Slain Militant Had Been Sought for Years." *Seattle Times*: 7.

Gunaratna, Rohan. (2002). *Inside Al-Qaeda: Global Network of Terror*. London: Hurst and Company.

Gunaratna, Rohan, Arabinda Acharya, and Sabrina Chua. (2005). *Conflict and Terrorism in Southern Thailand*. Singapore: Marshall Cavendish International.

Hefner, Robert. (1993). "Islam, State and Civil Society: ICMI and the Struggle for the Indonesian Middle Class." *Indonesia*. Volume 56: 1–37.

"The Hornets Are Disturbed." (31 August 2002). *Economist*. Volume 264, Issue 8288: 31.

Kadir, Suzaina. (June 2004). "Mapping Muslim Politics in Southeast Asia After September 11." *The Pacific Review*. Volume 17, Number 2: 199–222.

Kulick, Elliott, and Dick Wilson. (1994). *Thailand's Turn: Profits of a New Dragon*. New York: St. Martin's Press.

Liddle, R. William. (August 1996). "The Islamic Turn in Indonesia." *The Journal of Asian Studies*. Volume 55, Number 3: 613–34.

McGirk, Jan. (20 September 2006). "Billionaire Businessman Who Sparked His Own Downfall." *The London Independent*: 2.

Murphy, Dan. (2001). "The Philippine Branch of Terror." *Christian Science Monitor*. Volume 93 (October 26): 4.

Mydons, Seth, and Thomas Fuller. (20 September 2006). "With Premier of U.N., Thai Military Stages Coup." *The New York Times*: A1.

Pew Global Attitudes Project. (2007). "Rising Environmental Concern in 47-Nation Survey: Global Unease With Major Powers." *47-Nation Pew Global Attitudes Survey*. Washington, D.C.: Pew Research Center.

Qadir, Shoukat. (2001). "The Concept of International Terrorism: An Interim Study of South Asia." *The Round Table*. Volume 360: 333–43.

Ramakrishna, Kumar. (2005). "Delegitimizing Global Jihadi Ideology in Southeast Asia." *Contemporary Southeast Asia*. Volume 27, Number 3: 347–69.

Reardon, Lawrence C. (2005). "Interpreting Political Islam's Challenge to Southeast Asia: International Terrorism, Nationalism and Rational Choice." In *Democratic Development and Political Terrorism: The Global Perspective*. William Crotty, Editor. Boston: Northeastern University Press: 195–226.

Ressa, Maria. (2003). *Southeast Asia*. New York: Free Press.

Robles, Raissa. (2007). "Rebel Warns Abu Sayyaf Thrives on Conflict." *South China Morning Post*. (February 11): 9.

Scarpello, Fabio. (2007a). "A Severe Police Crackdown Last Month on Suspected Militants May Rekindle Sectarian Tensions." *Christian Science Monitor*. (February 5): 7.

Scarpello, Fabio. (2007b). "Crackdown on Islamists 'Could Backfire,' Militants Could Just Find New Base, Former Rebel Leader Says." *South China Morning Post*. (February 12): 10.

Shuja, Sharif. (Winter 2006). "Terrorism in Southeast Asia: Australia's Security Threat and Response." *Contemporary Review*. Volume 288, Issue 1633: 445–61.

Tan, Andrew T. H. (2005). "Singapore: Recent Developments in Terrorism and Japan's Role." *Asia-Pacific Review*. Volume 12, Number 2: 71–91.

United States State Department. (April 1998). *Patterns of Global Terrorism: 1997*. Department of State Publication 10535. Washington, D.C.: Office of the Secretary of State and Office of the Coordinator for Counterterrorism.

Vatikiotis, Michael. (2006). "Southeast Asia in 2005: Strength in the Face of Adversity." In *Southeast Asian Affairs 2006*. Daljit Singh and Lorriane Carlos Salazar, Editors. Singapore: Institute of Southeast Asian Studies: 3–14.

Vitug, M. D., and G. M. Gloria. (2000). *Under the Crescent Moon: Rebellion in Mindanao*. Quezon City: Ateneo Center for Social Policy and Public Affairs.

Wright-Newville, David. (March 2004). "Dangerous Dynamics: Activists, Militants and Terrorists in Southeast Asia." *The Pacific Review*. Volume 17, Number 1: 27–46.

CHAPTER 8

East Asia: A Lack of Sustained Terrorism

I N SHARP CONTRAST TO SOUTH and Southeast Asia are the East Asian nations of China, Japan, Mongolia, North Korea, South Korea, and Taiwan. These six states account for approximately one-fifth of the world's population, yet these same six states only accounted for 116 terror events during our nearly thirty-year period of study. Contrast that with Indonesia, which had 188 terror incidents, and India, which suffered 1,176 terror attacks during the same time period. Further, the great bulk of terrorist incidents emanate from one East Asian nation: Japan. Japan suffered a total of sixty-five terror attacks from 1975 to 2003. As one author states, "East Asia suffered fewer terrorist attacks than Europe or the Middle East" (Kurlantzick, 2001: 20).

Even where terror arises, the impact is not overly great. South Korea, for example, has suffered thirty-six terror attacks from 1975 to 2003, but these attacks have only accounted for less than fifty injuries and only ten deaths (MIPT-TKB). Further, South Korea has suffered no terror attacks since 1997. Therefore, whatever weak, disorganized terror campaign previously operated in South Korea, it appears to have collapsed.

The statistics on Japan can also be quite misleading if not examined carefully. The sixty-five terror attacks Japan has suffered produced 5,000 injuries and only nineteen fatalities (MIPT-TKB). Despite the high number of injuries, almost all of the injuries, and most of the fatalities, were produced in one major attack by Aum Shinrikyo.

On 20 March 1995, the Aum Shinrikyo cult unleashed a sarin gas attack upon unsuspecting commuters riding the through the Tokyo subway system. This single attack accounts for 5,000 of the total 5,107 total injuries reported from 1975 to 2003 and twelve of the nineteen fatalities. This means that the other sixty-four terror events produced very few injuries and almost no fatalities. This is one of the inherent shortcomings of any statistical measure of terrorism or terrorist events. Unfortunately, statistical measures often produce a very incomplete picture of the nature of terrorism or terrorist movements within a state or a region. This is one of the main reasons state and regional experts are, and will remain, important in studying and combating terrorism.

There is some terrorism occurring in East Asia. But the number of incidents is small; there are almost no coherent, sustained terror campaigns, and the terrorism that does occur often produces few injuries and almost no death. Explaining why East Asia is so unique in its lack of terrorism will be instructive toward an understanding of what prevents terrorism and what governments can do to successfully counter terror movements.

China and the Uygur Separatist Movement

China, the largest state in the world, with a population of over 1.3 billion, has experienced almost no terrorism. Given the size of China's population, this is an amazing feat. It must be noted that despite the large population, China is fairly homogeneous. Ninety-two percent of its 1.3 billion residents are Han Chinese.

Homogeneity is not the only factor keeping terrorism in check in China. One scholar argues that Chinese culture does not lend itself to the "mindset of terrorism." Suzanne Ogden points out that there is a social norm against violent outbursts. Children are often punished for fighting, even in self-defense, and in adult life, political protesters are generally supported in their efforts by the larger Chinese public unless the protesters become violent or engage in property destruction (2005: 238). The Chinese Communist Party (CCP) has shown a proclivity for handing out autonomous governmental regions to differing ethnicities (as well as states, like Hong Kong and Tibet, that have been subsumed by the People's Republic of China) and a penchant for economic development programs in these same regions. But as we show, not all autonomous regions were made or treated the same by the CCP.

Despite being an almost homogeneous Han nation, China is large enough in terms of both land mass and population to contain fifty-six distinct ethnic groups with distinct cultures, languages, ethnicities, and religions (Zhu and Blachford, 2006: 329). All of the ethnic minorities are small in comparison to the overall size of China's population. The largest ethnic minority, the Zhuang, comprise only 15.5 million of China's 1.32 billion citizens (Zhu and Blachford, 2006: 335). Having said this, 15 million is the equivalent population of some small European states; hence one must consider that proportional size gives way to absolute size at some point and that millions of ethnically distinct people within a state of any size could certainly pose a significant terrorist threat.

The Chinese government is fortunate in that twelve of the thirteen largest ethnic populations, those numbering in the millions, are fairly well dispersed throughout multiple provinces in China. Only one, the Uygur, are heavily concentrated in a single province. Further, of China's diverse ethnic minorities, only the Uygur have not demonstrated a predisposition to peaceful coexistence (Zhu and Blachford, 2006: 337).

There are many valid reasons underpinning the sometimes violent Uygur separatist movement. The Xinjiang province has been home to many ethnic groups and religions from ancient times. Since the Western Han Dynasty (206 B.C. to 24 A.D.), the Xinjiang province and its diverse people have been an almost inseparable part of the Chinese nation ("History and Development," 2004; Zhu and Blachford, 2006: 337). In fact, official histories written in China insist that "Uygurs and other non-Hans were made to be ruled by others" (Bovingdon, 2002: 46). Despite these written histories and almost unbroken Chinese rule, Xinjiang did know some brief periods of quasi-independence. Xinjiang was "the Turkistan Islamic Republic of Eastern Turkistan during 1933–1934 and the Eastern Turkistan Republic from 1944 to 1949" (Zhu and Blachford, 2006: 337). This makes logical sense as the Uygur people have more in common, ethnically and culturally, with the people of Turkistan than they have in common with the Han supermajority. Currently, separatist pressure is mounting as the independence of many Central Asian states has impacted Uygur thinking. As Bovingdon relates, the Uygur population now finds itself as one of the few Turkic people "with a substantial population but no state" (2002: 52).

Some concessions were made by the CCP in 1955 to keep the Uygurs from seceding when the Xinjiang Uygur Autonomous Region (XUAR) was created. The CCP has claimed, from the outset, that the diverse peoples populating XUAR are free to control their own political destiny. But the XUAR is, in reality, one of the least autonomous regions in China. While all the heads of governmental prefectures and other officials elected from the populace tend to be Uygurs, "virtually every Party organ, from the state level to the XUAR, is Han. It is common knowledge that the Party head at every level outranks the corresponding government official" (Bovingdon, 2002: 57).

Not surprisingly, the false governmental autonomy in XUAR and the unfulfilled promises of free speech for the Uygur people led to political unrest in the region. In February 2002, a small group of Uygurs protested in the streets of the city of Ghulja. The People's Armed Police reacted with violence in an attempt to stop the demonstration. Several police and dozens, possibly hundreds, of Uygurs were killed (Bovingdon, 2002: 39). The reaction from the Uygurs was a series of coordinated bomb attacks on three separate buses in Xinjiang's capital city (ibid.). As these events indicate, false promises of autonomy and freedom coupled with violent attempts to stop political protests led directly to Uygur terrorism.

Poor treatment of the people in the XUAR has led to bitter resentment and distrust between the Han and Uygur. Results from a recent survey (taken in 2001 in XUAR) are illustrative of this point. In terms of linguistic fractionalization, 99 percent of the Uygurs found the Chinese language to be either useful or very useful. Only 82 percent of the Han Chinese living in the XUAR felt similarly about the Uygur language (Yee, 2005: 38). Roughly 43 percent of the Uygurs surveyed felt that relations between Uygur and Han colleagues at work were poor, and 48 percent of the Hans also found these cross-ethnic working relationships were poor (Yee, 2005: 40). Only 34 percent of Hans surveyed reported being happy when working with Uygurs, while 44 percent of Uygurs were happy when working with Hans (Yee, 2005: 42).

These types of poll results point toward a discordant relationship between Han and Uygur ethnicities. Such a lack of congeniality between the ethnicities, coupled with hard feelings arising from violent police crackdowns and violent terrorist responses, indicates that the XUAR could continue to pose a terrorist threat in China for the foreseeable future.

There is some hope on the horizon that may lessen terrorist and separatist threats in China. The way the CCP is treating the Uygur and the XUAR is not the norm. China has survived as a multi-ethnic state largely due to CCP policies aimed at maintaining national unity (Zhu and Blachford, 2006: 338). Further, current Chinese leaders like Hu Jintao have inherited and maintained policies started by Deng Xiaoping that are aimed at quelling ethnic separatist sentiments through economic and social development (Zhu and Blachford, 2006: 339). The CCP, like the governments in Malaysia and Singapore, has had some success with efforts in provinces outside of Xinjiang. For example, CCP policies have produced a vibrant economy in Inner Mongolia that far outstrips the neighboring Mongolian economy. This has resulted in no secessionist rumblings in Inner Mongolia (Ogden, 2005: 233).

There is some evidence that CCP domestic policies are producing economic benefits for XUAR. In 2005, XUAR foreign trade amounted to $8 billion, which represented a 41 percent increase over the 2004 figure. Further, of the twelve Western Chinese Provinces, XUAR was number one in foreign trade (Bondarenko, 2006: 64). The XUAR also serves as an important conduit for an international pipeline to China. This pipeline produces 20 million tons of oil a year that feeds directly into the growing Chinese industrial complex (Bondarenko, 2006: 74).

In the end, China has some sizable ethnicities to contend with. But moderate or even conciliatory domestic policies have served to keep most violent terrorism at bay. Only in the XUAR has China experienced any sustained terrorism and even there the number of events is still quite limited. If the CCP continues to develop the XUAR economically, and if violent police repression can be reined in, it is very possible that even this minor terrorist threat will evaporate in the near future.

Japan's Surprising Terrorism Problem

Japan is one of the most stable and affluent democracies in the world. With a history of stable democratic governance since the end of World War II, the third-largest economy in the world, and a sizable middle class, it is surprising that Japan has suffered so many terror attacks. Terrorism seems to have hit Japan in two distinct phases. The first phase started around late 1960 or early 1970 and was a product of the Cold War. These terrorists pushed for a communist Japan and this type of terrorism has, for the most part, died out. Around 1980, a new phase in Japanese terrorism began with the development of extremist religious cults. Neither phase has been particularly effective in producing massive casualties through terrorism, with the exception of the Aum Shinrikyo (Supreme Truth) sarin gas attacks on the Tokyo subway system, nor has either movement produced any significant policy changes from the Japanese government. But both terrorism campaigns had longevity in a stable and affluent democratic system. Unfortunately, many scholars believe or are hopeful that affluence and democracy provide inoculation from sustained terror campaigns. This is why explaining the Japanese case is so crucial to our understanding of terrorism and the development of effective counterterrorism strategies.

The Japanese Left-Wing Terrorist Movement

Japanese terrorists are somewhat unique in that the overriding impetus is not religious, ethnic, or secessionist in nature. In fact, even the early communist movement had less to do with communism and more to do with a general discontent with Japanese government, Japanese ties to America, and a perception of unequal or inadequate education. Terrorists, too, tend to be the privileged in Japan (Crenshaw, 1981: 383), whereas in most of the other cases we have observed that terrorists tend to come from impoverished, repressed, and downtrodden classes in society. Japanese terrorists are also impatient. Political movements in Japan critical of Japanese government tend to skip attempts to find popular support for their movements and move directly into terrorist confrontation with the government (Crenshaw, 1981: 388). Much of the membership for these left-wing groups came from students dissatisfied with unequal educational opportunities. When radical student protests in Japan failed to bring any governmental policy change, these students quickly resorted to terrorist tactics (Jenkins, 1986: 775).

Japanese left-wing protests were numerous beginning in 1964, far outshadowing left-wing movements in Europe and the United States (Katzenstein, 2003: 743). Initially, students became increasingly militant as their demands went unmet. Many radical extremists began using *gebabo* or violence staves and donned native African helmets during demonstrations (Box and McCormack, 2004: 92–93). Some low-level violence was even perpetrated by these groups when they engaged in Molotov cocktail bombings of several police stations (ibid.).

All of the left-wing terrorist organizations recruited members from these early protests. The Japanese Red Army (JRA), for example, recruited its leaders from ex-student radicals (Shimbori et al., 1980: 141). Several small but increasingly violent left-wing groups formed in colleges and universities and actually perpetrated some violent acts against fellow students. Some very early left-wing groups, like Chukaku-ha (Middle Core Faction), which formed in 1957, began by attacking other groups with slightly different leftist philosophies. On 4 August 1970, members of Chukaku-ha beat to death a member of the far more left-wing group Kakumaru-ha (Revolutionary Marxist Faction). On 14 August 1970, members of Kakumaru-ha beat and stabbed several Chukaku-ha members but produced no fatalities (Beer, 1971: 80). On 8 November 1972, a student of Waseda University was lynched in a classroom full of students by members of Kakumaru-ha for allegedly spying on them for Chukaku-ha (Farnsworth, 1973: 119).

Chukaku-ha would go on to become a fairly formidable domestic terrorist group in Japan, perpetrating several notable terrorism events in Japan. For the most part, Chukaku-ha tried to produce property damage rather than casualties. However, Chukaku-ha seemed to ramp up frequency and violence in the 1980s, prior to largely dissipating with the other leftist groups after the Cold War ended. For example, in 1986, Chukaku-ha launched a rocket attack at the downtown palace residence where leaders from the major world economic powers were meeting for the Tokyo summit (Katzenstein, 2003: 744). The rocket attack missed the target and landed in the street near the Canadian embassy, causing no casualties, but it was clear that the intent was to kill or maim influential leaders meeting at the Tokyo summit. While not nearly as prevalent or strong as it was in the 1980s, Chukaku-ha remains a terrorist threat. The last attributable attack by this group occurred on 2 October 2001, when an improvised explosive device went off damaging the car of a Chiba prefecture governmental official who had been working on Narita airport (MIPT-TKB). Chukaku-ha had been attempting to bomb this particular airport and took umbrage at the official's work on the airport.

The Red Army Faction (RAF[1]) perpetrated few terrorist attacks as disorganization and internal bickering quickly led to this group splitting into three separate terror groups only three years after the RAF formed in 1969 (Steinhoff, 1989: 725; Box and McCormack, 2004: 95). But the Red Army represented the whole left-wing movement best with its constant declarations of "war on the bourgeoisie"; it used terrorist bombings and hijackings in an attempt to push the Japanese government toward communism (Box and McCormack, 2004: 95). Members of the Red Army Faction hijacked a plane on 31 March 1970 using swords. They did not use violence against any of the passengers and eventually diverted the flight to North Korea, where these terrorists remain to this day (Beer, 1971: 80).

Fleeing to another state in hopes of fighting another day, fighting for the communist cause abroad, or simply fleeing law enforcement was common among the left-wing extremist groups. When the RAF split into three factions in 1972, two of the three newly formed factions fled Japan. In fact, the several dozen or so RAF members who fled to North Korea immediately split from the RAF to form the Yodo Group. The Yodo Group immediately adopted Kim Il Sung's communist philosophy and narrowed its communist aspirations from a world revolution to simply liberating

Japan from capitalism and democracy (Box and McCormack, 2004: 95). But this group has yet to show that it has gained any ground toward this goal, and the Yodo Group poses very little in the way of a terrorist threat toward Japan.

The Japanese police were well aware of the growing left-wing militancy in Japan in the 1960s and 1970s. There was a conscious decision made to pressure, observe, and intimidate certain groups that were deemed most dangerous. The Japanese Red Army (Nihon Sekigun or JRA) was a group that police targeted for pressure. The tactic worked and JRA relocated to the Middle East, affiliating with terror groups there and helping to perpetrate the Tel-Aviv Airport attack in 1972. The members also blew up a Singaporean oil refinery in 1974, and helped to bomb the United States and Swedish embassies in Kuala Lumpur in 1975 (Katzenstein, 2003: 744). Additionally, they robbed banks in order to fund their operations (Box and McCormack, 2004: 96). The JRA was able to carry out international terror events and help domestic terror groups it was sympathetic to in the Middle East, but the main goal of overturning democratic rule in Japan went unrealized.

The JRA slowly waned in power and prestige as it languished in the Middle East. The Oslo Peace Agreement of 1993 accelerated the JRA withdrawal form the Middle East and significantly cut its base of support there (Katzenstein, 2003: 745). The U.S. war on terrorism further diminished its capacity until its terrorist, extremist threat has fairly well ended (ibid.).

The United Red Army (Rengo Sekigun or URA) was the only one of the three splinter groups to stay in Japan to fight for communism. The URA hoped to coordinate an international communist movement and "planned to serve as the guerillas of the Japanese revolutions, coordinating their activities with those of their comrades of North Korea and the Middle East" (Box and McCormack, 2004: 97). The URA targeted police and other governmental targets but the police were fairly apathetic toward the group (Steinhoff, 1989: 727). The URA was not very well supported, but it had an internal organization that boasted a weapons research division comprised of chemistry, medical, and physics students. This group produced the *pachinko ball* hand grenade, which was constructed of tightly packed dynamite forced into a round metal container in which Peace Brand cigarettes were sold and topped with a fuse (Steinhoff, 1989: 728). The URA self-destructed in 1972 when the leadership met in a hut on Asama mountain. The meeting was supposed to unify group ideology and organization but ended as a bloody purge where some members were tortured and killed. The police surrounded the hut and a firefight ensued that resulted in several dead police officers and URA members (Box and McCormack, 2004: 98). The group's activities ended soon after.

Religious Extremism in Japan

As most of the left-wing terrorism in Japan was ending, a new, far more dangerous brand of terrorism was taking root. Religious cult terrorism began to take hold in the 1980s, best exemplified by the Aum Shinrikyo (Aum Supreme Truth) religious cult. Aum Shinrikyo organized in 1987 and claimed to have as many as 10,000 members in Japan (and a like number in Russia and the United States by the mid-1990s) (Metraux, 1995: 1140). Despite being recognized as a legitimate religion by the Japanese government, Aum Shinrikyo bears all of the hallmarks of being a cult. As Daniel Metraux explained, Aum Shinrikyo "is a small voluntary group of strict believers who choose to live apart from the world" (1995: 1142). He went on to note that this cult totally dominates the lives of its membership (ibid.). Aum Shinrikyo slipped into the category of criminal cult when the attacks on government and civilians in Japan began. Besides engaging in terrorism, Aum Shinrikyo's leaders are alleged to have abducted and killed some members and enemies of the cult and manufactured and sold illegal narcotics (Metraux, 1995: 1143).

Prior to resorting to terrorism, Aum Shinrikyo attempted a peaceful takeover of the government through competitive election. In the 1990 Japanese general election, twenty-five Aum Shinrikyo candidates ran under their Sanskrit names and a platform of religious doctrine, including constant warnings of the apocalypse (Box and McCormack, 2004: 102). All candidates failed miserably and the blow to Shoko Asahara, the spiritual leader and founder, was great. A change in tactics was called for. Aum Shinrikyo became more militant and began to incorporate hard brainwashing tactics, including extreme sleep and food deprivation, that resulted in a few cult members' deaths (ibid.). The cult also began to produce AK-47 rifles and began a research division to develop biological weapons (Box and McCormack, 2004: 103). The biological research division began in 1990 and was able to culture and experiment with botulin toxin, anthrax, cholera, and Q fever (Olson, 1999: 514). By 1995, Aum Shinrikyo scientists had produced a fair amount of sarin gas as well.

All of the weapons research, development, and procurement was funded through savings turned over by cult members, fraud, narcotic sales, and extortion (Box and McCormack, 2004: 103; Metraux, 1995: 1143). Aum Shinrikyo's most famous and widely attributed attack occurred in March 1995, killing twelve and injuring an estimated 5,000 (Larimer, 2002: 23). The Japanese police had been suspicious of Aum Shinrikyo prior to the attacks. Authorities had uncovered and raided several hidden laboratories that contained toxic chemicals and decontamination chambers prior to the March 1995 attack (Fedarko and Kunii, 1995: 18). Further, members had attempted two biological attacks previous to the sarin gas attack — one in June 1993 in which members unsuccessfully attempted to spray anthrax spores from the roof of a building in Tokyo (Box and McCormack, 2004: 103).

Despite police involvement in the communist terrorist and the religious extremist terrorist waves, several scholars blame law enforcement officials for reacting too slowly and in a far too conciliatory a fashion. The Japanese government is loathe to cause alarm or move against a perceived threat in anything less than a slow, methodical fashion. In the case of Aum Shinrikyo, the government lacked public support, as most Japanese viewed the cult as too bizarre to actually pose a threat (Katzenstein, 2003: 747). The already slow predisposition of governmental officials became even more lethargic without public outcry or alarm.

Others point to a weak overall government that would do little even if there was popular outcry. The JRA hijacked a Japan Air Lines jet in 1977 and demanded money and the release of JRA terrorists from jail. The Japanese government eventually paid $6 million to the hijackers and released the convicted terrorists, showing weakness that was not shown by the United States or European governments when they dealt with their own left-wing terrorists (Pyle, 1982: 234). Weakness permeates the government currently as the Diet was unsuccessful in its bid to outlaw the criminal cult. Further, Aum Shinrikyo now derives most of its income from the sale of computers and software systems and has even acted as a subsubcontractor to the National Defense Agency and National Police Agency (Katzenstein, 2003: 747).

Terrorism of a Different Kind in South Korea

South Korea had thirty-six terrorism incidents between 1975 and 2003. This is high only in comparison to other East Asian nations. Thirty-six terrorism events for the states we examined places South Korea well into the bottom third. Further, according to the MIPT-TKB, these attacks produced only thirty-two injuries and seven fatalities. But this total, as well as what acts constitute terrorism, are in dispute. The South Korean case is important in shedding light on the massive problem of determining what is and is not a terrorist act. The South Korean case is also important because it is, ultimately, a success case. There have been no documented terror attacks since 1997. This does not mean that the threat of terrorism is nonexistent, but it does mean that something has intervened that has resulted in the end of a terror campaign or at least a long hiatus.

The vast majority of the terrorist threat for South Korea emanates from its neighbor to the north. Sang-Hyun Lee argues that agents sympathetic to the North Korean government and reunification of North and South Korea under a communist dictatorship have resorted to terrorism because communist sympathizers cannot force a regime change in South Korea through direct confrontation with South Korea's armed forces (2003: 30). A reliance on asymmetric warfare is a hallmark not only of North Korean sympathizers but also the North Korean government itself. An often overlooked reason underlying the pariah status of North Korea, especially now that Kim Jong-Il has embarked on a campaign to produce medium-range nuclear ballistic missiles, is the fact that North Korea has allegedly funded a long campaign of terror attacks against South Korea (Kurlantzick, 2002: 20).

The bulk of terror attacks against South Korea occurred in the 1960s. By the 1970s, the three major security concerns were "the possibility of another North Korean invasion; North Korean sponsored terrorism; and South Korea's gradual but increasingly costly participation in the Vietnamese conflict from the mid-1960s" (Chung Min Lee, 2003: 289). To a certain extent, all three of these threats have lessened considerably. The possibility of a North Korean invasion of South Korea seems very remote. The North Korean economy is failing under direct communist control and the weight of U.S. economic sanctions in response to Kim Jong-Il's nuclear weapons program. In fact, South Korean citizens have shown a great willingness to discuss a peaceful reconciliation between North and South Korea, which many citizens feel is being hindered by U.S. foreign policy that has placed North Korea on the "Axis of Evil" and continues to label North Korea as a sponsor of international terrorism (Anderson, 2005: 1–2). North Korean-sponsored terrorism has largely ended and the Vietnam conflict ended decades ago. As we discuss later, we do not mean to imply that the North Korean terrorist threat has completely dissipated.

The attacks that North Korea is alleged to have been involved with provide a particular conundrum for scholars and analysts studying terrorism. State sponsorship can be problematic when one attempts to classify a certain act as terrorist. Most scholars focus on the damage end of terrorism. If agents of the North Korean government or subnational organizations, or individuals sympathetic to the North Korean cause, attack civilian targets, then it is considered to be a terrorist event. We believe this is a dangerous practice and not helpful in the study of terrorism. In our discussion of the definition of terrorism in Chapter 2 of this book, we make the tacit argument that states cannot commit acts of terrorism. We outline why this is important in Chapter 2, and North Korean aggression is a perfect case in point.

Sang-Hyun Lee identifies three particularly heinous acts committed against South Korean governmental officials and civilians. Lee notes that in 1968 North Korean "commandos" infiltrated South Korea and attempted to attack the Presidential residence. In 1983, "Pyongyang" (meaning the North Korean government) successfully detonated a bomb and killed some of President Chun Doo's Cabinet, and a North Korean "agent" detonated a device that blew up a Korean Airlines passenger plane, killing all 115 people on board (2003: 30). The problem with these alleged terror events is that all are attributed, by Lee, as acts carried out directly by North Korean governmental or military agents. If Lee is correct in his attribution, then all of these events are more correctly labeled acts of war or crimes against humanity rather than terrorism. But the confusion over the alleged terror events in South Korea only begins with Lee's classification.

Kurlantzick describes the 1983 terrorist bombing of the Presidential Cabinet as being "funded" by the North Korean government (2001: 20). Chung Min Lee also asserts that North Korea has "sponsored" terrorism but not been directly acting in the alleged terror events in South Korea (2003: 289). States can and will continue to sponsor terrorist acts and organizations. State sponsorship does not invalidate the act as terrorist, so if Kurlantzick and Chug Min Lee are correct, then some, if not all, of these bombings, kidnappings, and assassination attempts could be correctly labeled terrorist.

There is a need for extreme caution when analyzing terrorist acts or it becomes a matter of taste or politics which determines whether an act is considered terrorist or not. This is damaging to the study of terrorism, as it becomes ever more difficult to determine counterterrorism strategies if the definition of terrorism is so subjective. Again, the need for state and regional analysts and scholars becomes of paramount importance in order that false conclusions are not drawn.

Assuming some of the terror events in South Korea were sponsored by North Korea supporting subnational groups and individuals (despite the loose way in which past scholars have classified North Korean aggression), when did the terror end and what caused it to cease? One answer is the end of the Cold War. Sang-Hyun Lee reports the last North Korean sponsored terror event occurred in May 1989 (2003: 31). Joshua Kurlantzick argues that North Korea "has not been conclusively linked to a terrorist attack since 1987" (2001: 23). By 1996, the U.S. State Department confirmed that there was no evidence directly linking North Korea to terrorism in that year. Our own research shows all terrorism ending in South Korea in 1997, whether it was sponsored by North Korea or some other clandestine group. The end of the Cold War may have prompted North Korea to end support for terrorist groups as the incentives for communist nations to engage democracies diminished (ibid.).

International pressure likely played a role as well. Both the United States and Japan have been pressuring North Korea to cease all aggression against South Korea. Former Japanese Prime Minister Junichiro Koizumi became an even stauncher proponent of the U.S. bid to keep North Korean terrorism and military aggression in check when, in September 2002, Kim Jong Il admitted that North Korea had kidnapped thirteen Japanese citizens (Anderson, 2005: 2). Japan and the United States have put increasing diplomatic and economic pressure on North Korea since the end of the Cold War, which may help to explain the North Korean government's reluctance to engage in further state sponsorship of terrorism.

The improving economy may also help to explain the end of terrorism. It may have become increasingly difficult to find safe houses and other local support in South Korea as the citizenry moved into a stable middle-class lifestyle. In 1960, supporting terrorism might have been more appealing to some South Korean sympathizers than it was in the 1990s or currently, when many more people are living comfortable middle-class existences.

South Korea currently fears international terrorism more than attacks from the north. After the 11 September 2001 attacks in the United States and the ensuing war on terror, the South Korean government became increasingly worried that its good relationship with the United States and other Western allies might make South Korea a target of Al-Qaeda. In 2002, when South Korea hosted the World Cup of soccer, the South Korean government devoted a 120-member force to guard the U.S. team and took extraordinary precautions to protect the players (Whiteside, 2002: 12c). These fears appear well founded, as Al-Qaeda deputy leader Ayman al-Zawahiri issued a call to Muslims to attack South Korea in reprisal for the South Korean government's support of the U.S.-led invasion of Afghanistan (Kilinger, 2004).

What worked to stop North Korean sponsorship of terrorism against South Korea may also help to inoculate her against Al-Qaeda attacks. Without a Muslim population and with wealth increasing within South Korea, it will be increasingly difficult for Al-Qaeda to find the domestic support it needs to complete terrorist operations. In fact, a reconciliation agreement with North Korea might be one of the best defenses against international terrorism, as North Korea would then be removed from the world stage as a pariah state, an "evil" state, and, most importantly, a potential future sponsor of terrorism.

Democracy, Poverty, Civilization, and Instability

Terrorism is largely lacking in East Asia, especially in a comparative sense. Compared to South and Southeast Asia, the amount of terrorism experienced in East Asia is fairly insignificant. Japan, with the worst case of terrorism in East Asia, has a fairly similar track record to some European states that experienced a similar amount of leftist terrorism during the early stages of the Cold War.

International terrorism is also largely nonexistent in the region. The only verifiable instance of a nation suffering a prolonged international terror threat is South Korea, and this threat did not emanate from a massive international terror movement, like Al-Qaeda, or a dangerous regional movement like JI. Instead, the threat was also created during the Cold War after Korea was split into two occupation zones at the end of World War II. Further, the threat from South Korea's communist neighbors to the north dissipated around 1997 and would surely be completely gone if North and South Korea reconciled into one state. South Korea has been added rhetorically to Al-Qaeda's hit list but nothing has come of that threat.

The terrorism that does arise in East Asia emanates from multiple sources. Despite Aum Shinrikyo being a splinter religious Buddhist/Hindu cult, the organization really is not motivated by religious hatred. The homogeneous nature of East Asian societies, in both ethnicity and religion, precludes the types of clashing civilizations that are at least partly responsible for terrorism elsewhere in Asia and Africa. Where differences in civilization do occur, like the Uygur separatist movement in China, we do see some terrorism, but even there the case may be better explained by CCP mistreatment of the Uygurs economically and culturally. However, ethnic differences may explain this mistreatment, as recent polls and historical records show many in the Han majority truly feel the Uygurs to be a lesser people.

Democracy is rich in East Asia. Four of the six, Mongolia, Japan, South Korea, and Taiwan, are incredibly stable, decades-old democracies. In fact, the most stable democracies in our study come from this region. Perhaps incredibly stable democratic systems do produce less terrorism. But it depends on how you look at it, as in East Asia the two states experiencing the most terrorism are Japan and South Korea. But relative comparisons are tricky, as Japanese and South Korean terrorism pales in comparison to terrorism experienced in many South and Southeast Asian nations.

Despite this, the democracy argument can only be taken so far, as China experiences very little terrorism, especially given her size, and, as far as we know, North Korea experiences no terrorism. Further, Japan seems to experience more terrorism because the well-established democratic government is reluctant to react quickly and harshly to terrorist threats. It is almost as if extremist groups know they can get away with a little terrorism and maybe even a few devastating attacks before the government and police react.

Poverty is not a good predictor of terrorism in East Asia either. While the Uygur terror campaign is clearly linked to poverty through CCP neglect, inadequate access to good schools, and inadequate employment opportunities, the terrorists in Japan tend to come from affluent families and have access to a solid education. In South Korea, the motivation for terrorists was to overthrow the democratic regime. Poverty does not even enter into the equation. In Mongolia, the standard of living is low overall, although improving rapidly and dramatically, and yet there is no terrorism.

The keys for understanding the overall lack of terrorism in East Asia are stability and homogeneity. Homogeneity in ethnicity, and largely in religion, removes two natural fault lines that extremists can use to motivate others to violent actions. The stability of a regime, regardless of whether it is democratic/capitalist or communist, also appears to play a role in keeping terrorism at bay. This is a key point, for if it is accepted that stability is one of the key factors in inhibiting terrorism, then the United States may be on the wrong foreign policy course in forcing democracy violently, and suddenly, onto historically dictatorial regimes. In fact, one could speculate that the instability from such a foreign policy action would increase terrorism exponentially rather than lower it.

Note

1. This is a separate group from Germany's Red Army Faction — the official name of the Baader-Meinhof Gang. Japan's RAF developed out of the Japanese Communist League.

References

Anderson, Desaix. (2005). "Who Is Losing Asia?" *American Foreign Policy Interests*. Number 26: 1–10.

Beer, Lawrence W. (January 1971). "Japan Turning the Corner." *Asian Survey*. Volume 11, Number 1: 74–85.

Bondarenko, Anna. (2006). "Xinjiang Uygur Autonomous Region's International Economic Ties." *Far Eastern Affairs*. Volume 34, Issue 4: 64–75.

Bovingdon, Gardner. (January 2002). "The Not-So-Silent Majority: Uyghur Resistance to Han Rule in Xinjiang." *Modern China*. Volume 28, Number 1: 39–78.

Box, Meredith, and Gavan McCormack. (2004). "Terror In Japan: The Red Army (1969–2001) and Aum Supreme Truth (1987–2000)." *Critical Asian Studies*. Volume 36, Number 1: 91–112.

Crenshaw, Martha. (July 1981). "The Causes of Terrorism." *Comparative Politics*. Volume 13, Number 4: 379–99.

Farnsworth, Lee W. (January 1973). "Japan 1972: New Faces and New Friends." *Asian Survey*. Volume 13, Number 1: 113–25.

Fedarko, K., and I. Kunii. (1995). "Japan: A Persistent Odor of Terror." *Time*. Volume 145, Issue 18: 72.

"History and Development of Xinjiang." (2004). *Chinese Journal of International Law*. Volume 3, Issue 2: 629–59.

Jenkins, Brian M. (1986). "Reflections for Providing 'The Common Defense.'" *Political Science Quarterly*. Volume 101, Number 5: 773–86.

Katzenstein, Peter J. (Autumn 2003). "Same War: Different Views: Germany, Japan, and Counterterrorism." *International Organization*. Volume 57, Number 4: 731–60.

Kilinger, Bruce. (15 October 2004). "South Korea Braces for Taste of Terror." *Asia Times Online*. http://www.atimes.com/atimes/Korea/FJ15Do3.html (accessed 7 July 2007).

Kurlantzick, Joshua. (Winter 2001). "Fear Moves East: Terror Targets the Pacific Rim." *The Washington Quarterly*. Volume 24, Issue 1: 19–29.

Larimer, T. (2002). "Why Japan's Terror Cult Still Has Appeal." *Time*. Volume 159, Issue 23: 8.

Lee, Chung Min. (July 2003). "Reassessing the ROK-US Alliance: Transformation Challenges and the Consequences of South Korea's Choices." *Australian Journal of International Affairs*. Volume 57, Number 2: 281–307.

Lee, Sang-Hyun. (Summer 2003). "Terrorism and Asymmetric War: Is North Korea a Threat." *East Asia: An International Quarterly*. Volume 20, Issue 2: 21–47.

Metraux, Daniel A. (December 1995). "Religious Terrorism in Japan: The Fatal Appeal of Aum Shinrikyo." *Asian Survey*. Volume 35, Number 2: 1140–54.

Ogden, Suzanne. (2005). "Inoculation Against Terrorism in China: What's In the Dosage?" In *Democratic Development and Political Terrorism: The Global Perspective*. William Crotty, Editor. Boston: Northeastern University Press: 227–54.

Olson, Kyle B. (July–August 1999). "Aum Shinrikyo: Once and Future Threat?" *Emerging Infectious Diseases*. Volume 5, Number 4: 513–16.

Pyle, Kenneth B. (Summer 1982). "The Future of Japanese Nationality: An Essay in Comparative History." *Journal of Japanese Studies*. Volume 10, Number 2: 223–63.

Shimbori, Michiya, T. Ban, K. Kono, H. Yamakazi, Y, Kano, M. Murakami, and T. Murakami. (March 1980). "Japanese Student Activism in the 1970s." *Higher Education*. Volume 9, Number 2: 139–54.

Steinhoff, Patricia G. (November 1989). "Hijackers, Bombers, and Bank Robbers: Managerial Style in the Japanese Red Army." *The Journal of Asian Studies*. Volume 48, Number 4: 724–40.

Whiteside, Kelly. (3 June 2002). "Security Forces Surround U. S. Team." *USA Today*: 12c.

Yee, Herbert S. (February 2005). "Ethnic Consciousness and Identity: A Research Report on Uygur–Han Relations in Xianjing." *Asian Ethnicity*. Volume 6, Number 1: 35–50.

Zhu, Yuchao, and Dongyan Blachford. (May 2006). "China's Fate as a Multinational State: A Preliminary Assessment." *Journal of Contemporary China*. Volume 15, Issue 47: 329–48.

CHAPTER 9

The Large and Constant Specter
of Terrorism in South Asia

ALTHOUGH EAST ASIA IS FAIRLY CALM, comparatively, on the terrorism front, the South Asian terrorism experience can only be aptly termed cataclysmic. Of the six South Asian states in our study, Bangladesh, Bhutan, India, Nepal, Pakistan, and Sri Lanka, only one is not currently grappling with a significant terrorist challenge. Other than the small, landlocked state of Bhutan, which experiences no terrorism, the rest of South Asia is teeming with terrorist groups and active, devastating campaigns. From 1975 to 2003, South Asian states experienced 282 international terror attacks and a staggering 1,622 domestic terror attacks from 1998 to 2003. Much of the international terrorism occurred in India and Pakistan, but a significant and growing number of attacks are either inspired or perpetrated by Al-Qaeda.

As Pyakuryal and Uprety state, "In view of the intense cross-boundary ethnic linkages, and the deep class and ethnic cleavages in most of the societies, each conflict in South Asia is interlocked with another in a number of ways" (2005: 475). This is a very accurate assessment of the situation, as colonial borders drawn by the British after the 1947 partition plan made little sense and soon came apart after the British colonizers left. There is at least some evidence the Indian security forces support terrorism in Bangladesh. Muslim terrorists in India are supported by Muslims and Al-Qaeda in Pakistan. Hence, there is a real cross-border aspect to terrorism in South Asia not seen to this degree in other regions of the world.

Layered on top of all of this postcolonial ethnic chaos is horrendous instability due to stalled, uneven, or, in the case of Pakistan, reversing democratization. Instability in government, crises of legitimacy, and coups d'état are the norm in South Asia. Further, even economic success stories like India's have to be viewed through the lens of incredibly uneven economic development. Several Indian provinces still largely rely on animal dung as the chief source of cooking fuel, while India, as a whole, produces roughly 400,000 engineers a year (Sengupta, 2006: A1). Even taking into consideration India's enormous population, this is still one of the best levels of engineer production in the world. In the end, South Asia is simultaneously a region of hope and despair, economic development and hardship, fledgling democracy and instability, and incessant violence and terrorism.

Lack of Development and an Incomplete Separation in Bangladesh

Bangladesh is a state that seems to deteriorate year after year. It is an unfortunate case of failing democratization that illuminates the many perils the democratization process brings. That the democratization process brings instability is an assertion that has a long history and consistent empirical underpinnings (Mansfield and Snyder, 1995; Thompson and Tucker, 1997; Ward and Gleditsch, 1998). But the period of instability during democratic transition is often longer than one might expect. Thailand, for example, has been undergoing the democratization process since 1931 and it has, unfortunately, recently suffered another military coup. Bangladesh is in a very similar situation, having won independence from Pakistan in 1971 (Hassan and Kundu, 2005: 34). Despite free elections in 1973, which elected the Awami League and Bangabandhu Sheikh Mujibur Rahman to power, the government of Bangladesh became increasingly autocratic (Murshid, 1995). Further, Bangladesh has been marked by short periods of democratic governance marred by longer periods of military or military-supported rule. Despite Rahman's attempts to force unity and a national identity on the people, Bangladesh has remained "divided by guns and the cacophony of ideologues" (Rashiduzzaman, 1997: 261).

Despite ethnic homogeneity, Bangladesh is about 98 percent Bengali, there is some religious division — 85 percent Muslim and 15 percent Hindu — and some of the Muslims are considered outcasts for their support of the Pakistani governmental claim over Bangladesh (Hassan and Kundu, 2005: 34). During the war for independence, it seemed as if there was a widespread nationalism taking root. However, some extremist parties within Bangladesh actually helped conduct an attempted Pakistani genocide undertaken in reprisal against the independence movement (ibid.). These extremists were not originally allowed to partake in politics, but that ban has been lifted. Unfortunately, Bangladesh allows for a unique political process that includes *hartals,* "the complete cessation of public activities during a political strike, which may be peaceful or violent" (Rashiduzzaman, 1997: 255), which have allowed extremist minorities the unusual ability to stop and eventually bring down majority governmental rule, whether it is legitimate or not. Hartals represent "uncompromising politics and demonstrated the hollowness of conventional party politics in Bangladesh" (ibid.). This has led to a system of governance that supports over one hundred different parties and has caused such a crisis of legitimacy in Bangladesh that all of the political institutions seem on the verge of collapse (Hassan and Kundu, 2005: 33).

Besides the failing democratic experiment and Bangladesh's bloody history with Pakistan and Pakistani sympathizers, there are issues of population density and poverty that only add to the chaos, anger, and instability. Bangladesh is one of the most densely populated states in the world. It is also a landlocked state and the track record for economic development of landlocked states has been very poor. Unfortunately, Bangladesh is no exception, where nearly half of the densely packed population lives below the poverty line (Yunus, 2007: 9).

In light of all of these negative inputs into the system and the overarching instability in Bangladesh, it is no surprise that violence and terrorism are rife within society. In fact, terrorism is growing at an exponential rate in Bangladesh (in a similar fashion to the Thai terrorism explosion). Bangladesh experienced fifty-four terrorist attacks (domestic and international) between 1975 and 2003, according to the MIPT-TKB, but from 2004 to 2006 another ninety-nine (or twice the amount for the previous twenty-nine years) were observed. Unlike Thailand, these attacks were not localized and encompassed almost the entire state of Bangladesh. On 17 August 2005, the Islamic extremist terrorist group Jammat-ul-Mujahideen coordinated the explosion of nearly 500 bombs in sixty-three of Bangladesh's sixty-four governmental districts, all within about the space of one hour ("All Over the Place," 2005: 35). Each bomb was simply the detonator portion of a larger explosive device, producing much less damage. While only two people were killed, this was commonly considered to be a show of force regarding what Jammat-ul-Mujahideen could have done if further provoked (ibid.).

Two Rival Parties and Slow Democratic Start

Despite gaining independence in 1971, Bangladesh suffered a series of repressive military governments that often took power through bloody coups. During this time period, two presidents were assassinated (Hassan and Kundu, 2005: 33). Starting in 1990, Bangladesh developed a fledgling democratic system and party politics began to form. Two major parties emerged as the political power brokers for the new democratic system (although both major parties often need the support of one or more of the smaller parties in Bangladesh to form a successful coalition government). The two major party players in Bangladesh are the Bangladesh National Party (BNP) and the Awami League (AL).

The BNP actually formed during the period of military dictatorship and the BNP won its first democratic election in 1978. General Ziaur Rahman and the BNP party he formed won a landslide mandate, but BNP's success was short-lived, as President Rahman was assassinated in 1981 and General Ershad took over control of the state in a military coup in 1982 (Smith, 1986: 796–97). AL formed around the same time, as an opposition to BNP, and the two have been bitter rivals through course of party politics in Bangladesh.

Political violence first emerged in Bangladesh in the 1980s but did not reach wide-scale proportions until after democracy began to take hold in the 1990s. The problem is that widespread corruption and promotion of violence on the part of both BNP and AL have alienated the electorate and caused bitter regional rivalries to form. As *hartal* politics prevail in Bangladesh, leaders and parties have to court the favor of political activists. No leader or party has risen to power without supporting activists who have committed criminal or violent offenses (Rashiduzzaman, 1997: 261). Further, some student activists end up wielding enough power that they can establish "parallel authority, dictating policies and offering protection to individuals or ethnic groups" (ibid.). Corruption spread through supposedly democratic society and a patron client system ruled the day (Hassan and Kundu, 2005: 33). BNP has had to court the favor of major Islamic extremist parties, like Jamaat-E-Islami Bangladesh, in order to retain power. As a result of these efforts, BNP has controlled Bangladeshi politics since the 1990s.

BNP under Khaleda Zia, wife of assassinated President Ziaur Rahman, has even been accused by opposition party AL and outside observers of fomenting Islamic extremism ("The Bothersome Little People," 2004: 43). But the truth is that both the BNP and AL have been involved in violence and terrorism against the people of Bangladesh ("All Over the Place," 2005: 35). Unfortunately, violence and terrorism have become staples of the Bangladesh political process. BNP may be more responsible for the terrorist reaction in Bangladesh, however, as the BNP government has engaged in highly unpopular "extrajudicial" killings of suspected terrorists and probably some opposition voices from at least 2005 onward (ibid.).

The Internal and External Terrorist Threat in Bangladesh

Jammat-ul-Mujahideen (JM) is currently the most dangerous terrorist organization in Bangladesh. It is estimated that this group can call on 10,000 full-time activists and 100,000 part-time supporters ("A Problem Shared," 2006: 45). This group is not only responsible for the 500 coordinated bomb attacks in August 2005, which resulted in few deaths and casualties, but JM has increasingly shown itself to be capable of deadlier and more destructive terrorist attacks. The lid is off in Bangladesh and the terrorist violence seems headed to produce ever greater fear, destruction, and instability.

But terrorism within Bangladesh seems to be supported by proximate sympathetic terror groups and international terror organizations. India accuses Bangladesh and the BNP government of harboring Islamic terrorist groups that help support domestic Islamic separatist terrorism in the remote northeastern provinces of India ("A Problem Shared," 2006: 45). India has been accused of fomenting terrorism in Bangladesh. From 1975 to the early 1980s, a pro-liberation terror organization, headed by Kadar Siddiqui, engaged in border outpost raids along Bangladesh's northern border and committed acts of terrorism within Bangladesh with the help of the Border Security Force of India (Hossain, 1981: 1123).

Al-Qaeda has also played a fairly active role in the Islamic terrorist movement in Bangladesh. Osama bin Laden created the International Islamic Front for Jihad (IIF) in 1998 and included the head of Bangladesh's Jihad movement (Stern, 2003). Al-Qaeda has also been active in its own separate terrorist strikes in Bangladesh and is alleged to have engaged in at least two terror attacks in Bangladesh in 2006 (MIPT-TKB).

With all of the domestic instability caused by the dense population of Bangladesh, extreme poverty, and a corrupt and incomplete deomcracatization, it is no wonder that terrorism is exploding there. When one adds the alleged impetus to violence from outside sources like the Indian government and Al-Qaeda, Bangladesh becomes a looming catastrophe. The United States and the international community should pay special attention to helping reverse this trend in Bangladesh before a historically secular, struggling democracy turns into an intolerant theocracy.

Chaos and Communism in Nepal

Nepal is a landlocked state nestled between two economic giants, India and China. Nepal has a low per-capita annual income of $1,500 (*CIA World Factbook Online*), and the Nepalese are highly dependent on trade with India and foreign assistance (Dash, 1996: 200). Nepal is a patchwork of ethnicities, with Chhettri (16 percent) and Brahman Hill (13 percent) being the two largest groups. Religion in Nepal is fairly homogeneous, with about 80 percent of the population being practicing Hindus. Nepal has a long history of independence, stretching back to 1759 when Nepal first emerged as a cohesive state (Khadka, 1986: 429). But Nepal also has a long history of dictatorial monarchical rule; hence it is not surprising to find that Nepal, like Bangladesh, is a recent entry into the democratization process.

Hindering the democratization process are a Maoist insurgency and an overly intrusive monarchy. Nepal is currently in the middle of a violent civil war, with a Maoist faction of the Communist Party of Nepal, that has lasted over a decade (Pyakural and Uprety, 2005: 459). Because of this civil war and the estimate that sixty-eight of seventy-five districts in Nepal are controlled by Maoist insurgents, some feel that Nepal is close to being a failed state ("The Bothersome Little People," 2004: 43). This sentiment is echoed by Suman Pradhan, who noted that over 1,500 people had died and thousands were left homeless over the course of less than one year after a ceasefire with Maoist rebels failed in 2003 (2004: 7). Since the "People's War" was initiated by the Maoists in 1996, an estimated 150,000 to 200,000 Nepalese have had to flee their homes as war refugees (Pyakuryal and Uprety, 2005: 470). Overall, the outlook for Nepal is not good and it will likely be a center of violence and terrorism for the foreseeable future.

A Struggling Democratic Process and a Meddling Monarchy

Like most states we have examined in this study, Nepal has a short history as a democratic experiment, and the instability that has arisen during the transition to democracy has caused violence and terrorism to erupt in society. Nepal held its first free, democratic elections in December 1960. Unfortunately, King Mahendra dissolved this elected government, citing that he believed the newly elected Congress could not provide security and would instill corruption into the political process (Khadka, 1986: 430).

The people of Nepal did not show a great deal of animosity toward the king's dissolution of government. According to Narayan Khadka, the reason for the lack of immediate response by the Nepalese populace is twofold. First, there was a centuries-long cultural acceptance of the king as a "benevolent reincarnation." Second, the king had sole control over the armed forces (1986: 431).

But this is not to imply that no response occurred. In fact, the communist movement in Nepal became intensified after the king dissolved parliament. This movement continued to gain steam, and it is estimated that the 5,000 members in various Communist parties in regions and localities doubled to 10,000 in the 1980s (Khadka, 1995: 57). During this time period, the king still exuded absolute control although, under increasing pressure from Nepal's democratic neighbor to the south, King Mahendra attempted to force a hybrid form of quasi-democracy on the people. This system, known as the Panchayat system, was a strange mix of monarchical authoritarianism and a pyramid of pseudo-democratic governance. Representatives in the Panchayat system were elected from a very narrow base of followers at the village level. Each village would elect eleven members to represent them, but those members elected the district members and the district representatives elected larger bodies until you had, at the apex, a national assembly (Khadka, 1986: 434–35). This is less a democracy and more an institutionalized patronage system with a supreme executive, in the form of the king, who could override anything that displeased him anyway.

True democratic reform was not instituted until April 1990, when Nepal became a constitutional monarchy with a multiparty democratic system (Khadka, 1995: 55; Pyakural and Uprety, 2005: 469). The first parliamentary elections were held in May 1991, in which the Nepali Congress (NC) party won a simple majority and the United Marxist–Leninist party (UML) occupied the minority opposition (Khadka, 1995: 55). The UML is generally blameless in the communist terrorism Nepal experiences. In fact, its acceptance of party politics and the willingness of UML to go to the voting box to win support caused a major rift within the communist movement.

Partly influenced by the success of Mao's Communist Revolution in neighboring China and partly influenced by perceived interference from India, the Maoist faction of the original Nepal Communist Party (NCP) split off into competing Communist party factions (Khadka, 1995: 60). The two most militant — the People's War Group (PWG) and the Maoist Communist Center (MCC) — began a civil war in 1996 and also began engaging in an aggressive terrorism campaign against civilians and governmental officials deemed unsupportive of the Maoist movement (Pyakuryal and Uprety, 2005: 469).

The Maoists view the National Army as a tool of oppression for the king, and the Nepalese government views the Maoist movement as having a penchant for terrorism (Hutt, 2007: 21). Both views are largely correct. Maoist groups have engaged in terrorism and the government has engaged in very heavy-handed military reprisals. In November 2001, King Gyanendra declared a state of emergency due to the civil war and incessant terror attacks. The dissolution of parliament and human rights abuses soon followed (Kramer, 2003: 208; Kumar, 2005: 285). Two hundred and twenty-seven people lost their lives in the first month after the royal coup (Kumar, 2005: 289). By February 2005, King Gyanendra had taken over all executive power and the democratic experiment was all but over in Nepal (Kumar, 2005: 285).

The Maoists are not without blame, however; terrorism from these Maoist extremist groups has been well planned and devastating. There were 135 terror incidents from 1975 to 2003, with most of these incidents occurring in the last decade. The Maoists have successfully hijacked planes, most notably the Indian Airlines hijacking of 1999. They have also attacked police and civilians. In one attack, they killed seventy police officers in the spring of 2001 (Baldauf, 2001: 1). But the most spectacular attack was the 1 June 2001 massacre of most of the royal family (Kumar, 2005: 285). This single act prompted King Gyanendra to dissolve parliament and use police and military personal to engage in extrajudicial killings of suspected Maoists and Maoist sympathizers (Baldauf, 2002: 1).

There is a glimmer of hope in Nepal as the Maoist insurgents did sign a peace accord with the central government in 2006 ("Maoist Rebels Sign," 2006: 7). But with thousands dead due to the civil war, terror attacks, and military reprisals and human rights abuses, this peace is tenuous at best. Also, with the amount of instability still present in Nepal and the penchant for kings to take over government at a moment's notice, the outlook remains grim. Unfortunately, Maoist terrorism will likely be a staple of Nepalese life for the foreseeable future.

Ethnic and Religious Strife and Terrorism and Civil War in Sri Lanka

Sri Lanka is another South Asian state caught in the throes of civil war. The Sri Lankan case is comprised of both an ethnic and a religious component, but terrorism in Sri Lanka cannot be solely explained by these factors. At its heart, the conflict in Sri Lanka is yet another in a long line of secession/separatist movements. Like most of the other secessionist movements we have discussed in this book, the government has played a pivotal role in fueling the drive for secession through unfair and inhumane treatment of the out-group. It seems that one surefire way to help prevent terrorism within a state is to ensure that the central government does not identify out-groups and exploit or mistreat them.

The Legacy of British Colonization

To only portray the economic deprivation as emanating from the current Buddhist Sinhalese-dominated government would be unfair. Economic deprivation and ethnic favoritism began during British colonization. The British colonizers favored the Muslim Tamil minority and often gave the Tamils privileged positions of power (Orjuela, 2003: 198). For example, in 1946 the Tamils comprised 33 percent of the civil service and 40 percent of the judiciary, while the Tamil population only comprised about 11 percent of the total Sri Lankan population (De Votta, 2000: 59). The British colonizers also attempted to convert locals to Protestantism and severely curtailed expressions of Sinhalese culture. As one author explains, "In keeping with Britain's divide-and-rule policies, her authorities in Sri Lanka badly favored minority communities [especially the Tamil] at the expense of the majority community's religion, language and culture" (De Votta, 2000: 58). In addition, the retribution that the Sinhalese majority sought against the Tamil minority was very harsh and restrictive.

In 1948, Sri Lanka gained independence from British colonization. The Sinhalese majority immediately took control of government and started a Sinhalese Buddhist revival. Immediately, Sinhalese was declared the only official language for Sri Lanka (Orjuela, 2003: 198). Tamil-speaking minorities were formally banned from certain employment opportunities in 1956, and in 1971, the government made it almost impossible for Tamils to gain admission to universities (ibid.). At first the Tamil community tried to peacefully protest. But by 1956, Sri Lanka experienced its first violent race riots (De Votta, 2000: 58). Some concessions were made by Prime Minister S. J. V. Chelvanayakam, who, through the Bandaranaike-Chelvanayakam Pact, recognized the Tamil language as a second but not equal national language (De Votta, 2000: 59). This meager concession drew heated opposition from Sinhalese nationalists and surprisingly from Buddhist elites.

Subsequent governments actually promoted economic oppression and Sinhalese colonization of northern provinces dominated by Tamils.

The government actually withheld money from international organizations that was donated for projects in Tamil-dominated northern provinces. At the same time, the government was sponsoring relocation of unemployed Sinhalese in northern lands that the Tamils saw as their historic homeland (De Votta, 2000: 61). This created an amazing amount of animosity and distrust in the minds of many Tamils.

By the 1970s, peaceful protest was beginning to give way to violent outbursts (Sprinzak, 2000: 70). During this time period, the Liberation Tigers of Tamil Eelam (LTTE or Tamil Tigers) emerged from competing secessionist groups as the voice and the violence behind the Tamil separatist movement (Pyakuryal and Uprety, 2005: 475).

The LTTE was immediately labeled a terrorist organization and, in fact, engaged in some heinous terrorist acts in the 1980s and 1990s. But this brings up an important point that we have already made with other separatist movements. It is difficult sometimes to distinguish among insurrection, insurgency, civil war, and terrorism.

Suthaharan Nadarajah and Dhananhayan Sriskandarajah argue that one of the key impediments to peace in Sri Lanka is the government's insistence on labeling LTTE a terrorist organization. Nadarajah and Sriskandarajah argue that LTTE is more correctly labeled a separatist movement. They note that the LTTE claims to be spearheading an independence movement against institutionalized racism and governmental violence (2005: 88). We do not disagree with this assertion or the implied assertion that institutionalized racism and governmental violence have been carried out against the Tamil minority. They go on to argue that the state has used the terrorist label to vilify the LTTE and largely ignore legitimate separatist claims and, finally, that "the state's sustained rhetoric of terrorism has become a serious impediment to reaching a permanent solution of the conflict" (Nadarajah and Sriskandarajah, 2005: 88). These accusations may be true, in part, but the conclusion that the Sinhalese-dominated government and the rest of the world should stop labeling LTTE and *some* of their actions as terrorist is as ridiculous as labeling all of their actions as terrorist.

Nadarajah and Sriskandarajah see the situation in Sri Lanka as an either/or conundrum. Either LTTE is justly labeled a terrorist organization or LTTE is a mislabeled insurgency. Unfortunately, terrorism is often found, as we have seen, in the midst of other violence (civil war, etc.). We believe terrorism in Sri Lanka and in other mixed cases (like Aceh separatism in Indonesia, MILF terrorism in the Philippines, and Uygur terrorism in China) is more of a mixed case, mixing with other forms of violence and criminality rather than being a blanket, clear-cut proposition. The points made by Nadarajah and Sriskandarajah are not to be dismissed lightly and they are hitting one of the core problems with terrorist studies: sometimes it is all in the eye of the beholder. That is why it is so important that a universal definition be agreed upon soon or scholarship cannot move forward. We will all be talking past one another. In our attempt to define terrorism (Chapter 2), we find that definition would conform nicely to many of Nadarajah's and Sriskandarajah's criticisms. For example, when LTTE attacked an army convoy in July of 1983 and killed thirteen soldiers, we agree with Nadarajah and Sriskandarajah that a politically motivated Sri Lankan government mislabeled those acts as terrorist (2005: 89), as terrorism can only be perpetrated against civilians. However, we would insist that LTTE's shooting and killing of civilian Buddhists worshipping at a Bo tree in the mid-1980s (Abeysekara, 2001: 18) be labeled as terrorism.

By 1983, most scholars had determined that the Tamil separatist movement had become extremely violent (Abeysekara, 2001; De Votta, 2000; Nadarajah and Sriskandarajah, 2005; Orjuela, 2003), and many international organizations and outside state observers recognized both the civil war and the terrorism carried out by LTTE. By the time Junius Richard "JR" Jayewardene ascended to the presidency in 1978, things were getting very tense between the Tamils in the north and the southern Sinhalese. President Jaywardene began with a conciliatory tone toward the Tamils and Tamil claims of discrimination. In fact, even after the 1983 LTTE attack on the military, President Jaywardene refused to immediately embrace heavy-handed tactics. Initially, the United National Party (UNP), which was the dominant Sinhalese party in Sri Lanka, and President Jayewardene recognized that colonization was a legitimate gripe for Tamils and included it in the UNP election manifesto (Peebles, 1990: 46). But President Jayewardene did not follow up on this once in office. In fact, he may have been between a rock and a hard place, as almost no concession went over well with the majority of Sinhalese voters. Still, in 1984, several prominent Buddhist monks were advocating full-scale war to eradicate the terrorism problem and President Jayewardene insisted that he would not "kill innocent people" or turn into an Idi Amin or a Hitler (Abeysekara, 2001: 16). In fact, he admonished Buddhist leaders for what he perceived to be an anti-Buddhist embracing of violence (Abeysekara, 2001: 17). When terrorist attacks began targeting Buddhists and Buddhist places of worship in the mid

1980s, Buddhist leaders actually called for President Jayewardene's ouster (Abeysekara, 2001: 18).

The problem is that both LTTE and the Buddhist leaders had very strong points. LTTE and all of the Tamil population had been treated horribly by the Sinhalese-dominated government. Tamils and the LTTE had been subjected to open institutionalized racism, a government-backed resettlement of their lands, an attack on Tamil culture and religion, and horrible human rights abuses, including pogroms carried out by the Sinhalese-dominated military in which thousands of innocent civilians were killed. In fact, by 1990 the Sri Lankan army was essentially 100 percent Sinhalese and the police force for the entire nation was 96 percent Sinhalese (Burger, 1992: 751). Where can Tamils turn for safety and security under such conditions?

Buddhists, too, had been subjected to horrible, inhumane acts of terrorism that sought to remove Sinhalese from certain areas, kill Buddhists and Sinhalese, and destroy religious places of worship and religious artifacts. In one case in 1987, the LTTE captured and systematically decapitated thirty-two Buddhist monks on a pilgrimage (Abeysekara, 2001: 19). In a more recent attack on 25 January 1998, the LTTE ran an explosives-laden truck into the most revered Buddhist temple in Sri Lanka, killing sixteen civilians and almost damaging the religious relic the Tooth of Lord Buddha housed inside (De Votta, 2000: 55). Sri Lanka has one of the most active suicide terrorism campaigns in the world. One author estimates the total number of suicide attacks from 1983 to 2000 to be 171 (Sprinzak, 2000: 69). All of these attacks, plus the damage that has been done to the civilian populace and Buddhist places of worship, have led scholars to observe an unending spiral of mistrust and fear in Sri Lanka (Orjuela, 2003: 198).

India's Role in Sri Lanka

Like the other two states discussed thus far experiencing terrorism in South Asia, India seems to play a predominant role and have vested domestic and international interests that draw the Indian government to intervene. Early in the conflict, India played the role of aid giver to the Tamils and LTTE who were suffering under governmental pogroms. In one case, India actually violated Sri Lankan airspace to deliver food and medicine to LTTE (Jenkins and Bond, 2001: 23). But by 1987, Indian forces had entered the state formally and at the request of the UNP-dominated government to act as an international peacekeeping force (Peebles, 1990: 46). Indian troops did, on occasion, have to fight LTTE forces (Pyakuryal and Uprety, 2005: 475). But

Indian troops did not stay long and when they left in 1990, the government felt it had a green light to hunt down and kill LTTE members and sympathizers. This not only caused Tamils to hate their own government even more, but they now felt betrayed by India on two accounts (Burger, 1992: 753). The Liberation Tigers felt so betrayed that they staged a suicide attack against Rajiv Gandhi on 21 May 1991. A woman bearing flowers for Rajiv met him on the campaign trail as he campaigned to retake the Prime Minister's position (which he had held in 1987 when India sent troops to Sri Lanka to stop the fighting). She was strapped with explosives and in a suicide bombing attack killed Rajiv, herself, and sixteen other civilians (Phillips, 1991: 26). LTTE eventually developed a military network with separatist groups in India, which forced India to stay engaged with LTTE even though India had left Sri Lanka (Pyakuryal and Uprety, 2005: 475).

Overall, the situation looks grim in Sri Lanka. There was an attempt at peace in 2002 with a formal truce signed, but little has changed. The animus each group holds toward the other is so deep that peace movements cannot even draw more than 1,000 participants (Orjuela, 2003: 200). Further, Tamils who attempt to engage in politics are viewed with suspicion by the Sinhalese and their own people (ibid.). Finally, Sinhalese leaders, like President Jayewardene, who attempt reconciliation are often rewarded with ridicule, suspicion, and may eventually be elected out of office. The terrorism, which is particularly vicious in Sri Lanka, will most likely continue for some time to come.

A Multi-Ethnic, Multireligious India in Turmoil and Transition

India is the fourth state in South Asia to experience a significant and devastating amount of domestic violence and terrorism. India, unlike the three South Asian nations mentioned thus far, also experiences a good deal of international terrorism. Most of the international terror attacks emanate from Pakistan and the Al-Qaeda network operating in northeastern Pakistan, but some instability is also coming from separatist and insurgent terrorist groups in Bangladesh, Nepal, and Sri Lanka (Dash, 1996: 190). India is a patchwork of ethnicity, religion, caste, and economic development. Whole regions in India are experiencing poverty so great that there is often no easily accessible, potable water or access to electricity. Other regions are on the cutting edge of First World development, and India produces a great deal of the world's scientists, technicians, and engineers.

A state containing 1.12 billion people and a diverse mix of ethnicities, religions, languages, and cultures is bound to experience some friction. The predominant ethnicity is Indo-Aryan and over 70 percent of the nation belongs to this group. The other major ethnicity is Dravidian and 25 percent of Indians belong to this group. Most Indians practice Hinduism (80 percent), but there is a significant Muslim population (13 percent) and smaller Christian (2 percent) and Sikh (2 percent) populations. India has fifteen official languages and even the majority of Hindus in India do not speak Hindi, creating fault lines even among what appears to be a majority in India (Bose, 2004: 101). With all of the ethnic, religious, cultural, and linguistic differences layered over great disparities in wealth and income, it is not surprising that violence and terrorism has erupted in India. One must also consider that with such a large population, even smaller ethnic or religious divisions could pose a significant problem for the central government. For example, adherents to the Sikh religion comprise only 2 percent of the total Indian population. But 2 percent of 1.12 billion is roughly 22 million people, which is a larger population than many states in the world. As one author states, India is "the most heterogeneous and complex society on earth" (Manor, 1996: 459).

The Mess the British Left for India

Colonization plays a particularly pivotal role in explaining much of the current terrorism that India is experiencing. Colonial borders were drawn up in Africa and Asia by the European colonizers based on international economic agreement with no consideration for the indigenous cultures, religions, and ethnicities that occupied the colonized territory. This often leaves competing hostile groups within the same postcolonial borders, causing a great deal of instability and setting the foundation for violent interaction between these competing groups.

India broke away from British colonization in 1947 after a bitter struggle with British colonizers who had ruled over the state for ninety years. However, the dissolution of British rule and transition into a new, unified Indian nation was anything but smooth. In fact, the old colonial borders drawn by the British immediately gave way to two new states. The British partition plan would have encompassed three-fifths of the subcontinent, but Pakistan and India separated as soon as Great Britain ceded colony rights in 1947 (Schendel, 2002: 117). During the relocation, millions of Hindus, Muslims, and Sikhs immigrated to the state of their choice. Many Muslims attempted to enter Pakistan and most Hindus immigrated to India. Many wayfarers were waylaid on the road and an estimated one million people died in the mass exodus (Bose, 2004: 96).

The new border between India and Pakistan, especially East Pakistan, was one of the most ridiculously drawn borders in history. The result was the biggest enclavization of indigenous populations in the world. A true enclave is actually rare in international relations. In order for an area to meet the true definition of an enclave it must be a "portion of one state completely surrounded by another state" (Schendel, 2002: 116). The enclaves that existed between India and East Pakistan (now Bangladesh) represented over half of the world's enclaves. The 197 enclaves that were created through negotiation between India and Pakistan have created lasting political tensions between India and Bangladesh, not to mention the animosity that the indigenous populations feel in being thrust into such a ridiculous situation (Schendel, 2002).

Separatism and Terror from India's Minority Populations

Most of the violence and terrorism that India experienced did not come from this unlikely, landlocked archipelago of indigenous enclave islands. One ethnic minority and two religious minorities have been the root of domestic terrorism in India. The Tamil ethnic minority in the province of Tamilnadu, the Sikhs in the Punjab province, and the Muslims in Kashmir are three of the most contentious subgroupings of people in India. The Kashmir situation is somewhat special and is discussed later in this chapter; Tamil and Sikh violence and terrorism are the focus here.

The situation for the Tamils and Sikhs in India is eerily similar to those of the minority Tamil population in Sri Lanka, the minority Muslim population in the Philippines, the Aceh population in Indonesia, and the Uygurs in China. When Jawaharlal Nehru took control of India in 1947, there were already significant democratic institutions in place for him to use to create a unified India (Kohli, 1997: 331). It had been both Mahatma Gandhi's and Nehru's wish that a pluralist democracy be developed that accommodated all ethnic, religious, and cultural groups in a unified state (Bose, 2004: 96). Nehru was far more conciliatory to outgroups because of his personal ideology and secure position in government (Kohli, 1997: 332). But even during his reign from 1947 to 1964, the Preventative Detention Act of 1950 was enacted and the Indian Constitution was not significantly rectified to democratic ideals. One scholar determined that both democracy and dictatorship are consistent with the sometimes confounding ideals present in the Indian Constitution (Mathur, 1992: 341).

In the 1950s, the Indian Congress actually pushed to redraw Indian boundaries along ethnic and linguistic lines. Nehru resisted this, fearing that if all Tamils were pushed into one province, then the call for separatism would grow louder (Manor, 1996: 466). There was just cause to fear Tamil secession in the 1950s and 1960s as leaders demanded from Delhi's central government autonomy at the least or, in the best-case scenario, secession (Kohli, 1997: 333). The Tamils in India are defined linguistically rather than ethnically. Tamils in India are defined by the Dravidian-derived Tamil language even though early Tamil separatists insisted that all Tamils were ethnically and culturally different from the rest of Indians (Kohli, 1997: 333–34). Despite Nehru's concerns, the Congress, in 1956, did follow the wishes of the majority of Indians and drew provincial borders along linguistic lines. This was quite a victory for Tamils as they now had their own pseudo-state called Tamilnadu.

When Nehru died in 1964 his daughter, Indira Gandhi, took over as Prime Minister. She was far less conciliatory and feared challenges to her power, and she attempted to consolidate as much power as she could in the executive branch (Kohli, 1997: 332). She and other Indian national leaders attempted to again impose Hindi as the national language for all states, and the Tamils reacted most violently to this attempt (Kohli, 1997: 334). Actions like this and others gave steam to a new secessionist movement started by Jayaprakash Narayan (Upadhyaya, 1992: 828). About this same time, the call for Tamil separatism was stronger than ever and Tamil nationalists started to use the local Dravida Munnetra Kazhagam (DMK) party in an attempt to drive separatism through politically (Kohli, 1997: 334).

To combat militancy, terrorism, and political protest, Indira Gandhi and the Indian Congress passed the Internal Security Act of 1971, which allowed for arbitrary arrest and detainment (Mathur, 1992: 342). A state of emergency was declared by Gandhi four years later, in 1975 (Forrester, 1975: 296). The police and Indian military felt comfortable using heavy-handed and coercive techniques to quell militancy and protest (Kohli, 1997: 335). Indo-Aryan militancy also began to rear its head in India. The Rashtriya Swayamsevek Sangh (National Volunteers' Union, RSS) began to gain legitimacy both as a voice for Hindu-only cultural acceptance and as a political party in the form of Jana Sangh (Upadhyaya, 1992: 828–29). While in political power as part of the larger Janata Party starting in 1977, Jana Sangh attempted to ban secular textbooks and religious conversion (Upadhyaya, 1992: 829).

A state of crisis was reached in 1977 and the Indian government actually suspended democratic rights for two years while rebellious groups were sanctioned. Indira Gandhi returned to power in 1980 and became even less populist, starting to speak openly about the problems religious minorities, especially Sikhs, were causing (Kohli, 1997: 332). In 1980, the National Security Act was enacted, making it easier to arrest and detain individuals than ever before (Mathur, 1992: 342). Part of the reason Indira Gandhi had to embrace Hindu nationalism had to do with the growing popularity of the Bharatiya Janata Party (BJP), which was founded in 1980 and, soon after, attempted to combine forces with the RSS (Upadhyaya, 1992: 829).

This group is associated with the Indian history of Aryan supremacy. Even Gandhi embraced the notion of unification on the subcontinent through a shared ancient national heritage or Aryan blood, race, and nationality. But she "managed to reconcile these visionary themes with ideals of harmony among the many different religions, regional cultures, and linguistic groups of the subcontinent" (Bayly, 1993: 13). Unfortunately, the Indian National Congress had retained links with Hindu revivalists and quickly began attacking Muslims and non-Hindus (ibid.). The BJP is also closely linked to this movement and members are proposing rebuilding Ram's Temple on the demolished remains of the Muslim Ayodhya mosque, much to the chagrin of India's Muslims (ibid.).

All of this Hindu revivalism was occurring at the same time the Tamils in Sri Lanka were attempting to secede from the Sinhalese-dominated state. Indira Gandhi wanted to help broker a peace agreement but found she was unable to take a hard line against LTTE and the Sri Lankan Tamils, as the coalition government was worried about upsetting the Indian Tamils in Tamilnadu (Rao, 1988: 424). In fact, after riots broke out in July 1983 in Sri Lanka, Sri Lanka President Jayewardene asked Indira Gandhi to stop Tamil militant groups in Tamilnadu from supporting LTTE and other Sri Lankan Tamil separatists, but she refused (Rao, 1988: 420). It was no secret either that Tamil Tigers from LTTE had a safe harbor in Tamilnadu (Oberschall, 2004: 36). In fact, the Tamils in Tamilnadu were allowed "to build up arsenals of sophisticated arms, ship them to Sri Lanka, run training camps, and set up communication facilities" (Rao, 1988: 424).

But with the death of Indira Gandhi, the free reign in Tamilnadu was short-lived. Rajiv Gandhi wanted to take a harder line against terrorist activities and Tamil separatism so he began, in 1985, to intercept ships carrying Tamil arms and rebels, and later he took action to remove Tamil militants from their bases in Tamilnadu (Rao, 1988: 426). Rajiv Gandhi also promised to establish a *Ram Rajya* or "Perfect State," which sounded idyllic and egalitarian but actually ended as a policy courting the favor of Hindu revivalists who, among other things, wanted the Muslim mosque at Ayodhya replaced with a temple commemorating the Hindu god Ram (Upadhyaya, 1992: 829).

Ironically, at the same time Rajiv Gandhi was cracking down on minority groups and BJP was ascending to power, they would form a winning ruling coalition in parliament in 1991, and the Tamil separatist movement lost steam. It lost steam mainly because concessions were made. Tamilnadu was created out of primarily Tamil-speaking Indians, giving this minority a strong political voice. Further, concessions on the standing of the Tamil language were made and for a short time, Tamil militants were allowed free rein to support and help militant separatism, which included a good deal of terrorism in Sri Lanka.

India was far from free of militant separatism and terrorism, however. Punjab is one of India's most populous states. Half of the state is comprised of Sikhs and the other half are Hindus. Sikh nationalism is still a very powerful force in Punjab but in the 1980s, it hit a high point (Kohli, 1997: 355). Here, too, we have the first instance of Pakistan taking an active role in supporting insurrection and terrorism in India, as the Sikhs found willing support from their neighbors to the northeast.

Early in Punjab's electoral history, the Hindu Congress party was able to use a fractured Sikh population with a Hindu voting block to secure political power in the Punjab province, which contained a Sikh majority. However, the Akali Dal party (which represented the Sikhs) found that it could galvanize Sikh support through militancy and appeals to religion, and in 1966 Akali Dal took control of the Punjab state (Kohli, 1997: 336). Indira Gandhi countered this growing militancy through repression (ibid.). Terrorism was especially brutal in Punjab. One estimate puts the total dead at about 12,000 (Kohli, 1997: 335), while other estimates have terrorist acts responsible for 25,000 civilian deaths ("Peace at Last," 1993: 45). A minor religious figure, Sant Jarnail Singh Bhindranwale, rose to head the terrorist movement (Wallace, 1986: 363). Most interestingly, a good deal of the terrorism was aimed at Sikhs in an attempt to drum up unified support for Sikh nationalism.

Reaction by the central government to growing secessionism, which Indira Gandhi labeled as treasonous (Kohli, 1997: 336), was swift and harsh. At first, the parliament passed the Terrorist and Disruptive Activities (Prevention) Act (TADA) in 1984, which allowed anyone to be held for six months without trial and individuals to be tried in a designated court outside normal jurisprudence (Mathur, 1992: 343). In the 1980s, the Central Reserve Police Force (CRPF) had its powers expanded, as well as the size of its force. Now the CRPF could arrest a person or search a home without a warrant and detain suspects with impunity (Mathur, 1992: 345). Eventually, the government started to crack down and the Sikhs of Punjab were subjected to wide-scale extrajudicial killings (Pyakuryal and Uprety, 2005: 471).

The response by the Sikh separatists was equally violent. In 1984, the Indian government had cornered some Sikh separatists in the sacred Golden Temple and Indira Gandhi gave the order for tanks to attack, demolish portions of the temple, and the military to proceed with killing the Sikhs inside. This heavy-handed tactic prompted Sikhs to retaliate by assassinating Indira Gandhi a few months later ("The Lessons of History," 1993: 42).

A combination of brutal tactics and conciliation ended the Sikh separatist movement, which died in the early 1990s. In this case, brutal state repression went a long way toward stopping horrendous and widespread terrorism. But accommodations by President Rao in the early 1990s helped as well. President Rao's most significant contribution was to allow state-level elections (Kohli, 1997: 335). This caused the war-weary Sikh and Hindu populations to get down to the business of government again.

The Special Case of Jammu and Kashmir and the Indo-Pakistan Problem

Currently the worst terrorist threat lies between Muslims and Hindus, especially in the contested state of Kashmir. This is also the most internationalized terrorist effort India has had to deal with yet, involving both Pakistani cross-border raids and support as well as participation by Al-Qaeda. Kashmir finds itself in a situation very similar to that of Northern Ireland. Although the terror groups in Northern Ireland generally tried to stay away from causing civilian casualties, Pakistani terror groups, international and domestic, have no aversion to causing civilian death and maiming. The Indo-Pakistan conflict has resulted in open war twice (in 1948 and 1965) over control of the Kashmir region (Dash, 1996: 190), in addition to a dangerous nuclear arms race. It has also resulted in the Hindu community in Pakistan and the Muslim minority community in India being viewed with suspicion and treated as a lesser class of citizen (Pyakuryal and Uprety, 2005: 474). Among the reasons the conflict continues is a dispute over the Jammu and Kashmir regions, Pakistan's increasing emphasis on Islam as the basis of the state, and India's Hindu nationalist tendencies, which have produced, at various times, mistreatment of Muslims, a history of violence, and Al-Qaeda's growing presence in Pakistan. Many of these impetuses for conflict cannot be readily remedied.

Kashmir joined India out of necessity. After Partition in 1947, the British gave separate princely states the right to choose to join either India or Pakistan. Pakistan coveted the Kashmir region and the Muslim majority contained within. Instead of waiting for Kashmir to choose, Pakistan invaded Kashmir in October 1947. The ruler of Kashmir signed on to become part of India if only to save his kingdom from Pakistani aggression (Jafa, 2005: 143). A majority of Muslims had originally wished to merge with Pakistan but now felt safer taking their chances in a secular India (ibid.).

Despite several attempts at political secession and constant goading by forces inside Pakistan, a real, sustained terror campaign did not ensue in Jammu and Kashmir until 1989. There have, however, always been terror attacks in the Kashmir region. For example, members of the Kashmir National Liberation Front attempted to murder a policeman in 1967 and their leader, Maqbool Butt, was tried and convicted for murdering an Intelligence Bureau officer (Swami, 2004: 148). But it was not until the beginning of the Kashmiri *intifada* in 1989 that the true and extremely violent terror campaign began (Alavi, 2002: 29). This crisis fell on an Indian parliament (Lok Sabha) during the reign of the Hindu supremacist party BJP, which dominated Congress from 1991 until the Congress party took back control in the 2004 elections.

The three major underlying causes of the 1989 *intifada* were economic deprivation, cultural repression, and an influx of mujahadeen fighters from Afghanistan. Kashmiri Muslims had been alienated from India, lost political rights, and faced high unemployment (Jafa, 2005: 142). About 10,000 college graduates could not find gainful employment just preceding the *intifada* (Jafa, 2005: 145). A few years preceding the 1989 *intifada*, Mujahadeen veterans from the Afghanistan conflict with the Soviet Union began showing up in Kashmir and increased the "reach and lethality" of terror groups operating (Acharya, 2006: 299). The Pakistani government has taken a direct role in sponsoring terrorism in Kashmir, as the Pakistan's Inter-Services Intelligence (ISI) agency has had a hand in attempting to transplant the successful Mujahadeen in Afghanistan to Kashmir (Chalk, 2001). As further evidence of the international sponsorship of the Kashmir terror campaign, Yateendra Jafa noted that three of the four major terror groups operating in the Kashmir region were nonindigenous organizations

(Jafa, 2005: 147). Of the four terror organizations operating in Jammu and Kashmir, Harkat ul-Mujahideen (HUM), Jaish-e-Mohammed (JEM), Lashkar-e-Tabia (LET), and Hizb ul-Mujahidin (HM), only HM is an indigenous terror organization (ibid.). LET, for example, is one of the best-trained and most active terror organizations in the Kashmir region. This group relies almost solely on foreign fighters, however. Most of the fighters come from Pakistani madrassahs or were recruited directly as veterans from the Afghan War (Jafa, 2005: 148).

The Indian governmental reaction was very similar to the Indian reaction in Punjab. Indian security forces attacked the terrorists with hard military aggression. Between 1990 and 2003, almost 17,000 terrorists have been killed by security forces (Jafa, 2005: 149). Yet the terrorism continues in the Kashmir region and none of the four significant terror groups have been dissuaded from their separatist cause. In fact, many worry that the confrontation over Kashmir between India and Pakistan is escalating, and with the introduction of nuclear weapons,[1] is particularly dangerous. Both sides are under serious delusions. The Pakistani government feels that it can force India to the bargaining table by constant and continuous use of asymmetric force, mainly through terror attacks, and the Indian government feels that it can defeat militancy in Kashmir through superior military might (Shankar, 2003). By 2000, India had over 700,000 troops jammed into a valley populated by a large Muslim majority in an attempt to keep a lid on the growing terror problem (Marquand, 2000: 7). That same year, then Prime Minister Atal Behari Vajpayee broke with Indian foreign policy history and went with hat in hand to ask the United States for help in dealing with the separatist violence (ibid.). Neither side is making any real progress except to escalate tensions and the stakes of the Indo-Pakistan conflict.

India is the center of all conflict and all economic expansion in South Asia. India is a confounding dichotomy of successful economic and democratic development juxtaposed against extreme poverty and instability. India is involved, usually in a negative way, with most of its neighbors. The terrorism that results as India attempts to address all of the international and external destabilizing forces will only continue to grow. The United States is caught in an interesting foreign policy situation when it comes to India and the terrorism there. Caught between two allies, Pakistan and India, the U.S. government must continue a very unstable balancing act to keep both parties satisfied. While U.S. foreign policymakers might be inclined to side with India, given the democratic and economic development there and India's increasing importance as a military counter-weight to Chinese military expansion, Pakistan is of prime importance in the war on terrorism and especially the counterterrorism strategy against Al-Qaeda. There are no easy solutions to India's terrorism problem, and the extreme terrorist violence in Kashmir appears destined to continue.

The Prime Importance of Pakistan

In our opinion, Pakistan is the most important state in terms of terrorism. Unfortunately, we also find Pakistan to be one of the least-stable polities in the world. In this nation suffering from internal terrorism, external military threats, an unstable and fairly recent dictatorship, significant out-group animosity, uneven economic development, and growing Islamic funda-mentalism, it is amazing that dictatorial President General Pervez Mushar-raf held power as long as he did. Pakistan had been on its way toward be-coming a democratic republic, being rated very highly in the Polity IV database on the democracy scale until 1999, when General Musharraf took control of government in a bloodless military coup. Musharraf was a long-time ally of the United States and pledged to help in the U.S. war on terror. But as Musharraf's strength waned, Al-Qaeda and other fundamental Is-lamic terrorist groups gained importance and power over an increasingly dissatisfied public. Despite having suffered a serious and destabilizing set-back in governance less than ten years ago, it seems as if Pakistan is again facing a looming governmental catastrophe that could result in the installa-tion of a semi or fully theocratic government. This does not bode well for India, the United States, or the world.

Pakistan has suffered more terror attacks than any South Asian state. During our time period of study, 1975 to 2003, there were 188 international terror events, and between 1998 and 2003, 273 domestic terror events were reported. Many of these terror attacks were aimed at governmental offi-cials and supporters, including President Musharraf, who vowed rhetori-cally to help the United States in the war on terrorism and have instituted policies aimed at breaking at least some of the domestic terror groups within Pakistan. President Musharraf was targeted for assassination by Al-Qaeda, and in December 2004 he had two near misses. On 14 Decem-ber 2004, his motorcade narrowly missed the remote detonation of a bomb, and on 26 December 2004 two trucks ran into his motorcade in ex-cess of 80 miles per hour, killing four in his entourage with Musharraf es-caping injury (Priest, 2004: A1).

An Inauspicious Beginning

At the same time India was shaking off the yoke of colonial rule, so too was Pakistan. But it had been agreed that India and Pakistan should not stay joined as one state soon after the British departure. As a result, the 1947 Partition Plan was enacted and two new states were born. But the birth was hard for both new states. Prior to independence, the notion of an independent state of Pakistan had only been brought in open debate starting in 1940, seven short years before actual independence (Bose, 2004: 97). The lack of planning and debate prior to the split was endemic to the problems that occurred post-Partition.

There had been a serious proposal by some key political players to plan an orderly separation of Muslims and Hindus prior to the states of Pakistan and India formally coming into existence. But this proposal was categorically opposed by Gandhi, and Nehru opposed all but a plan to remove Muslims from the state of Punjab (Papanek, 1972: 5). Despite the powerful political figures against religious and ethnic separation, the act of separating a Muslim-dominated Pakistan from a Hindu-dominated India, which had shown serious nationalist/supremacist tendencies, created the factors necessary for a wide disorganized exodus of Muslims to Pakistan and Hindus to India (ibid.). Yet, as we have already stated, because the exodus was not planned, refugees were waylaid and ethnic and religious riots broke out that resulted in an estimated one million dead. Partition for India, Pakistan, and Bangladesh is the event of the twentieth century for these states, "equivalent in terms of trauma and consequence to the First World War (the 'Great War') for Britain" (Pandey, 1992: 31). In India the memory and perhaps implied responsibility are so painful that textbooks, histories, and movies all depict 14 August 1947, the day Pakistan became independent, as a mistake for which unnamed others were responsible (Pandey, 1992: 33).

Regardless of who is to blame for all of the bloodshed, Pakistan gained independence and, as Sumantra Bose states, independence is a time of exceeding, if short-lived, joy for Pakistani nationalists who are willing to accept the massive casualties, and the fact that numerous Muslims did not make it out of India, in exchange for a Muslim homeland (2004: 97). P. G. Robb warns us that we cannot look at Muslim separatism as simply a religious phenomenon, however. Robb explains that while religion did play a role, calls for Islamic separatism in South Asia have to be viewed against the backdrop of an increasingly hostile and rising Indian nationalism (1991: 105). Unfortunately, in the very first year of the Pakistan's existence it became painfully obvious the price Pakistan had paid from the Hindu exodus. An economic vacuum was created in Pakistan when the Hindus left en masse in 1947. West Pakistan was particularly devastated, and in January 1948 the Karachi riots broke out, further destabilizing portions of Pakistan's economy (Papanek, 1972: 5). Pakistan has recovered a great deal, economically, from this inauspicious beginning, but politically, one could argue that Pakistan is regressing.

From Partial Democratization to Dictatorship

Democracy has never established a strong foothold in Pakistan. The problem is that the vast majority of the Pakistani populace was predisposed to some kind of theocratic, or at the very least autocratic, rule in 1947 when it became and independent state (Bose, 2004: 104). Another problem, which we have previously stated, is that the movement for an independent Pakistan was less than ten years old — meaning that a foundation for government had not been properly laid. This left a very thin layer of intelligentsia at the top stratum of Pakistani society pushing for democratic reform, while the vast majority of the populace was more traditionally Muslim (ibid.). The two main proponents of the modernization and democratization process in Pakistan suffered early, untimely deaths. In 1948, the chief architect of the democratization and modernization movement in Pakistan, Muhammad Ali Jinnah, died of natural causes, and his close associate Liaqat Ali Khan was assassinated in 1951 (Maley, 2003: 207).

Pakistan limped toward democracy, attempting free and fair elections, but the vacuum left by these two untimely deaths ultimately resulted in a military coup and dictatorship from 1958 to 1962. Only very short periods of quasi-democracy would exist until 1989, as Pakistan suffered military dictatorship from 1969 to 1972 and again from 1977 to 1988 (Maley, 2003: 207). It seemed that Pakistan was on the path toward becoming a stable democracy and economy from 1989 to 1998. During these years, the Polity IV data set scores Pakistan's democracy at roughly an 8 out of 10 or a very stable and deep democracy. But this, too, was eventually interrupted in October 1999 when General Musharraf took control through a military coup. He led Pakistan as a dictatorial leader until the summer of 2008.

The picture would be grim enough, but two other factors are also leading to destabilization in Pakistan. First, during the military dictatorship of General Zia-ul Haq (1977 to 1988), "Islamization" policies were forced upon the nation (Bose, 2004: 104). This pleased radical Muslims and Muslim leaders as much as it angered pro-democratic forces. These policies also allowed radical Islamic extremists to grab a foothold in the military (Maley, 2003: 207). Islamic extremists gained further prestige and power when the Pakistani government decided to back the Taliban Mujahadeen resistance movement during the Soviet invasion in the late 1980s. This not only created an explosion in Islamic extremist Madrassahs in Pakistan (Haleem, 2005: 146) but also infused a proliferation of arms into private hands, usually into the hands of extremist and terrorist groups (Maley, 2003: 206). The Madrassahs sprang up, in part, to train insurgents in Afghanistan and Southeast Asia and, in part, as a check to Shiite activism after the Iranian revolution in 1978–79 (ibid.). For these reasons, militancy was infused into the fundamentalist Islamic teachings from the very start.

The Indo-Pakistani Conflict and the Looming Specter of Kashmir

In some ways it was unfortunate that the Soviet Union was so easily expelled by an ill-armed, ragtag group of jihadists backed by Pakistan and the United States. Cold War tensions made strange bedfellows and emboldened the Pakistani government to support the exporting of jihad and Islamic terrorism against the Indian government in Kashmir. For almost three decades the export of Islamic extremism has been used by the Pakistani government as "a cheap way to bleed India continually" (Chellaney, 2002: 104).

Tensions between India and Pakistan have been present since the inception of the two states in 1947. The long march out of India for many Muslims did not go well and resulted in many deaths and injuries. Tensions escalated when India backed the secession of East Pakistan. The state of Bangladesh was formed in 1971 out of this successful secession, and Pakistan is certainly partly to blame for the cavalier and noninclusive attitude displayed toward the Bengal Muslims, but the Pakistani military has long been determined to find revenge for this perceived Indian meddling (Stern, 2000: 115).

The opportunity the Pakistani military and government sought took the form of the Kashmir dispute. India controls the Jammu and Kashmir region through legitimate means by the acquiescence of the nobility in 1947 when nonaligned princely states were allowed to choose which state, India or Pakistan, they wished to join. But this has lent no legitimacy to India's claim in the eyes of the Pakistani government, people, or the Muslims living in Indian-controlled Kashmir. Worse still, the larger area that would have been Kashmir is divided between India and Pakistan. India controls two-thirds of this area (in the form of Jammu and Kashmir) and Pakistan controls one-third, known as Azad Kashmir or Free Kashmir (Yasmeen, 2003: 189). Both lay claims to the other's portion, but the fiercest fighting is over the Indian-controlled Jammu and Kashmir region. Unfortunately, both the Indian army and the Pakistani terror groups have killed thousands of civilians in the conflict (Stern, 2000: 115). While the Indian army's actions are not terrorist in nature, they are no less heinous, illegal, or unjust.

The *intifada* uprising in Kashmir in 1989 was supported by both the Pakistani government and Al-Qaeda. This low-level insurgency was viewed by the Pakistani military as a low-cost tactic that might destabilize India internally. The low-level insurgency continued for ten years, until people became battle fatigued and the specter of nuclear warfare reared its ugly head in 1998, when both Pakistan and India successfully tested multiple nuclear devices. In order to revive the conflict, the Pakistani government began supporting suicide terrorist raids, starting in 1999, that targeted governmental offices and officials (Chellaney, 2002: 104).

The recent invigoration of terrorism in Kashmir, spurred on by the Pakistani government, has produced some horrendous terror incidents. In one incident (October 2001), thirty-one Indian assembly members were killed and sixty injured when militants detonated a bomb in the legislative assembly building in Kashmir (Lavoy, 2002: 29). Terrorism has increased in frequency and destructiveness since 1999, and today, India and Pakistan are further apart on the Kashmir issue than in any time in recent history.

General Musharraf in the Middle

General Musharraf's days in office are over. No one could have maintained the delicate balancing act in which he was entangled. Musharraf was caught between the United States, India, and domestic, militant Islam. Given the extent to which the Pakistani government has backed and continues to back terrorism in Kashmir, harsh words between leaders in India and Pakistan, and the nuclear posturing, it would seem that Musharraf would have liked nothing better than to win back Jammu and Kashmir for Pakistan. But the ties between Pakistan and the United States were never stronger than under the Musharraf regime, and the U.S. government was not only also allied with India, but wanted Pakistan to join wholeheartedly in the war on terrorism, specifically Al-Qaeda. The U.S. government had even threatened an Afghanistan-style invasion of part or all of Pakistan (Raghavan, 2004: 151). Pressure also emanated from Indian Prime Minister

Atal Vajpayee, which caused General Musharraf to publicly ban five militant Islamic groups in January 2002 (Evans, 2002: 94). Ironically, Musharraf used and backed some of these same groups in order to continue to foment terrorism in Kashmir. In fact, in the same speech in which he banned these five fundamentalist groups, Musharraf said that Pakistan would continue to support the Kashmir freedom struggle (Lavoy, 2002: 31).

Such contradictory behavior had angered local terror groups, especially Al-Qaeda, which sought to assassinate General Musharraf on at least two occasions. Domestic terrorism was spreading in Pakistan at an alarming rate. The northwest frontier province of Peshawar, where Al-Qaeda is assumed to be based, attempted to break free of Musharraf's control through a particularly brutal terror campaign. On 14 July 2007, a deadly rocket attack aimed at governmental buildings and security installations killed twenty-four people (Ismail Khan, 2007: 12). In the capital, Islamabad, a militant cleric and some students who had committed acts of terrorism in the capital took refuge in a famous holy site known as the "Red Mosque" and held off Pakistani security forces for weeks. Over one hundred people died in retaliatory terrorist strikes after Musharraf made the decision to end the stand-off by force. As one observer simply stated, "Musharraf's leadership is failing" (Andan R. Khan, 2007: 30).

The problem is that since the dictator fell, Pakistan will likely turn into the world's first nuclear, fundamental Islamic theocracy, with heavy influence from Al-Qaeda shaping the government and foreign policy initiatives. In fact, a recent U.S. intelligence report claims that Al-Qaeda has restructured its central organization in Peshawar and is now stronger than ever (De Young and Pincus, 2007: A1).

Pakistan's Uncertain Future

Pakistan is arguably the most important regional and world player in terms of terrorism. The problem is that governmental instability and the incomplete democratic reform in Pakistan have laid the groundwork for a future Pakistan that is even more brazenly militant, fundamentally Islamic, and a promoter of regional and international terrorism. Pakistan is also being destabilized, regionally, through Indian military pressure and, domestically, through an increasingly strong Al-Qaeda and larger fundamental Islamic movement. Pakistan is the number one priority in the war on terror, but the prospects for dealing peacefully with Pakistan dwindle every day. The U.S. military seems to realize this, as the chairman of the Joint Chiefs, Admiral Mike Mullen, has made overtures to the Pakistani government emphasizing "America's eagerness to help Pakistan in the fight against foreign terrorists and homegrown militants" (Shanker, 2008: 6).

In South Asia, Instability Means Terrorism

From an ill-thought decolonization and partition plan to current instability borne from ethnic and religious hatred, sputtering, incomplete, or dead democracy movements, poor treatment of minority out-groups, Al-Qaeda's involvement, and widespread poverty, South Asia contains every single destabilizing factor in spades. It is no wonder that terrorism flourishes in the region. Worse still, there is no light at the end of the proverbial tunnel as none of these problems has been dealt with effectively. If anything, the two giants of South Asia, India and Pakistan, continue to ramp up the violence on a weekly basis. With spillovers across borders and between groups, it will take a regional effort to stem the terrorist tide. But cooperation seems last on everyone's list, and the United States seems to vacillate between intermittent and unproductive meddling and periods of neglect as the U.S. government remains bogged down in Iraq. The future for South Asia and the world does not look bright at this point.

Much of the instability in South Asia can be traced through horrendous Partition decisions and post-Partition treatment. Bangladesh might not have suffered so much terrorism if it had been allowed to form its own nation from the onset or if Pakistan had treated the Bengal Muslims as equal (in which case Pakistan might have retained East Pakistan). The princely states, especially Jammu and Kashmir, have caused a perpetual Northern Ireland type of situation between India and Pakistan. However, unlike Northern Ireland, terror groups are much more unrestrained in their targeting and killing of civilians. The British colonizers favored the Tamil minority in Sri Lanka, and that has led to long-term resentment, violence, and terrorism.

But a failed colonial withdrawal is not the only explanation of terrorism in South Asia. Ethnic hatred plays a role in Sri Lanka, Pakistan, and India. In fact, a resurgent Indo-Aryan supremacist movement has gone a long way toward fueling domestic and regional terror aimed at Indian civilians and governmental officials.

Democracy has mainly brought instability to the region, which has fueled terrorism and, in the case of Nepal, provided the impetus for a Maoist terror campaign. The international community, as a whole, and the United States and Europe, in particular, missed an opportunity to infuse aid and support to the region as fledgling democracies arose. The opportunity still exists in many states and especially India, which is very close to stabilizing politically. But in Pakistan it is an opportunity lost, and the U.S. government's convoluted relationship with Musharraf will probably lead to a Pakistani rebuffing now that Musharraf is out of power.

Economically, poverty and terrorism do seem somewhat linked. But the link is part of a larger central government mistreatment of people in South Asia. Separatism is strong in many South Asian nations, as it is in Southeast Asia, and these larger separatist movements are often fueled by economic and human rights mistreatment by central governments in South Asia.

Unfortunately, South Asia is a Gordian knot of terror and terror groups that will not be easily untied. One panacea, like spreading democracy, will not work in combating the complex domestic, regional, and international roots of terrorism in the region. South Asia may be the focus of attention in the "war on terror" in the not too distant future.

Note

1. Both India and Pakistan tested a number of nuclear weapons in 1998; each successfully exploded six nuclear devices in a show of force.

References

Abeysekara, Ananda. (2001). "The Saffron Army, Violence, Terror(ism): Buddhism, Identity, and Difference in Sri Lanka." *Numen*. Volume 48, Number 1: 1–46.

Acharya, Arabinda. (2006). "India and Southeast Asia in the Age of Terror: Building Partnerships for Peace." *Contemporary Southeast Asia*. Volume 28, Number 2: 297–321.

Alavi, Hamza. (Spring 2002). "Pakistan Between Afghanistan and India." *Middle East Report*. Number 222: 24–31.

"All Over the Place." (27 August 2005). *Economist*. Volume 375, Issue 8441: 35–36.

Baldauf, Scott. (1 August 2001). "After Unrest, Nepal Tries to Regain Safe, Friendly Image." *Christian Science Monitor*. Volume 93, Issue 173: 1.

Baldauf, Scott. (8 May 2002). "In Nepal's Maoist Hunt, Villagers are Hit Hardest." *Christian Science Monitor*. Volume 94, Issue 115: 1.

Bayly, Susan. (April 1993). "History of the Fundamentalists: India After the Ayodhya Crisis." *Bulletin of the American Academy of Arts and Sciences*. Volume 46, Number 7: 7–26.

Bose, Sumantra. (2004). "Decolonization and State Building in South Asia." *Journal of International Affairs*. Volume 58, Number 1: 95–113.

"Bothersome Little People Next Door, The." (11 June 2004). *Economist*. Volume 373, Issue 8400: 43–44.

Burger, Angela S. (August 1992). "Changing Civil–Military Relations in Sri-Lanka." *Asian Survey*. Volume 32, Number 8: 744–756.

Chalk, Peter. (2001). *Pakistan's Role in the Kashmir Insurgency*. Washington, D.C.: Rand Corporation.

Chellaney, Brahma. (Winter 2002). "Fighting Terrorism in Southern Asia: The Lessons of History." *International Security*. Volume 26, Number 3: 94–116.

Dash, Kishore C. (Summer 1996). "The Political Economy of Regional Cooperation in South Asia." *Pacific Affairs*. Volume 69, Number 2: 185–209.

De Votta, Neil. (Spring 2000). "Control Democracy, Institutional Decay, and the Quest for Eelam: Explaining Ethnic Conflict in Sri Lanka." *Pacific Affairs*. Volume 73, Number 1: 55–75.

De Young, Karen, and Walter Pincus. (18 July 2007). "Al-Qaeda's Gains Keeps the U. S. at Risk, Report Says." *The Washington Post*: A1.

Evans, Alexander. (May/June 2002). "India Flexes Its Muscles." *Foreign Policy*. Number 130: 94–96.

Forrester, Duncan. (March 1975). "Factions and Filmstars: Tamil Nadu Politics Since 1971." *Asian Survey*. Volume 16, Number 3: 283–96.

Haleem, Irm. (2005). "Pakistan, Afghanistan, and Central Asia: Recruiting Grounds for Terrorism?" In *Democratic Development and Political Terrorism*. William Crotty, editor. Boston: Northeastern University Press: 121–46.

Hassan, Monirul, and Indrajit Kundu. (2005). "Reaching Social Integration or Consensus: Bangladesh as a Case Study." *International Social Science Review*. Volume 80, Issue 1: 29–40.

Hossain, Ishtiaq. (November, 1981). "Bangladesh-India Relations." *Asian Survey*. Volume 21, Number 11: 1115–28.

Hutt, Michael. (March 2007). "A Nepalese Triangle: Monarchy, Maoists and Political Parties." *Asian Affairs*. Volume 38, Number 1: 12–20.

Jafa, Yateendra. (2005). "Defeating Terrorism: A Study of Operational Strategy and Tactics of Police Forces in Jammu and Kashmir." *Police Practice and Research*. Volume 5, Number 2: 141–64.

Jenkins, J. Craig, and Doug Bond. (February 2001). "Conflict Carrying-Capacity, Political Crisis, and Reconstruction: A Framework for the Early Warning of Political System Instability." *Journal of Conflict Resolution*. Volume 45, Number 1: 3–31.

Khadka, Narayan. (Autumn 1986). "Crisis in Nepal's Partyless Panchayat System: The Case for More Democracy." *Pacific Affairs*. Volume 159, Number 3: 429–54.

Khadka, Narayan. (Spring 1995). "Factionalism in the Communist Movement in Nepal." *Pacific Affairs*. Volume 68, Number 1: 55–75.

Khan, Ismail. (15 July 2007). "Deadly Violence Surges in the Tribal Regions of Pakistan." *The New York Times*: A12.

Khan, Andan R. (23 July 2007). "Pushing Pakistan to the Brink." *MacLean's*: 30.

Kohli, Atul. (May 1997). "Can Democracies Accommodate Ethnic Nationalism? Rise and Decline of Self-Determination Movements in India." *The Journal of Asian Studies*. Volume 56, Number 2: 325–44.

Kramer, Karl-Heinz. (2003). "Nepal in 2002: Emergency and Resurrection of Royal Power." *Asian Survey*. Volume 43, Number 1: 208–14.

Kumar, Ram Narayan. (May 2005). "King Gyanendra and Democracy in Nepal." *Contemporary Review*. Volume 286: Issue 1672: 285–89.

Lavoy, Peter R. (Autumn 2002). "Fighting Terrorism, Avoiding War: The Indo-Pakistani Situation." *Joint Force Quarterly*. Issue 32: 27–34.

"Lessons of History, The." (23 October 1993). *Economist*. Volume 329, Issue 7834: 42.

Maley, William. (June 2003). "The 'War Against Terrorism' in South Asia." *Contemporary South Asia*. Volume 12, Number 2: 203–17.

Manor, James. (July 1996). "'Ethnicity' and Politics in India." *International Affairs*. Volume 72, Number 3: 459–75.

Mansfield, Edward D., and Jack Snyder. (Summer 1995). "Democratization and the Danger of War." *International Security*. Volume 20, Number 1: 5–38.

"Maoist Rebels Sign Peace Accord in Nepal." (22 November 2006). *International Herald Tribune*: 7.

Marquand, Robert. (22 March 2000). "India Seeks Clinton's Help in Combating Terrorism." *Christian Science Monitor*. Volume 92, Issue 83: 7.

Mathur, Kuldeep. (April 1992). "The State and the Use of Coercive Power in India." *Asian Survey*. Volume 32, Number 4: 337–49.

Murshid, Tazeen. (July 1995). "Democracy in Bangladesh: Illusion or Reality." *Contemporary South Asia*. Volume 4, Issue 2: 193–214.

Nadarajah, Suthaharan, and Sriskandarajah Dhananhayan. (2005). "Liberation Struggle or Terrorism? The Politics of Naming LTTE." *Third World Quarterly*. Volume 26, Number 1: 87–100.

Oberschall, Anthony. (March 2004). "Explaining Terrorism: The Contribution of Collective Action Theory." *Sociological Theory*. Volume 22, Number 1: 26–37.

Orjuela, Camilla. (March 2003). "Building Peace in Sri Lanka: A Role for Civil Society?" *Journal of Peace Research*. Volume 40, Number 2: 195–212.

Pandey, Gyanendra. (Winter 1992). "In Defense of the Fragment: Writing About Hindu-Muslim Riots in India Today." *Representations*. Number 37, Special Issue: Imperial Fantasies and Postcolonial Histories: 27–55.

Papanek, Hanna. (October 1972). "Pakistan's Big Businessmen: Muslim Separatism, Entrepreneurship, and Partial Modernization." *Economic Development and Cultural Change*. Volume 21, Number 1: 1–32.

"Peace at Last in Punjab." (22 May 1993). *Economist*. Volume 327, Issue 7812: 45.

Peebles, Patrick. (February 1990). "Colonization and Ethnic Conflict in the Dry Zone of Sri Lanka." *The Journal of Asian Studies*. Volume 49, Number 1: 30–55.

Phillips, A. (3 June 1991). "India's Danger." *MacLean's*. Volume 104, Issue 22: 26–31.

Pradhan, Suman. (May 2004). "Nepal Is South Asia's Worst Trouble Spot." *New Internationalist*. Issue 367: 7.

Priest, Dana. (3 January 2004). "U. S. Aids Security of Musharraf: Efforts Build After Attacks in Pakistan." *Washington Post*: A1.

"Problem Shared, A." (25 March 2006). *Economist*. Volume 378, Issue 8470: 45–46.

Pyakural, Bishwambher, and Kishor Uprety. (Winter 2005). "Economic and Legal Impact of Conflict on States and People in South Asia with Specific Reference to Nepal." *Journal of Social, Political, and Economic Studies*. Volume 30, Number 4: 459–84.

Raghavan, V. R. (Autumn 2004). "The Double-Edged Effect in South Asia." *The Washington Quarterly*. Volume 27, Number 4: 147–55.

Rao, P. Venkateshwar. (April 1988). "Ethnic Conflict in Sri Lanka: India's Role and Perception." *Asian Survey*. Volume 28, Number 4: 419–36.

Rashiduzzaman, M. (March 1997). "Political Unrest and Democracy in Bangladesh." *Asian Survey*. Volume 37, Number 3: 354–68.

Robb, P. G. (1991). "Muslim Identity and Separatism in India: The Significance of M. A. Ansari." *Bulletin of the School of Oriental and African Studies, University of London*. Volume 54, Number 1: 104–25.

Schendel, William Van. (February 2002). "Stateless in South Asia: The Making of the India–Bangladesh Enclaves." *The Journal of Asian Studies*. Volume 61, Number 1: 115–47.

Sengupta, Somini. (17 October 2006). "Skills Gap Threatens Technology Boom In India." *The New York Times*: A1.

Shankar, Bajpai K. (May/June 2003). "Untangling India and Pakistan." *Foreign Affairs*. Volume 82, Issue 3: 112–26.

Shanker, Thom. (4 March 2008). "Joint Chiefs Chairman Asks Pakistanis What They Need." *New York Times*. A6.

Smith, Thomas B. (July 1986). "Referendum Politics in Asia." *Asian Survey*. Volume 26, Number 7: 793–814.

Sprinzak, Ehud. (September/October 2000). "Rational Fanatics." *Foreign Policy*. Number 120: 66–73.

Stern, Jessica. (November/December 2000). "Pakistan's Jihad Culture." *Foreign Affairs*. Volume 79, Issue 6: 115–25.

——. (July/August 2003). "The Protean Enemy." *Foreign Affairs*. Volume 82, Issue 4: 27–40.

Swami, Praveen. (April 2004). "Failed Threats and Flawed Fences: India's Military Responses to Pakistan's Proxy War." *India Review*. Volume 3, Number 2: 147–70.

Thompson, William R. and Richard Tucker. (June 1997). "A Tale of Two Democratic Peace Critiques." *The Journal of Conflict Resolution*. Volume 41, Number 3: 428–54.

Upadhyaya, Prakash Chandra. (October 1992). "The Politics of Indian Secularism." *Modern Asian Studies*. Volume 26, Number 4: 815–53.

Wallace, Paul. (March 1986). "The Sikhs as a 'Minority' in a Sikh Majority State in India." *Asian Survey*. Volume 26, Number 3: 363–77.

Ward, Michael D., and Kristian S. Gleditsch. (March 1998). "Democratizing for Peace." *The American Political Science Review*. Volume 92, Number 1: 51–61.

Yasmeen, Samina. (2003). "Pakistan's Kashmir Policy: Voices of Moderation?" *Contemporary South Asia*. Volume 12, Issue 2: 187–202.

Yunus, Muhammad. (11 June 2007). "Give Bangladesh Duty-Free Access to US Markets." *Christian Science Monitor*. Volume 99, Issue 136: 9.

CHAPTER 10

Central Asia and the Role of the Soviet Union

T HE DISSOLUTION OF THE SOVIET UNION in 1992 brought to casual observers a perception of an era of peace in international affairs with the effective end of the Cold War that had dominated global politics for four decades. The most visible threat to the United States had been nuclear conflict with a large, organized, and well-armed antagonist. Whether the Soviet collapse was brought on by unsustainable, centrally planned economics or a fundamental failure of ideas, the impact on U.S. national security seemed obvious.

Time soon exposed the underlying reality, which was that the powerful socialist and communist governments had suppressed internal political tensions across Eastern Europe, Eurasia, and Central Asia. The dissolution of Yugoslavia and that of Czechoslovakia were prominent examples of what could happen. With the end of the Soviet government, rivalries between and within the former Soviet republics were soon to emerge.

While the organizing power of the Soviet government was gone, the factors that made the region an economic, political, and military power remained. Tremendous resources are scattered across Eurasia, including arable land, oil, gas, and a well-educated populace. Though significant problems existed (and remain) within the military, the conventional weapons became even more dangerous as control devolved to multiple state and non-state actors.

This chapter considers three states—Tajikistan, Afghanistan, and Uzbekistan—that are each very different, yet they have commonalities in their history that are illuminating. Two of these states' political experiences—those of Tajikistan, and Uzbekistan—were shaped by Soviet-style communism, their economies are not particularly prosperous, and national identity is troubled. These three states are important because of their potential impact on broader regions, but also because their similarities and differences provide an opportunity to understand some of the underlying factors in terrorism.

Afghanistan, while not formally part of the Soviet satellite state orbit, owes much of its current instability and terrorism to the Soviet invasion of December 1979. The subsequent Islamic Mujahadeen and fundamentalist Taliban government were direct results of the Soviet invasion. The Soviets removed forests as they retreated in the late 1980s, further destabilizing the economy of Afghanistan. But it was the relocation of Al-Qaeda from Sudan to Afghanistan that prompted the current U.S. invasion and the greatest increase in terrorism.

Uzbekistan Terrorism

Uzbekistan is a large state, about the geographic size of California, with a population of 26 million. It is landlocked, sitting between Afghanistan and Kazakhstan. Islam has been important in the local culture for centuries, variously promoting pan-Islamism and opposing Soviet domination in the early 1900s (Ilkhamov, 2001). While repressed by the communist government, significant parts of the population held onto the notion of Islam as part of their independent political identity (although knowledge of the Koran and Islam may have been limited).

Islam Karimov has been president of Uzbekistan since independence in 1991, and the government is generally characterized as authoritarian. His first term was extended by two years, and constitutional manipulations have kept him eligible for, and in control of, the presidency ever since. Long-standing tensions between the urban and rural areas form the basis of political division in the state. But competition between former Soviet power holders and independent-minded but disenfranchised groups is also a factor.

Political competition has also played out along regional lines, leaving the Fergana Valley region out of meaningful participation in the central government. The Fergana Valley, which holds about one-third of Uzbekistan's population, sustained Islamic institutions during Soviet rule, and became home to terrorist training schools in the 1990s (Olcott and Babajanov, 2003). The political uncertainty and economic dislocation of the 1990s created an environment for opposition groups to act against the state.

President Karimov worked to accumulate the government power into the executive, and moved power also from the provinces to the central government (Ilkhamov, 2001). In his efforts to combat the opposition, Karimov labeled all opposition movements as terrorists developed and backed by foreign influences. There is some truth to this claim, stemming from connections between Islamic groups in Uzbekistan and Afghanistan, as well as Uzbekistan's role in drug trafficking between Afghanistan and Russia. However, there is clearly a strong domestic opposition to the government that goes beyond "foreign control."

In some parts of Fergana, the government lost legitimacy to the point that Sharia law (fundamentalist Islam) was enforced by nongovernmental actors in the early 1990s. Although the government has reasserted power, the organization Hizb Ut-Tahrir continues to work toward an Islamic polity. The group describes itself as nonviolent, but interconnections between nongovernmental political organizations underscore the need for specific expertise in analyzing the linkages between policy and violence.

Given the political setting of an authoritarian regime, economic decline, and a geographically based opposition minority, it is no surprise that the MIPT-TKB lists many acts of terrorism in Uzbekistan. In 2005, a group attempted to detonate a bomb outside the Israeli embassy. In 2004, a suicide bomber linked to the Uzbek Islamic Jihad Group killed himself and two other people at the Israeli embassy in Tashkent. That same year, a bomb and gunshots were used against police at a checkpoint outside of Tashkent. Three people were killed in another suicide bombing at a marketplace in Tashkent in March 2004, the day after another suicide bomber killed six people in a residential area. In an example of a coordinated act of terrorism, the Islamic Movement of Uzbekistan detonated six car bombs at about the same time outside of government buildings in the same city (February 1999).

These acts reflect consistency with our definition of terrorism. Each of these acts was in the capitol city (Tashkent), representing the provincial opposition to the central government. Several bombings near the Israeli embassy likewise align with Islamic Jihad opposition to Israel. Political, financial, and tactical connections between opposition groups in the Fergana Valley and Afghanistan support the notion of international forces at work, but long-standing political conflict between the central government and rural populations are at the center of the terrorist acts.

Tajikistan and the Soviets

Soviet policies of *perestroika* and *glasnost* were important factors preceding independence in Tajikistan. The former, meaning restructuring, resulted in economic dislocation and declining state investment. Political power in the north (which includes part of the Fergana Valley) and the capital of Dushanbe claimed the limited resources, thereby increasing hardship in the south. As in Uzbekistan, however, geography was but one factor in internal politics.

The southern regions were home to growing political opposition at the time of independence in 1991 (Akbarzadeh, 1996). The northern areas, which had control of the central government, were more inclined to conservatism that sustained the Soviet-style politics. This approach by the leadership at the time of independence ceded the banner of nationalism to the opposition, which enabled it to attract support on the basis of anticolonialism.

Political maneuverings in the central government sparked opposition protests, which in turn triggered pro-government demonstrations in the streets. Skirmishes led to battles, and by 1992, Tajikistan was in civil war. A peace agreement was reached in 1997, and for the past decade the state has been trying to establish a viable economy and a stable government. However, it is the poorest of the former Soviet Republics, which undermines political and economic development in the state.

In 2006, Imomali Rakhmanov was re-elected president of Tajikistan in what was reported to be the latest in a series of unfair elections (Gorst, 2006). The opposition continues to struggle against the central government, but opposition leaders are imprisoned and intimidated.

Terrorist acts in Tajikistan may be an expression by the opposition that they do not have confidence in the system. MIPT-TKB reports a series of bombs in June 2006 in central Dushanbe. Government offices were the target of a bomb in September 2003. In 2001, the Minister of Culture was shot and killed by an assassin, as was an advisor to President Rakhmanov.

The authoritarian government in Tajikistan would seem to preclude significant acts of terrorism, but the physical landscape of the state makes much of the population very isolated. Attempts to disrupt the government or rally supporters occur periodically, such as those acts already cited. Islamic leaders escaped Tajikistan in the early 1990s to refuge in Afghanistan, which established links with Al-Qaeda and other groups with the training and resources necessary to support terrorism.

Invasion and Instability in Afghanistan

Afghanistan has never been a shining example of economic development. Much of the rural population lives in what many describe to be fifteenth- or sixteenth-century living conditions. The major cities are not much better, lacking a modern sewage disposal system, running water in parts of the city, and other amenities taken for granted in First World states. While Afghanistan does have significant natural gas reserves and some mineral resources, the Soviet Union, historically, took advantage of Afghanistan by bullying the state into selling these resources at a much reduced rate (Wafadar, 1982: 152). Afghanistan also has a booming opium drug trade, which has made it difficult for any central government to exert control over all of Afghanistan, adding further destabilization to the mix (Haq, 1996: 950).

The first major disruption to an already fragile, some might even say failing, government and economy came in the form of the December 1979 Soviet invasion of Afghanistan. The immediate economic result of the invasion was a 50 percent drop in economic production (Wafadar, 1982: 152). Pakistan and the United States were the two most interested states backing the Mujahadeen and the expulsion of the Soviets. The United States wanted the Soviets to lose because the USSR was its prime Cold War adversary, while the Pakistani government, in the form of General Zia, was looking to appease the Pashtun minority in northwest Pakistan (Hilali, 2002: 291). The solution was backing the Mujahadeen. Unfortunately for the United States, Osama Bin Laden played a large role in funding the Mujahadeen in Afghanistan in their conflict with Soviet invaders. His larger-than-life status was made in a single battle in which Arab Afghans stopped advancing Soviet forces in fierce fighting. Benjamin and Simon note, "Bin Laden took part, and while the details of his actions are clouded in myth, his reputation as a fighter was made there" (2002: 100).

Another unintended consequence of United States intervention was the effect on the Afghan economy. U.S. support for the local resistance movement further destabilized the economy as the U.S. Central Intelligence Agency (CIA) poured millions into funding the Mujahadeen and supplying arms to the fighters; the Mujahadeen began making even more money with the newly acquired arms to provide security for local opium producers (Haq, 1996: 951). By the late 1980s, Afghanistan and Pakistan were producing the lion's share of the world's heroin (Hilali, 2002: 302). Al-Qaeda had learned it could fund its terrorist campaign through illicit drug trafficking, and this lesson has spread to neighboring Pakistan and even into Southeast Asia.

The fundamentalist Taliban government attempted to impose strict interpretations of the Quran on the Afghan populace. In an attempt to control the people further, the Taliban destroyed much of the meager infrastructure in Afghanistan (Emadi, 2006: 430). Both the Soviet invasion and brutal occupation and the human rights abuses at the hands of the Taliban-led government led to an exodus of Afghans into neighboring Pakistan (Wafadar, 1982: 152). This destabilized Pakistan to some degree and helped to build ties between the states that could be later exploited by drug traffickers and terrorist organizations.

The legacy of the Taliban is a particularly grim one. Today, despite U.S. intervention and aid from international organizations, roads in the capital city of Kabul are still littered with men with disabilities begging for money (Emadi, 2006: 434). Kabul also still has to ration insufficient electricity, and the majority of people in Kabul do not have access to basic necessities like clean drinking water (Emadi, 2006: 438). The rural areas of Afghanistan are still not controlled by the central government, and the people in these areas do not feel particularly compelled to follow the U.S.-backed government, which is accused of being corrupt (Emadi, 2006: 439) and continually demands a cessation in opium production, which is one of the major money-producing endeavors in the state.

The most incredible thing about Afghanistan is that terrorism did not rear its head in any meaningful sense until the Taliban were removed by force through the U.S. military invasion in 2002. The MIPT-TKB reports that Afghanistan had experienced six or fewer terror attacks a year. However, in 2002, Afghanistan experienced sixty-five terror incidents. As the United States settled into occupation mode in 2003, the number of terror attacks more than doubled to 148. In 2004, there were 146 terror attacks and the campaign continues to ramp up. In 2005, there were 207 terror attacks and 2006 saw 352.

The Afghanistan case is very instructive. It does not seem to matter whether a communist dictatorship is forced on a state or whether a benevolent democratic leader unseats a human-rights-abusing regime. The resultant instability caused by invasion and overthrow lays the groundwork for terrorist groups to exploit. The fact that the United States is nobly attempting to rebuild and stabilize Afghanistan after a horrendous two decades of Soviet and Taliban destruction has proved to be no inoculation against terrorism. In fact, terrorism is burgeoning in Afghanistan and terror groups seem to gain strength in Afghanistan with each passing year.

The Soviet Legacy of Instability in Central Asia

The dissolution of the Soviet Union left fifteen new states in Eurasia to find their way. New states are prone to conflict and chaos (Horowitz, 2003), which provide the environment for terrorism when a motivated group loses hope that their aims can be achieved through broadly accepted political means. Tajikistan and Uzbekistan each entered independence with uncertainty, a divided polity, and no recent experience in democracy.

But telling differences help identify issues behind terrorist activity. A central issue is the faith that people have in the political processes of their state. When people believe that their concerns can be addressed through "legitimate" political activity such as voting or protests, they are more likely to work through such mechanisms.

Other acts, such as intimidation of political campaigns and journalists, could be connected to political outcomes. However, the pattern of attacking journalists who challenge the elected leadership or threatening opposition candidates would point to political groups that seek stronger association with Russia or more conservative (authoritarian) politics. That would mean the party holding the presidency in the late 1990s and early 2000s — which was losing popular support — was the intended beneficiary of terrorism, rather than the opposition. This, in the end, is quite consistent with the notion that those who do not believe the status quo political system can achieve their agenda are the ones likely to engage in terrorism.

Uzbekistan had the lowest terrorist incident score, as well as the lowest democracy score. There are two theories that could explain this. The first is that a highly authoritarian regime has intelligence services and law enforcement agencies that effectively bar terrorist groups from significant action. This situation can be found in several states around the world at any one time — proving its possibility — but is likely not the primary factor in Uzbekistan's situation, given our at least partial knowledge of terrorist events. The second theory is that, following the tradition of Soviet government, the state controls information tightly to ensure the best face possible on the international stage. This may be a partial explanation of the low terrorism scores in Uzbekistan.

A third factor may be that the opposition in Uzbekistan is concentrated in the Fergana Valley, where it had some autonomy during the data analysis period of 1975 to 2003. The imposition of Sharia law in the early 1990s was one indicator of this. Drug trafficking and connections to terrorist or resistance training camps in Afghanistan give the Uzbek opposition considerable resources for violent acts of terrorism.

Tajikistan had a high domestic terrorism score, and the highest international terrorism score for Central Asia. In part, this may be attributed to the civil war and continued political alienation of the opposition (hence the low democracy score). The opposition's geographic connection to the Uzbek opposition in the Fergana Valley, as well as other resources in Afghanistan, creates the international underpinning for terrorism.

An important issue to raise is the democratic orientation of the Tajik opposition, which broadly sought liberal reforms since independence. Political maneuverings by the central government undermined faith in the system, and pro-government responses to public protests pushed the opposition away from peaceful or legitimate politics and descended into civil war. But the idea that terrorism can be linked to authoritarian politics does not endure.

Afghanistan suffered from a lack of economic development, an extremely disruptive and damaging Soviet invasion in 1979, a fundamentalist Taliban regime, the introduction of the most dangerous international terror group, Al-Qaeda, and a second invasion by U.S.-led forces, which triggered a titanic increase in terror activity. Afghanistan is a prime example of how terrorism seems to breed and thrive in an atmosphere of prolonged chaos and governmental interruption.

Instability and the Soviet Legacy

Political uncertainty at the end of the Soviet era left political and power vacuums across Eurasia and Central Asia. Violence was used — and continues to be used — as a means of achieving economic or political agendas, but it had different causes and different forms. Criminal entities used both targeted and blunt acts to influence enemies, groups associated with government interests used violence to intimidate opposition, and political opposition forces used violence to affect policy and rally supporters.

Common to each of the three situations explored in this chapter were issues of legitimacy, either in the political or criminal justice processes. With varying understandings of fundamental societal values, the former Soviet republics did not have long-standing traditions to moderate and resolve political differences. Soviet invasion of Afghanistan proved to be costly not only to the Afghanistani people but, with the rise of Al-Qaeda under Taliban rule, to the world.

All of these cases conform to a common theme seen throughout our study: instability is closely associated with terrorism. Again, it does not matter whether the instability is grounded in virtuous motives or not. Instability creates the backdrop that terror groups use to exploit their position, often against much stronger military or governmental foes.

John Locke wrote that the formation of government is a decision by individuals to cede authority to a political body. People do this when they see greater good in a government, and they act against a government when they see no value and no hope in the status quo. Terror groups exploit citizens' feelings of confusion and mistrust when instability arises, giving prophetic credence to Locke's statement.

References

Akbarzadeh, S. (1996). "Why Did Nationalism Fail in Tajikistan?" *Europe-Asia Studies*. Volume 48, Number 7:1105–29.

Benjamin, Daniel, and Steven Simon. (2002). *The Age of Sacred Terror*. New York: Random House.

Emadi, Hafizullah. (Winter 2006). "Rebuilding Afghanistan Five Years After the Collapse of the Taliban." *Contemporary Review*. Volume 288, Issue 1683: 430–40.

Gorst, Isabel. (7 November 2006). "Tajik President Set for Easy Poll Win." *Financial Times*: 11.

Haq, Ikramul. (October 1996). "Pak-Afghan Drug Trade in Historical Perspective." *Asian Survey*. Volume 36, Number 10: 945–63.

Hilali, A. Z. (2002). "The Costs and Benefits of the Afghan War for Pakistan." *Contemporary South Asia*. Volume 11, Issue 3: 291–310.

Horowitz, S. (2003). "War after Communism: Effects on Political and Economic Reform in the Former Soviet Union and Yugoslavia. *Journal of Peace Research*. Volume 40, Number 1: 25–48.

Ilkhamov, A. (2001). "Uzbek Islamism: Imported Ideology or Grassroots Movement?" *Middle East Report*, Number 221: 40–46.

Olcott, M., and B. Babajanov. (March/April 2003). "The Terrorist Notebooks." *Foreign Policy*, Number 135: 30–40

Wafadar, K. (February 1982). "Afghanistan in 1981: The Struggle Intensifies." *Asian Survey*. Volume 22, Number 2: 147–54.

CHAPTER 11

Terrorism in Northern Africa

TERRORISM ON THE AFRICAN CONTINENT is unique. Just as each African state is unique in its history and culture, each state has a unique terrorist situation. In this chapter we address terrorist activity in the region, focusing on the states with high incidences of terrorism.

Terrorism in Africa is misinterpreted and misunderstood when compared in analyses with the rest of the world. The most common tendency when studying any subject is to find commonalities within the subject and then draw conclusions from those common traits. When looking at terrorism in Africa, it is difficult to find a common trait other than terrorism itself. The first difficulty lies in the common misunderstanding of the continent. David Lamb said it best: "No continent has been more mistreated, misunderstood and misrepresented over the years than Africa" (Lamb, 1987: 12). The climates, cultures, ethnicities, geography, and governments vary tremendously, yet we still tend to group the region under the single heading — Africa — and assume there is a single, easily understandable culture and governance under that heading.

To keep the discussion of terrorism on the African continent manageable, we divided the analysis into two chapters by region: northern Africa and Sub-Saharan Africa. This is not a division of the continent by terrorist activity or groups but purely by geographical boundaries commonly accepted in the literature. There are five major states of interest in northern Africa: Algeria, Egypt, Ethiopia, Somalia, and Sudan. In Sub-Saharan Africa (Chapter 12) we explore the four states experiencing the highest levels of terrorism: Uganda, Angola, Kenya, and South Africa. These nine states account for 75 percent of all regional international terrorism and 91 percent of all domestic terrorism.

North African Terrorism

North Africa is comprised of those countries north of the Sahara Desert. Their main cities stretch along the coastal waters from the Atlantic Ocean, around the waters of the Mediterranean Sea, past the Red Sea to the Indian Ocean. Behind these cities and separating these states from the remainder of the continent is a vast emptiness of the Sahara Desert, which forms a formidable obstacle and separates the northern states from their central and southern neighbors.

Given their high volume of terrorist activities, we focus on five North African states, which account for 63 percent of international terrorism and 72 percent of domestic terrorism on the continent (Table 10). Because of recent attacks and increased activity by Al-Qaeda in northern Africa, the George W. Bush administration designated northern Africa as a key region in combating the spread of global terrorism (Lyman and Morris, 2004). This region of Africa does deserve the most attention in the international war on terrorism, and the state with the highest number of terrorist incidents, Algeria, is of special interest. Sudan is also of special interest not only for the massive instability revolving around the genocide being perpetrated by the Muslim-dominated, dictatorial government but also for the fact that Sudan was the state that initially harbored Al-Qaeda and allowed it to grow and thrive.

Secular or Sharia Law in Algeria?

In Algeria in December 1991, the political party of the Islamic Salvation Front (FIS) was poised for victory after the first round of elections (Hall, 2005: 73). The rise to power of this Islamic-based political party threatened the power base of the more secular National Liberation Front (FLN). In January 1992, "a group of military officers led by Khaled Nezzar, the Defense Minister, stepped in and engineered a coup d'état" (Volpi, 2006: 555). This prompted a decade of violence, 1992–2002, that resulted in the loss of at least 100,000 lives from fighting between the emergence of armed religious and ethnic groups (Testas, 2002: 161).

Recorded during this same time period were 181 terrorist incidents in Algeria. This leaves only six incidents prior to the coup. This, by far, ranks as the highest terrorist rate on the continent and is triple the number of incidents in any other state in Africa except Egypt (MIPT-TKB).

Table 10 ■ Breakdown of the Highest Terrorism-Experiencing States in Africa by Frequency of Events and Casualties

State*	International terrorism, 1973–2003	Domestic terrorism, 1998–2003	Injured (all available dates)	Fatalities (all available dates)	Total casualties (all available dates)
North					
Algeria	74	113	1,426	1,039	2,465
Egypt	109	2	855	330	1185
Somalia	60	3	187	127	314
Ethiopia	46	8	298	197	495
Sudan	36	2	42	102	144
South					
Angola	65	6	216	358	574
South Africa	30	25	194	12	206
Uganda	27	16	462	546	1,008
Kenya	10	1	5,166	242	5,408
Total	457	175	8,846	2,953	11,799
Total North	289	126	2756	1,693	4,603
Percent in North	63.24%	71.59%	31.27%	57.33%	39.01%
Total South	168	50	6,080	1,260	7,196
Percent in South	36.75%	28.40%	68.73%	42.67%	60.99%

* These 10 cases represent roughly 80% of the total terrorist incidents for the African Region.

The response of the Algerian government was not democratic, but the government was facing a very real terrorist threat. The secular government was, and is, caught between a rock and a hard place. As the government cracks down on Islamic terrorism, the legitimate political arm representing Islamists gains ground. If FIS was able to gain a majority in the ruling assembly, then Sharia law and an anti-Western stance could be instituted formally through democratic governmental initiatives. Thus, democracy does not insure either that Western allies will be created or that terrorism will be repelled.

The world has seen the rise of two radical Islamic governments: the rule of the Ayatollah Khomeini in Iran after the fall of the Shah; and the rule of the fundamentalist Taliban in Afghanistan, which ended with the American invasion and occupation in 2002. Numerous documentaries and articles have expressed the harsh treatment of women, the strict conformity to Islamic teaching and Islamic law, and the fertile ground for the exportation of radical Muslim fundamentalism. Hence it is evident why the government of Algeria took the steps that it did in preventing the rise to power of the Islamic Salvation Front. The result, however, was the emergence of a violent, armed wing of the Islamic Salvation Front—the Armed Islamic Group (GIA). The GIA targeted business, economic, private citizen, and diplomatic targets until 2001 (MIPT-TKB). Its violent attacks against civilians "began to alienate some of the members of the Islamic Salvation Front, many of whom were subsequently granted immunity after separating themselves from the GIA. Hence one tactic to end terrorism is to begin to split opposition groups and then co-opt the less militant faction" (Hall 2005:73). This governmental tactic of divide and conquer illustrates the necessity to at least consider negotiating with the rational and moderate factions within terror groups in order to erode the power and the threat posed by the main terrorist organization.

All organizations mutate as events unfold over time. For the GIA, its membership has opted for pardons offered under the "Peace and Reconciliations Charter" or moved on to a splinter group — the Salafist Group for Call to Combat (GSPC). One also finds members of the GSPC linking up with the current, most significant terrorist group in Algeria, the Al-Qaeda organization in the Islamic Maghreb. Algeria now faces a renewed energy in terrorism that emanates from an outside force. With the number of terror attacks increasing, it will now be the challenge of the new Algerian government to provide stability. Algeria's terrorist threat continues to be deadly and connected to the larger issue of international terrorism through Al-Qaeda's increased presence.

Egypt's International Terror Problem

As mentioned earlier, the Sahara Desert has been one of the major factors in the differing development between north and south Africa. The one place where the regions tend to blend together is the eastern portion of northern Africa, which is the focus of much of the terrorist activity on the continent. In the Horn of Africa, Egypt is the political and economic power. Its biggest challenge as a regional leader is controlling international terrorism.

In terms of international terrorism, Egypt ranks at the top of the list in the region with 109 incidents between 1975 and 2003. This contrasts with only two domestic terror incidents in Egypt from 1998 to 2003, highlighting the extent to which international terrorism is indeed a problem for this state. The development of the different terrorist organizations in Egypt is based on the dissatisfaction with the government since President Sadat. President Sadat's predecessor, President Nasser, was viewed as a tough politician who was willing to stand up to Israel and the Western powers. Upon Nasser's death in 1971, President Sadat was elected to power and made great changes in economics, politics, and Egypt's view of, and foreign policy with, Israel. Because of the government's growing tolerance and foreign policy engagement with Israel and the United States, violent fundamental Islamic groups emerged. Fundamentalism also gained traction as popular socialist promises given by Sadat's successor, Gamal Nasser, failed to materialize and many Egyptians grew disenchanted (Benjamin and Simon, 2002).

The basic stated goals of the terrorist organizations in Egypt vary slightly. These goals include: the establishment of a fundamentalist Islamic state in Egypt; militant Egyptian nationalism; opposition to any Middle Eastern governments that these groups deem to be aligned with the West and the injustice of the Egyptian government under President Mubarak; and opposition to all U.S. foreign policy engagement and intervention in the Middle East.

One of the initiatives sought by President Sadat was greater political freedom and forgiveness of past transgressions, which included the release of many members of the Muslim Brotherhood. The Muslim Brotherhood, founded in 1928, is an officially banned political movement in Egypt. Although its stated political agenda is nonviolent, members with a more violent predisposition carried out or supported violence as a means of changing policy, which helped to fragment the Muslim Brotherhood. One of these splinter groups is al-Gama'a al-Islamiyya (GIA).

GIA was linked to thirty-seven terror incidents between 1992 and 1998. Recently, the spiritual leader of GIA, Sheik Umar Abd al-Rahman, has been arrested and is serving a life sentence for his involvement in the 1993 World Trade Center bombings. This all but ended GIA's terrorist activities. With the fading of GIA, Abdullah Azzam Brigades of Al-Qaeda Egypt and the Levant has surfaced and has been associated with recent attacks in Egypt. This group has been linked to one particularly devastating terror attack in July 2005, which killed at least sixty-seven people vacationing at the popular Red Sea resort of Sharm el-Sheikh ("The Bombers Stir," 2005: 40). Despite the new name, Martyr Abdullah Azzam is very similar to GIA. Both have stated goals that are very similar and both have heavily targeted the tourist industry. Both also have ties to the Al-Qaeda network.

Tourism has consistently been the target of choice for terrorist groups in Egypt. Attacks on tourists account for only 37 percent of all incidents but, at the same time, account for 79 percent of the casualties (MIPT-TKB). Unless targeting a specific individual or activity, tourism has provided the best source of casualties for the myriad organizations operating in Egypt.

Terrorists target tourism for two main reasons: Egypt has a unique combination of ancient sites, and Red Sea beach resorts attract Westerners by the thousands. Tourists spending time at resorts and visiting ancient ruins generated $6 billion in 2004 for the Egyptian economy (Wells, 2006: 48). Attacking tourists not only harms the economy, but could destabilize or even topple the government (Spencer, 2006: 16). Basically it disrupts a multi-billion-dollar industry, discredits the government by showing how ineffective the police force is in its ability to protect the foreign tourists, and forces the government to dedicate more resources toward protecting this economic interest.

Tourism also has a "Clash of Civilizations" aspect to it. On the one side are the visiting Westerners, who bring with them social behavior that involves alcohol, gambling, and showing far more skin on the beaches than allowed by fundamental Islamic beliefs (Spencer, 2006: 16). On the other side are the Islamic fundamentalists, who want to rid Egypt of Westerners, their money, their influence, and these abhorrent social behaviors.

Another point of tension within the tourism industry is the existence of pre-Islamic statues or ancient artifacts. In Afghanistan, the ancient Buddha statues at Bamuyan were destroyed by the Taliban in 2001 because of their strict Islamic beliefs and the emphasis by the Taliban on the primacy of Islam. Similar opinions and actions could prompt targeting of Egypt's ancient structures as some can be viewed as un-Islamic. These structures were "neglected by Egyptian Muslims until British colonists arrived and began both to restore them and show the Egyptians how lucrative they could be" (Spencer, 2006: 16). For the terrorists, tourism becomes a high-payoff target—that is, they view it as an opportunity to kill "infidels," to cause chaos and economic problems for the government, and to receive the desired attention for their causes and agendas.

Egypt has a long history of a surrogate role in terrorism for foreign terrorist organizations. Egypt's role is unique as it is not a state sponsor of terrorism but local fundamental populaces provide the backdrop for Egypt as a participant in the execution of domestic terrorist acts carried out by outside, international organizations. This was evident when Hezbollah planted mines in the Suez Canal causing damage to nineteen ships in August 1984 (MIPT-TKB). Also reported is the Lebanon-based organization, Amal, which also ventured into Egypt with attacks in 1990 and 1992. The list continues with Al-Fatah, Al-Saiqa, Native-African September, and the Palestine Liberation Front. These foreign, group-based organizations are significant for Egypt as they account for a sizable number of the total incidents in the state.

The Muslim Brotherhood has also been linked to numerous terrorist incidents and organizations throughout the Middle East. For example, Sheik Ahmed Yassin began his career in the Egyptian Muslim Brotherhood but went on to found Hamas in the Israeli occupied territories in 1987 (Amiel, 2004: 38). He was instrumental in crafting the unwavering Hamas party line that Israel must be wiped off the earth and no compromise solution could be accepted (ibid.).

Domestic groups, especially the Muslim Brotherhood, still pose a significant threat, but in the post-9/11 period the United States has increased its support for the Egyptian government led by Hosni Mubarak. In this position, the U.S. government remains the main donor ally to Egypt and has looked the other way as Mubarak has arrested hundreds, if not thousands, of Muslim Brotherhood activists (Black, 2007: 20). Jeffrey Black worries that the semidemocratic institutions in place in Egypt are taking a significant hit in order to wipe out the remaining remnants of the Muslim Brotherhood (2007: 23). Laying the debate over dwindling democracy aside, the Muslim Brotherhood is waning but outside terror threats continue to pose a significant problem for Egyptian stability. Further, as in any dictatorial or semidictatorial regime, there is significant doubt over the stability of the fragile Egyptian government when Mubarak steps down or is forced from office.

Egypt is somewhat unique in that an unusually large number of foreign groups are conducting and claiming responsibility for terror incidents within the state. These groups appear to have the same goals, yet there seems to be no major organizational coordination in their efforts. As a whole, Egypt has a significant amount of terrorist activity, but most of it emanates from outside the state itself. Despite this fact, Egypt also has a clear history of domestic fundamentalism in the form of the waning Muslim Brotherhood.

Further, one can conclude that international terror groups would have a much more difficult time operating and succeeding if a significant portion of the domestic populace did not support these groups and their actions. Currently, there are two rising specters on the horizon that threaten the stability of Egypt. Workers in Egypt have recently begun protesting the deteriorating wages and the economy. These protests have been met with threats and arrests by the government, further enraging the angry workers (Slackman, 2008: 1). The instability caused by the deteriorating economic situation in Egypt is exacerbated by Palestinians in the Gaza Strip blowing up the border wall between Egypt and the Gaza Strip and flooding in as refugees ("Fenced In," 2008: 5). Despite the fact that Egypt forced the refugees back into the Gaza Strip and repaired the wall, it is unlikely these actions will result in a long-term solution to the problem. Considering all of this, the future of a post-Mubarak Egypt looks potentially chaotic and it might provide a power vacuum that resurgent fundamental groups will attempt to fill.

Significant Separatist Movements in Ethiopia

Ethiopia has faced a far different terrorist threat than Egypt. In fact, Ethiopian terrorism more closely resembles secessionist-inspired terrorism present in South and Southeast Asia. Ethiopian terrorist attacks are marked by a long series of incidents by the Eritrean People's Liberation front (EPLF). These attacks targeted the government and businesses with the goal of bringing attention to the issue of an Eritrea separate from Ethiopia. The EPLF felt it had no choice but to fight, as the United States had taken a foreign policy stance in the 1980s that made it clear it wanted Ethiopia to remain unified at all costs (Cliffe, 1987: 82). The Ethiopian government used this opportunity to establish a brutal regime of repression and neglect of all Eritreans. Unification of disparate groups was justified by the Ethiopian government because Italian colonization had forced these groups to coexist for so many years. The Ethiopian government claimed "historic rights" to a unified Ethiopia but often resorted to repression to contain and coerce these groups into a larger union (Sorenson, 1991: 302).

The EPLF rebelled and in a two-pronged insurgency, it fought directly with military forces and committed acts of terrorism against non-Eritrean Ethiopians, almost daring the army to respond (Cliffe, 1987, 81). What followed was a classic war of liberation, from insurgency to armed conflict and terrorism to independent state. In 1991, the EPLF troops defeated the Ethiopian Army and, in 1993, forced a referendum that created an independent state of Eritrea.

What remained in Ethiopia were two terror groups. One separatist terror group was based on the goal of carving out an Oromo state or home-land for the Oromo people. The Oromo are culturally distinct from the Ethiopian majority and have a distinct language, placing further barriers between realistic reconciliation and integration into a larger Ethiopia (Blackhurst, 1980: 55–56).

The other group is made up of people from the Tigray region, which is comprised almost entirely of Tigray people. Besides being distinct cultu-rally from the Ethiopian majority, the Tigray people are pressuring the Ethiopian dictatorship toward a more democratic form of governance. This is not sitting well with the Ethiopian government and has been met with governmental repression (Reid, 2003).

The success of the Eritrean movement in breaking away from Ethiopia has provided a model for success for other separatist terrorists to emulate. This is compounded by a state that ranks as one of the twenty poorest in this study, with an average GDPpcPPP of 671 and with one of the highest terror-ist incident rates (Table 9). Without proper funding, the government has no capital to counter the terrorist threat or to improve the infrastructure and economy, which separatists use as a rallying cry against the government. Separatism should continue to be a leading cause of instability and terrorism in the future for Ethiopia. It will be largely justified through the continuing brutal repression perpetrated by the central government. An independent Eritrea also harbors ill-will against its former oppressors and often takes the opposite foreign policy stance on contentious issues if Eritrea feels it will cause pain and instability to the central government. A key example of this involves the Islamic Courts Union movement in Somalia. The Ethiopian government openly backs the fragile central government, while the Eritrean government backs and supports the Islamic Courts Union despite having no ideological or religious affinity toward the group (Mushtaq, 2007: 19).

Chaos and Civil Unrest in Somalia

Somalia is a state without a stable or recognized government. "Warlords and political factions control territories, and factional fighting continues unabated" (Dagne, 2002: 63). When the statistical analysis from MIPT-TKB is examined, one finds a long list of unknown groups attacking the people and infrastructure of the state. From a total of sixty-three attacks, only five incidents are associated with five different named groups; the re-maining ones are attributed to unnamed groups. This is likely the result of conflict between clans, warlords, and rival factions, or just general lawlessness, which is endemic in Somalia. It is difficult to distinguish which, because reporting out of Somalia is so sparse. There is no unified cause or objective, just a struggle for power and control in Somalia, which has been historically, and is currently, marked by periods of tenuous dictatorial rule followed by chaotic and bloody power vacuums.

This was evident as early as 1984, when the U.S. military conducted part of its humanitarian exercise "Bright Star" in Somalia. Fourteen hundred U.S. troops were airlifted into Somalia from Egypt to help deliver food and restore order under operation "Bright Star" starting in 1980 (Volman, 1984). By 1984, food supplies were still being left sitting to rot on the loading docks because Somalia lacked adequate infrastructure and cohesiveness to deliver the food to the people. When offers were made by the United States to assist in the distribution of those supplies, these offers were declined. Somalia started a downward spiral toward chaos despite having gained some strategic status in U.S. Cold War foreign policy (Volman, 1984). This decline culminated in total anarchy in 1992 and a second U.S.-led peacekeeping mission under a mandate from the United Nations Security Council was enacted. Somalia has both a long history of chaos and a long history of poor interactions with the United States and Western aid organizations.

What raises the most concern in Somalia today is not the level of terrorism in the state but the spread of Islamic fundamentalism. What is found is that "the absence of central authority in parts of Somalia has created an environment conducive to fostering terrorism and extremist groups, and analysts do not doubt that they are present in Somalia though their current strength and numbers are uncertain" (Dagne, 2002: 64). Increasingly, terrorists and insurgent groups seem to have a fundamental Islamic predisposition. This is particularly evident in the recent Islamic Courts movement, which attempted to seize power in 2006 and establish a fundamentalist theocratic government.

After General Said Barre's dictatorship fell in 1991, Somalia has been in chaos, fighting a fragmented civil war involving dozens of warlord led tribal factions (Mushtaq, 2007: 17). In 2006, the Islamic Courts Union renamed itself the Supreme Islamic Courts Council and waged war on the warlords of Mogadishu in an attempt to divide and conquer the warring factions. By June 2006, the Supreme Islamic Courts Council had defeated the warlords in Mogadishu and had taken control of Somalia's capital city (Mushtaq,

2007: 17). The Supreme Islamic Courts Council continued to consolidate power in 2006 and began to attack and defeat warlords outside of Mogadishu, eventually wresting control of much of the fertile land and Somalia's lucrative southern ports (Dealey, 2006: 50).

In 2007, Ethiopian forces invaded Somalia with the prodding and help of the United States and with the support of the United Nations ("A Brittle Western Ally," 2007: 31). The United States provided air attacks supporting the Ethiopian invasion, which local Somalis found to be "nothing short of humiliating catastrophe," as Ethiopia has long been a mortal enemy of Somalia (Mire, 2007:23).

U.S. involvement in Somalia is not surprising as Somalia is a state containing nearly nine million Muslims, many of whom back the Islamic Courts movement and the fundamental laws and practices that have been enacted (Dealey, 2006: 50). Recently, public execution of murderers, usually conducted not by a governmental official but by a family member of the murdered victim, banning of traditional folk music and other "un-Islamic material," and strict enforcement of modesty on Somali women have become common in areas controlled by the Supreme Islamic Courts Council (Mushtaq, 2007: 18).

The United States has also asserted that the Supreme Islamic Courts Council is sympathetic to the Al-Qaeda movement and may even be supporting it. There is a clear indication that Osama bin Laden wants influence over Somalia. He has recently released an audiotape lauding the Islamic Courts' victories in Somalia (Mushtaq, 2007: 18), and he has openly urged Al-Qaeda followers to "open up shop there" (Perry, 2007: 17). The George W. Bush administration accused the spiritual leader of the Islamic Courts movement, Hassan Dahir Aweys, of giving refuge to at least some of the terrorists responsible for the bombings of the U.S. embassies in Kenya and Tanzania (Mushtaq, 2007: 18). The U.S. military has even recently targeted and killed Saleh Ali Saleh Nabhan, a mastermind of the embassy bombings who was hiding in Somalia (Carter, 2008: 1).

Given all of this, it is no coincidence that the U.S. government has invested in the security force of Kenya, which is a southern neighbor to Somalia. From a military perspective, the region would make an excellent training, staging, and deployment area for international terrorists. Training in Somalia, supported by Islamic fundamentalist and clan leaders, combined with international travel through the economic center of Kenya, makes Somalia, potentially, a prime location for international terror groups.

A Long Conflict in Sudan

Terrorism in Sudan is twofold, encompassing acts of terrorism in the state itself as well as Sudan's historical and current support to outside terrorist organizations. Both have had a significant impact on the state's ability to achieve some form of stability and growth. Internal terrorist incidents in Sudan have created an environment where new ideas and individual talent have been lost to violence. Infrastructure is destroyed or damaged to a point where time and money are spent on protecting or repairing rather than improving the state's often bleak economic condition.

In Sudan, one cannot ignore the fact that the state has been in almost constant armed conflict for several decades. This long-term conflict finds its roots in a state with a major ethnic division. This is a classic "Clash of Civilizations" situation. This clash is a result of poorly drawn colonial lines and even worse implementation of colonial rule by the British. British colonizers decided on a bifurcated colonization of Sudan. The British ruled the mostly Arab, Islamic north and the non-Arab south as two separate entities but the British never created two separate states. The northern partition of Sudan has always held a large Muslim and Arab majority. Islam penetrated Sudan in the seventh century, when Islamic conquerors attempted to create a broader Middle Eastern caliphate under Osman Ibni Affan (Ousman, 2004: 89).

The southern partition of Sudan practiced largely indigenous beliefs, along with a small but significant grouping that practiced Christianity. The Islamic forces built power during the Cold War as the United States backed any organization willing to at least rhetorically disavow communism (Ousman, 2004: 91). Islamic fundamentalism gained strength and by the 1970s it had become a powerful political force (ibid.). The British failed to protect the southern portion of Sudan as they disengaged from and ultimately left Africa. The result was that the southern provinces were overrun with Arab teachers and Islamic clergy backed by Muslim police and military personal. The heavy-handed tactics practiced by these interlopers led to a decades-long civil war that has recently escalated into a state-sponsored genocide of Sudanese Christians (O'Balance, 2000).

A breakdown of terrorist incidents in Sudan shows a predominance of incidents by southern groups protesting repression by the northern Islamic government. The main organization responsible is Sudan's People's Liberation Army (SPLA). The SPLA was formed in response to the southern region's alarmed reaction to the attempt to institute Sharia law. There is an international dimension to the SPLA as well, as Uganda is openly backing its fight against the Sudanese government and Islamic fundamentalism (Peterson, 1998: 1).

The conflict between Afghanistan and the Soviet Union produced Osama bin Laden as a myth and allowed him to create Al-Qaeda. Many people are under the mistaken assumption that Al-Qaeda then set up shop in Afghanistan after the Soviets were expelled. This is not the case. It turns out Al-Qaeda was originally headquartered in Sudan, where a growing Islamic movement and Islamic military dictatorship welcomed the money and development offered by bin Laden's organization. Al-Qaeda quickly developed a close relationship with the Islamic military dictatorship in the form of the National Islamic Front, and among the first things Al-Qaeda operatives received from the government were "several hundred valid Sudanese passports" (Benjamin and Simon, 2002: 112). As Benjamin and Simon note, "there was hardly a battle anywhere involving Islamic radicals in which Al-Qaeda was not involved" (2002: 113). Al-Qaeda spent $100,000 to support Eritrean Islamic Jihad in Ethiopia, provided equipment and training to MILF and Abu Sayyaf Group in the Philippines, and supported the fundamentalist Jamit Ulema Islamiyya party in Pakistan (Benjamin and Simon, 2002: 112–13). Al-Qaeda operatives also successfully attacked U.S. embassies in Kenya and Tanzania while operating out of Sudan, and this prompted U.S. President Bill Clinton to bomb a suspected chemical weapons manufacturing facility in Khartoum (Peterson, 1998: 1). Despite repeated attempts at intervention by the United States, J. Stephen Morrison believes "the United States will not be able to eliminate the threat to its security interests posed by Sudan and Somalia expeditiously or reliably in the near future. Both states are highly porous, fractured, and weak (or wrecked) states; both welcomed Al-Qaeda in the past and retain linkages to it today" (2002: 192). Again, prolonged instability seems closely linked with terrorism.

Sudan has been a hotbed of violence, chaos, and terrorism. Islamic fundamentalism gained a foundation under British colonial rule and only expanded from there. Somalia and Sudan are marked by unstable political systems and internal and external conflicts. Shaul Shay believes this is one of the key preconditions for terrorism in these two states (2005), and we agree with that assessment. Sudan is particularly distressing because of its past harboring of the entire Al-Qaeda organization, its current ties with Al-Qaeda and international terrorism, and the destabilizing genocide that is still ongoing there. Sudan is one of the most important states that must be watched if the United States is going to have any sort of effective global counterterrorism strategy.

A Continuing International and Domestic Threat in Northern Africa

Terrorism in northern Africa will continue to be the biggest concern for the continent for the foreseeable future. If terrorism continues, many states' infrastructures will never have an opportunity to grow and develop, and neither will their people. The climate of chaos and terrorist violence will hinder adequate agricultural production, and international aid will continue to be difficult to execute. The magnitude of the problem could compound itself in armed violence that creates more economic hardship, which, in turn, creates more dissatisfaction that results in more terrorism.

There is also a significant separatist/"Clash of Civilizations" component to much of the terrorism in northern Africa. In both Ethiopia and Sudan, historical mistreatment of minority populations by central governments has created a domestic terror problem. The success of EPLF and the creation of a separate nation of Eritrea only embolden separatist terror groups in northern Africa. The prolonged war between the National Islamic Front government in Sudan and the SPLA forces in the south has created instability and linkages with Al-Qaeda that will not soon be dealt with effectively. With so much poverty and so many different ethnicities, tribes, and clans in Africa, combined with the destabilizing influence of Al-Qaeda, terrorism could continue to grow at an alarming rate.

Nonetheless, the terrorist forecast in northern Africa is not all negative. Several groups have become inactive due to the arrest of key leaders or through mediation and the resolving of the indifferences. As in the cases of the Baader-Meinhof Gang or the Red Brigade, both terrorist organizations active in Europe in the 1980s, when key leaders are arrested or otherwise taken from power, then the organizations tend to lose their focus, drive, and effectiveness.

References

Amiel, Barbara. (5 April 2004). "Justifiable Homicide." *MacLean's*. Volume 117, Issue 14: 38.

Benjamin, David, and Steven Simon. (2002). *The Age of Sacred Terror*. New York: Random House.

Black, Jeffrey. (July 2007). "Egypt's Muslim Brotherhood in Crisis." *Middle East*. Issue 380: 20–23.

Blackhurst, Hector. (1980). "Ethnicity in Southern Ethiopia: The General and Particular." *Africa: Journal of the International Africa Institute*. Volume 50, Number 1: 55–65.

"Bombers Stir a Toxic Brew, The." (30 July 2005). *Economist*. Volume 376, Issue 8437: 40.

"Brittle Western Ally in the Horn of Africa, A." (3 November 2007). *Economist*. Volume 385, Issue 8553: 31–33.

Carter, Sara A. (4 March 2008). "U. S. Strike Kills Terrorist; Target Found in Somalia." *The Washington Times*: 1.

Cliffe, Lionel. (September 1987). "Congress in Eritrea." *Review of African Political Economy*. Number 39: 81–83.

Dagne, Theodros. (Fall 2002). "Africa and the War on terrorism: The Case of Somalia." *Mediterranean Quarterly*. Volume 13, Issue 4: 62–73.

Dealey, Sam. (27 November 2006). "Terror's Playground." *Time*. Volume 168, Issue 22: 50–53.

"Fenced In." (5 April 2008). *Economist*. Volume 387, Issue 8574: 4–7.

Hall, Gardner. (2005). *American Global Strategy and the "War on Terrorism*. Burlington, Vt: Ashgate Publishing.

Lamb, David. (June 1987). *The Africans*. New York: Vintage Books Edition, Random House.

Lyman, Princeton N., and J. Stephen Morrison. (January/February 2004). "The Terrorist Threat in Africa." *Foreign Affairs*. Volume 83, Issue 1:19–31.

Mire, Amina. (March 2007). "Grim Future: Ethiopia's Invasion of Somalia Ha US Fingerprints." *New Internationalist*. Issue 398: 23.

Morrison, J. Stephen. (Spring 2002). "Somalia's and Sudan's Race to the Fore in Africa." *Washington Quarterly*. Volume 25, Issue 2: 191–205.

Mushtaq, Najum. (January/February, 2007). "Divide and Conquer." *Bulletin of the Atomic Scientists*. Volume 63, Issue 1: 17–19.

O'Balance, Edgar. (2000). *Sudan, Civil War, and Terrorism, 1956–99*. New York: St. Martin's Press.

Ousman, Abdek. (Fall/Winter 2004). "The Potential in Islamist Terrorism in Sub-Saharan Africa." *International Journal of Politics, Culture, & Society*. Volume 18, Issue 1: 65–105.

Perry, Alex. (2 July 2007). "Somalia's Al-Qaeda Link." *Time*. Volume 169, Issue 27: 17.

Peterson, Scott. (4 September 1998). "Why Can't We Be Friends?" *Christian Science Monitor*. Volume 90, Issue 198: 1.

Reid, Richard. (2003). "Old Problems in New Conflicts: Some Observations on Eritrea and Its Relations with Tigray, From Liberation Struggle to Interstate War." *Africa: Journal of the International Africa Institute*. Volume 73, Number 3: 369–401.

Shay, Shaul. (2005). *The Red Sea Terror Triangle: Sudan, Somalia, Yemen and Islamic Terror*. Rachel Liberman, translator. Piscataway, N. J.: Transaction Publishers.

Slackman, Michael. (7 April 2008). "Day of Angry Protest Stuns Egypt." *International Herald Tribune*: 1.

Sorenson, John. (June 1991). "Discources on Eritrean Nationalism and Identity." *The Journal of Modern African Studies*. Volume 29, Number 2: 301–17.

Spencer, Robert. (May 1, 2006). "Tourism Jihad in Egypt." *Human Events Online.com* (http://www.humanevents.com/article .php?id=7591): 16.

Testas, Abdelaziz. (2002). "The Roots of Algeria's Religious and Ethnic Violence." *Studies in Conflict and Terrorism*. Volume 25, Number 3: 161–84.

Volman, Daniel. (March 1984). "Africa's Rising Status in American Defense Policy." *The Journal of Modern African Studies*. Volume 22, Number 1: 143–51.

Volpi, Frederic. (June 2006). "Algeria's Pseudo-democratic Politics: Lessons for Democratization in the Middle East." *Democratization*. Volume 13, Number 3: 442–45.

Wells, Rhona. (April 2006). "Middle East Destinations Lead the Field." *The Middle East*:48–53.

CHAPTER 12

The Terrorist Experience
in Sub-Saharan Africa

INSTABILITY AND TERRORISM ARE NOT confined to northern Africa. Almost every state south of the Sahara Desert has had some form of terrorist incident—with the exception of one, Malawi. The remaining Sub-Saharan states have had varying degrees of instability that have resulted in terrorist attacks. This chapter focuses on the four states that have experienced the highest levels of terrorism within the Sub-Saharan region: Uganda, Angola, South Africa, and Kenya. Malawi is also included as one of the rare examples of an African nation-state not in perpetual chaos, as it has a terrorism-free history.

Sub-Saharan African states have suffered countless governmental changes since the region gained its independence from colonial masters in the 1960s during the "Springtime of Freedom." Since that time, most states have experienced leadership changes initiated by military coup or prolonged civil war. Violent conflict seems to be a part of everyday life in Sub-Saharan Africa. Explanation for some of this can be found in the colonial era of the continent. Some states colonized under the French now experience a system "very centralized, unified, and bureaucratic and based on direct rule and assimilation. In contrast to the British system which was regarded as very decentralized, pragmatic and based on indirect rule, which means the respect of native customs and chiefs" (Ousman, 2004: 67). Additionally, the creation of arbitrary boundaries between colonial powers resulted in ethnic problems. Prior to colonial rule, ethnic groups lived in regions recognized by each other. With poorly drawn colonial boundaries, traditional enemies have been forced to live together in close proximity or ethnic groups are spread across multiple borders, creating tensions between states (Kalipeni, 1992: 4).

Another aspect of Sub-Saharan African life is a general acceptance of death. Ancient history teaches us the differences in the ways cultures develop based on the environment. Mesopotamia developed more of the "live for today" philosophy based on the random flooding of the Tigris and Euphrates rivers. Egypt was a more planned society because of the annual flooding of the Nile. For Sub-Saharan Africa, life was harsh with disease taking a large toll, particularly among newborns and children. Infant mortality rates were, and remain, high, and created a society where death is common and an almost daily part of a tribal life. In Rwanda, personal accounts of brutal killings — where ethnic Hutus stood in line and waited their turn — emphasize an acceptance of the harshness of life in Sub-Saharan Africa.

Tribalism is another common aspect of Sub-Saharan life. Tribalism is ethnic heritage that creates common links between like-minded people. Ethnicity plays a key role in much of the violence in Sub-Saharan Africa. For example, the brutal killings in Rwanda show how deep ethnic hatreds can run. But "tribalism is one of the most difficult African concepts to grasp and one of the most essential in understanding Africa" (Lamb, 1987). Tribalism and other ethnic differences bring a usable dynamic to African terrorists. As seen in the Lord's Resistance Army (LRA) in Uganda, the issue is partially about members of the Choia ethnic group following a Choia-centric national vision and perpetrating acts of terror against ethnic opponents who do not share in the LRA vision. If a strong tribal group exists, it becomes a natural link for recruiting and identifying an organization's friends and enemies.

Lord's Resistance Army—A Brutal Terrorist Campaign in Uganda

The Lord's Resistance Army (LRA) has exhibited a particularly brutal brand of terrorism through rape, torture, and murder. This movement is one of the newest on the continent but has proven to be one of the deadliest. In existence since 1986, the LRA has been linked to thirty-three incidents of terrorist activity (MIPT-TKB). Most of these attacks, 57 percent, were directed against private citizens and property (MIPT-TKB). The founder of the organization, Joseph Kony, began his movement as an armed rebellion against the government of Uganda with the goal of establishing a new government under his control (MIPT-TKB).

The recent history of Uganda has been the setting for violence and brutality. Action by the LRA could be perceived as a continuation of the violence the state has experienced over the years. It is difficult to determine where the state changed, as Uganda started as a state with no settlers trying to monopolize the economy and no political struggle between rival groups (Byrnes, 1992: 3–4). The most notable change comes with the brutal history of Idi Amin Dada. He has been linked to the torture and murder of over 100,000 Ugandan citizens (Melady and Melady, 1977: 175). Several accounts of village massacres and prison murders have been reported (Melady and Melady, 1977: 173). Additionally, his brutal reign was not limited to the people of Uganda. It appears that no one was safe from his brutality, as even twenty-two members of the Catholic Church, who were later declared saints by Pope John Paul VI, were killed by this erratic ruler (Melady and Melady, 1977: 135). Unfortunately, this level of violence did not end with the removal of Idi Amin. During the four years from 1981 to 1985, the Milton Obote UNLA government attempted to remove Yoweri Museveni as a political rival. This armed conflict resulted in more violence and death than under Amin's regime (Byrnes, 1992: 34). The Obote government was backed mainly by military forces made up of the Acholi and Langi people of northern Uganda. The UNLA troops also conducted operations in northern Uganda, which had been the ethnic base of Idi Amin (ibid.). This provided the perfect opportunity for the Acholi-based military to take revenge against Amin's supporters for past wrongs under Amin's rule. In 1985 and 1986, the state witnessed the eventual overthrow of Yoweri Museveni. This move to power forced the Acholi-based military to flee to their ethnic base in northern Uganda (ibid.). It should be no surprise that with the change of political power in 1986, and with the loss of military power by the Acholi, the LRA rose to power.

The LRA has been terrorizing northern Uganda and has been linked to three recent attacks in Sudan. The attacks by the LRA have been notable for their brutality and their pointlessness or ineffectiveness (MIPT-TKB). There have been frequent questions as to how coordinated the LRA is. One author asks, how can there be a coordinated effort when the leadership of the organization displays no clear political agenda (Quaranto, 2006:137)? Still, thirty-three attacks, from 1992 through July 2006, resulted in 848 casualties, with approximately twenty-five casualties per incident—the largest casualty statistic for any African terrorist group (Table 10). We understand that guerilla warfare might use terrorist tactics in coordinated efforts to accomplish the goals of the movement, as seen by terrorist acts in Angola by UNITA. But it is difficult, in Uganda, to determine where armed conflict and guerilla warfare ends and terrorism begins.

Uganda is also a case where the secondary effects of terrorism may soon become a major issue. In Uganda's case, the impact has been on the social infrastructure — namely, the children. The LRA's army has been well publicized as an army of children. It has been estimated to be comprised of 80 percent children (McKay, 2005: 390). Long-term effects from children living a life of violence will still be seen for years, even if a peace agreement is signed by the Joseph Kony government. These young children have seen violence on a brutal scale, and Susan McKay worries that young women abducted into rebel forces will be particularly hard to reintegrate into society (2005: 394). She describes how young girls not only are abducted into the force but grow into motherhood and adulthood in this environment (ibid). There will also be a difficult judicial question, attempting to define criminal acts and terrorist acts that are carried out by abducted children between the ages of seven and seventeen (Quaranto, 2005:140).

Recently, the Sudanese government has pulled its support for the LRA and has forced the movement to shift its operation back to northern Uganda and to the Democratic Republic of Congo. Pressure from the military and lack of public support has prompted talks between the LRA and the United Nations. These talks are aimed at negotiating a lasting solution between the LRA and the Ugandan government. Because of the brutality of the attacks and the possibility of arrests, trial by international criminal courts becomes a distinct possibility. It becomes, ultimately, a choice of allowing the members of the LRA to come out of hiding and return to their homes without fear of arrest or continuing the threat of more violent acts until the LRA can be cornered, eliminated, or forced into negotiations.

Two major points arise from Uganda. First is the concept of continuing struggle, of which the Acholi people appear to be the focus. This began with the rise to power of Amin, where one of his first actions was the mass execution of Acholi and Langi troops he felt were loyal to the previous government (Byrnes, 1992: 26). It continued with the return of Acholi soldiers to the new government and then their eventual loss of power. In all stages of this transition, brutality and mass atrocities were committed by all sides. It would be logical to propose that the protracted war and terrorist acts by LRA are a continuation of events beginning almost a half century ago. The second point for Uganda is the issue of children warriors and their return to some semblance of a "normal society." It will take a concerted effort on the part of the world community to not only end the terrorism in Uganda, but somehow provide a new beginning for this lost generation.

Fading Terrorism in Angola

Angola is one of the best examples of a nation suffering from a negative colonial experience. Angola is also ironically blessed with an abundance of easily accessible oil, diamonds, and other precious metals, yet Angola's lack of stability and the resultant poverty make it one of the worst places in the world to live (Malaquias, 2001: 521).

The struggle against Portuguese colonization in Angola began in 1956 with the formation of the Popular Movement for the Liberation of Angola (MPLA). The National Front for the Liberation of Angola (FNLA) formed soon after in 1961 and began fighting alongside the MPLA. A third group, UNITA, formed shortly after the MPLA and FNLA took up the struggle against Portugal (Ndumbe and Cole, 2005: 53). The MPLA emerged as the clear victor in 1965, when independence was achieved from Portugal. Portugal designated the MPLA as the anointed successor after the Portuguese withdrawal from the state. This designation left out other major players, like the FNLA and UNITA, and helped to create an atmosphere in postcolonial Angola that led to a degeneration into chaos. As one author aptly puts it, postcolonial Angola "quickly turned into a collective nightmare as the nationalist movements that led the anti-colonial struggle failed to find peaceful mechanisms to share power in a postcolonial state" (Malaquias, 2001: 522). Worse still, the MPLA quickly exploited its position as head of the Angolan state, creating an oligarchical dictatorship in which the members "transformed the few remaining viable portions of the state into their own private fiefdom" (ibid.).

Ethnic differences and Cold War rivalries added two more dimensions to conflict in Angola. UNITA disliked the *mestizo* (mixed Portuguese/Angolan race) aspect of most of the MPLA leaders considering themselves (free of Portuguese racial mixing) to represent pure or true Africans in Angola (Ndumbe and Cole, 2005: 53). This use of racial superiority by UNITA added a strong racial component to the violence and terrorism present in Angola since its independence.

Although the MPLA degenerated into a corrupt, ruling oligarchy that grew spectacularly rich by "embezzling billions of dollars in revenues originating from exploration of offshore oil" (Malaquias, 2001: 522), the MPLA was originally oriented to Marxist/Leninist ideals. Despite having quickly lost their Marxist/Leninist ways, Cuba and the Soviet Union backed and supported the MPLA-led government. The Cold War often made the two superpowers overlook the superficial commitment of dictatorial regimes to the causes of capitalism and communism, respectively, opting instead to find friends where the two powers felt it was strategically expedient. It is, therefore, no surprise that the Soviet Union backed the MPLA. It should also not be surprising that the U.S. government immediately chose the side of the UNITA rebels against an MPLA government that had become heavily reliant on Soviet monetary support and Cuban troops to remain in power (Ndumbe and Cole, 2005: 54).

The problem for the United States in the short and long term was that it had become complicit in sponsoring a group that drew no boundaries in its struggle against the MPLA and the civilians perceived as supporting it. The civil war that began almost immediately after independence in 1976 has claimed over half a million Angolan lives and has been fueled, in part, by a UNITA rebel movement that "degenerated into a powerful private guerilla force whose primary objective is inflicting unrelenting and indiscriminate suffering upon defenseless civilian populations while obliterating all infrastructures as a means to render the state ungovernable" (Malaquias, 2001: 523). Such actions by UNITA, which clearly target civilians with the express purpose of toppling the MPLA-led government, cannot be defined as anything other than terrorism. Donald Snow agrees with such a conclusion, noting that UNITA uses guerilla warfare, terrorism, and political mobilization to achieve its political ends (1998: 228). Further, Victoria Brittain notes that for twenty years after a failed U.S./South African attempt to expel the MPLA by force, the CIA backed Jonas Savimbi as the leader of UNITA. As Brittain aptly put it, "The CIA embraced Savimbi as warmly, and as unthinkingly, as it did Osama bin Laden. Both were dependable anti-communists. Both became terrorists" (2001: 24).

There is clear evidence that UNITA has increasingly used terrorism as its modus operandi in modern times. The *UN Chronicle* reports that on 16 August 2001, UNITA attacked the Angolan civilian railway system with a series of bombs, resulting in over 150 civilian deaths ("UNITA Attacks," 2001: 69). This attack was immediately condemned by the UN and then UN Secretary General Kofi Anan. The total number killed in this terror attack was later upgraded to 250 ("UNITA — Down but Not Out," 2001: 35). In May 2001, UNITA attacked just outside of the Angolan capitol of Luanda, in a town named Caxito. In this massive attack, UNITA rebels killed over 100 civilians, raided civilian stores, and abducted sixty children (ibid.).

More worrisome still are the increasing links discovered between terrorism and radical Islamic movements in western Africa and movements found in the Middle East. Daniel Morris observes that religious radicalism is on the rise in many western African nation-states (2006: 228). While there is no automatic correlation between religious extremism and terrorism, Morris found a clear link between western African extremism and Middle Eastern nation-states supporting or condoning such extremism. Morris argues that most western African states "have significant Muslim populations if not outright majorities whose communities have increasingly begun to welcome the training and funds provided by Iran, Saudi Arabia, and Pakistan" (ibid.). In Angola, Jonas Savimbi, the former leader of UNITA, sold diamonds from his rebel-controlled mines to Hezbollah, linking the two groups and causing speculation about how deep the coordination and cooperation between Hezbollah and UNITA ran (Ndumbe and Cole, 2005: 54).

Despite Jonas Savimbi's death in February 2002, at the hands of the MPLA military, UNITA continues to carry out guerilla and terror attacks against the MPLA government and innocent civilians. Angola is a state that bears close scrutiny going forward, as its natural resources not only can provide funding for terror within Angola but, because of ties with Middle Eastern terror groups and movements, can supply fuel for terrorism around the world. It should also be remembered that Al-Qaeda first set up shop in Sudan, and an Angola controlled by UNITA or fundamentalist elements in Angolan society could turn into a safe haven, a conduit, or material supporter for global and regional terror groups. The lack of stability, long and almost unbroken history of governmental abuses and rebel terrorism, and history and magnitude of death, all lead to instability that can continue to breed a significant terror threat.

South Africa, the African National Congress, and a Limited Form of Terrorism

The key to economic growth in Sub-Saharan Africa lies in South Africa. This country is a regional economic powerhouse that produces nearly a third of the income in all of Sub-Saharan Africa. South Africa is also a state that owes its success to early colonization and an abundance of natural resources, including gold and diamonds. The early colonization by European states became the foundation for success but also the friction point between competing interests that has generated political instability.

South Africa is a state where each racial group has had a significant impact in formation and development, and each has a stake in its future. This brings up the question of which group has the strongest claim to the land (Leach, 1986: 1). South Africa is a "racial cauldron" made up of native Africans, white Europeans, and Indians (ibid.). To understand terrorism in South Africa it is important to understand the historical background of South Africa and the historical friction between groups. The region traces its colonization back to the early settlement by the British and Dutch in the eighteenth century. Early Dutch settlements were first formed in 1652 as a supply point to assist ships of the Dutch East India Company in their travel around the southern tip of Africa. This early outpost expanded as men released from their contracts were allowed to develop farms in the area.

By the early 1700s, immigrants and independent farmers had imported slaves and began to expand their area of influence to the north and east of the Cape (Cape of Good Hope). These groups of settlers were known as "trekboers." By the late 1700s, events in Europe had shifted the balance of power in favor of the British and also control of the Cape in South Africa. By the mid-1800s, British settlers had arrived, pushing the descendants of the early Dutch settlers, "Boers," further to the north and east sending them clashing with the expansion of the Bantu tribes in the east, mainly the Zulu tribe.

To add to the confrontational issues, the discovery of diamonds and gold in the 1880s created conflict between the British and the Boers. The other significant aspect of the discovery of mineral wealth is the need for labor and the migration of native African workers to the area.

If you look at the armed conflicts during the history of South Africa, you will see wars that pitted Boers against Zulu, British against Boers, and British against Zulu. Each group has fought and died for the right to live and prosper in this land. For the Europeans, their presence has been an integral part of the colonization and modernization. For the native Africans, their labor has provided the workforce that has operated the mines and worked in the factories. What is common to all is that they all feel they have had the only legitimate claim to the land. Graham Leach sums it up in his examination of how South Africa was founded and its current status of interaction between native-Africans and whites by saying, "There is far more racial tension in the big cities of Britain, where there are a large immigration population, or in America. Maybe that is because each race knows that the other is here to stay. Perhaps, also, over 300 years of living together has established a common African consciousness in the minds of native-Africans and whites which even the harshest aspects of apartheid have failed to obliterate" (1986:18).

What makes this state interesting is that it is not a traditional struggle for power by one group trying to expel the other (as found in other states). In Egypt, it is the Muslim Brotherhood trying to gain political control of the state. In Angola, it was the competing interests of the MPLA and UNITA. What is left then is not a struggle for power but a struggle for equality.

Despite a rough start, South Africa has reached a turning point in terrorism, with its last reported incident in 2002 (MIPT-TKB). It is also important to note that of the fifty-five incidents, twenty-nine are by unknown groups and fall mainly between 1999 and 2002 (ibid.). This leaves the bulk of the incidents — and the focal point of terrorism in South Africa — to the ANC (African National Congress). The ANC was founded in 1912, shortly after the Union of South Africa was formed in 1910 (Davis, 1987: 1). Because of the laws restricting the lives of a native-African majority in the state, the ANC evolved as a political voice of the native-African population in a quest for equality. This series of laws that became the reason for political unrest was known as apartheid.

The basic method of action for the ANC was for change through peaceful and political means (Mandela, 1986: 162). This changed in 1961 with the formation of the armed wing of the ANC — the Umkhonto we Sizwe (Spear of the Nation) (Boehmer, 2005: 48). Why did the ANC switch from peaceful to violent means in order to achieve its stated political goals? Nelson Mandela, in his second court statement in 1964 during the Rivonia Trial, stated that he planned sabotage as a method to achieve political goals because peace was not working and he wanted to prevent the organization from escalating to violence against civilians. Mandela went on to say that the goal of the ANC was always for a nonracial democracy and that escalated violence would only pit white Europeans against native Africans in a continuous violent struggle. In lieu of allowing a violent terrorist response that would claim the lives of innocent civilians, the ANC chose sabotage because it was a method that should not involve the loss of life (1986: 161). In his statement, Mandela outlined the targets and limitation of Umkhonto. The main targets would be infrastructure such as rail, power, and communication facilities in order to hinder the economy and thus, force people to reconsider their position (1986: 168). Members of Umkhonto were given strict instructions that "on no account were they to injure or kill people in planning or carrying out operations" (1986: 168).

Mandela continued in his elaboration of the command structure and specified that Region Commands had authority to select targets but were restricted to guidelines laid out by the National High Command (ibid).

The end result to this is evident in reviewing the number of terrorist incidents in South Africa (Table 10). As shown in the table, South Africa has had fifty-eight terrorist incidents. The key is that there have been only twelve fatalities. This accounts for less than 1 percent of total casualties on the continent. Of the fifty-eight incidents, the ANC accounts for sixteen of these and only five fatalities (MIPT-TKB). What should also be noted in this statistic is that Umkhonto conducted several other operations, but these bombs created no destruction. This is important to the ANC in that the desired effect was still achieved without too much destruction or death. It would appear from these statistics that Umkhonto was fairly successful in achieving its goals for violent action without taking human life. In effect, the ANC achieved its goals by conducting a limited form of terrorism. Regardless of ANC's intent or methods of control, violence did occur and this violence is rightly categorized as terrorism. Since apartheid rule ended in 1987, it appears that South Africa has entered into a quiescent period in terms of terrorist activity.

Kenya: An Enticing Target for International Terrorists

Kenya has had very little problem with terrorist activity compared to the remainder of Africa. Despite some violent riots and bitter disagreements between rival political and ethnic groups, terrorism has not become the method of choice of the politically dissatisfied. During the 1950s, Kenya underwent one of the most violent times in the history of the state with the rise of the Mau Mau warriors. This reign of violence saw brutal attacks on people and property but has not been the basis of a long-term reign of terror. What Kenya does have, however, is a geographically central location and a stable form of government that offers economic growth, accessible transportation hubs, and tourism. Nevertheless, cross-border trade and ease of movement due to a heavy reliance on tourist trade, coupled with friendly relations with the West, especially the United States, makes Kenya a prime target for anti-Western international terrorists.

Kenya is in a unique geographical position. Its location at the bottom of a very unstable northern Africa makes it susceptible to problems and issues simply because of location. Surrounding Kenya on three sides are four states with some of the highest terrorism rates on the continent. The four states of Somalia, Ethiopia, Sudan, and Uganda have averaged 49.5 terrorist incidents over a three-decade span beginning in 1968 (Table 10). What merits attention in Kenya is not the frequency of attacks but the fact that they lead the continent in the number of casualties at well over 5,000 (ibid.). This statistic alone makes it important for scholars to examine not only the frequency of terror events but the ramifications thereof.

Of the eleven incidents in Kenya, eight have produced no casualties and one of the incidents had only two. This leaves two incidents: the bombing of an Israeli-owned hotel in Mombasa by Al-Qaeda (where ninety-three people were killed or injured), and the bombing of the U.S. embassy in Nairobi by Al-Qaeda in 1998 (where over 5,000 people were reported as injured or killed) (MIPT-TKB). With these two attacks, Al-Qaeda is responsible for over 40 percent of the total casualties in the region (ibid.).

Evidence recovered in 2004 details the methods of surveillance used by Al-Qaeda. The evidence recovered shows a "meticulous approach to terrorism" (Lipton and Weiser, 2004). Targets were photographed, sketched, and studied for years before an attack was carried out by operatives. Court records show that Ali A. Mohamed traveled to Kenya as early as 1993 to conduct surveillance on targets for bin Laden. Mr. Mohamed testified in court that he presented to bin Laden the pictures and diagrams from which he designated the location for the truck bomber (Lipton and Weiser, 2004).

The surveillance would have detailed the embassy located in a crowded area near the center of the city. Large buildings surrounded the embassy, and the daily population in the area guaranteed a large crowd. It was determined that the force of the explosion would be more effective in an enclosed area and that this would also result in a greater casualty rate.

On the morning of 7 August 1998, a truck laden with explosives approached the back gate of the American embassy in Nairobi (Helling, 2004: 872). Unarmed security guards stopped the truck and shots were fired from the terrorists. In the engagement, the truck drove into the parking area in the rear of the embassy, which was surrounded on three sides by large buildings. Personnel in the embassy went to the windows to observe what was happening and were injured or killed when the bomb was finally detonated (ibid.). The end result was massive casualties and damage, which included the collapse of the Ufundi Cooperative Building.

Kenya was not only targeted for the American embassy there. Kenya has a significant Muslim minority of 3.7 million or 10 percent of the total population, which provides a significant base that could be recruited to carry out terrorist acts or support them. Further, the government has engaged in an ill-advised program of systematic discrimination, which makes it a good place for militant Islam to grow and prosper (Hammer, 2007).

Further, Kenya was a popular tourist stop for many Africans and foreign travelers. The economy actually rebounded to a growth rate of around 7 percent thanks in large part to a billion-dollar tourism industry (Gettleman, 2008a). What has been the recent downfall of the tourist industry has not been the terrorist attacks but the internal unrest as a result of the violence over shared political power. The images of machete-wielding mobs have caused numerous cancellations very recently, and this will probably cut deeply into the 7 percent GDP growth rate (Gettleman, 2008b). Bookings are down 80 to 90 percent, and it was estimated by Rose Musonye, of the Kenya Tourist Board, that business for the year could be down 50 percent (ibid.). Even if the politically motivated riots that have occurred in the recent months are not categorized as terrorist acts by the press, the end results have had a significant impact on the people and the economy. When tourism slows or stops, the effects are felt within multiple levels of the economy. Tourism employs guides, drivers, cooks, waiters, masseuses, wood carvers, and bead stringers, and these professionals support larger extended families, many of whom are unemployed (Gettleman, 2008b).

Varying motivations surround the terrorist incidents in Kenya, but what is absent are incidents from terrorist organizations indigenous to the state. Kenya has remained free of internal terrorist activity while, at the same time, remaining vulnerable to international attacks. Free trade, cozy relations with Western nations, and internal instability have made Kenya prime target of international terrorists. A significant local population of Muslim fundamentalists has only added fuel to the fire. Kenya bears watching, with its heavy reliance on tourism and proximity to states in league with Al-Qaeda; the largely terrorism-free state could face an onslaught of future violent instability.

Malawi: Surprising Quiet on a Chaotic Continent

Within the continent of Africa lies the landlocked state of Malawi, situated between the domestic terrorism of South Africa and the international terrorism of Kenya. Part of the explanation for the lack of terrorism in Malawi lies in recent events of the state and also in the historic events that begin with colonial and precolonial time periods. With a brief look at the history it is possible to see that many preconditions necessary for terrorism are not present in this state.

Malawi had a disruptive precolonial history. Prior to the 1800s, the area around Lake Nyasa (now called Lake Malawi) was a place where several different ethnic groups settled and established a presence. But by the early 1800s, the arrival of groups supporting the Arab slave trade spread through the area. This disruptive force, along with the influence of the Ngoni a warlike people fleeing the expansion of Shaka Zulu — totally disrupted the quiet tranquility and any chance of political or economic development of the area (Kalipeni, 1992: 2). The work of Dennis Venter describes this time, saying, "The pattern of endemic tribal conflict and disruption caused by the slave trade, however, to a great extent promoted social instability and even detribalization in precolonial Nyasaland," (1995: 152). This, coupled with the arrival of British explorers, most notably David Livingstone, set the stage for future events.

David Livingstone was so shocked by the conditions present and the inhumane nature of the slave trade that he convinced British organizations to send missionaries with the intent to "end the slave trade in central Africa and in its place introduce legitimate commerce, education and Christianity" (Kalipeni, 1992: 2). This effort proved so successful that missionaries and settlers began to move into the area and establish plantations and a stable economic system. Threatened by the Portuguese, the British settlers convinced the British government to form "the British Protectorate of Nyasaland" in 1891. From the early efforts of the missionaries and British administration, what evolved from this region of chaos was a sense of peace and order and the rise of a national identity that circumvented traditional ethnic and tribal boundaries (Venter, 1995: 153). This new order set the stage for Malawi's future and possible explanations for the lack of terrorism.

What was found in Malawi at the beginning of colonial times was the lack of a dominant ethnic or tribal group or the presence of competing groups. In current state studies of Malawi, the dominant historical ethnic populations are listed by tribe. Kalipeni identified the fractured nature of tribal cleavages in Kenya and noted, "Today, no less than fifteen ethnic groups can be identified in Malawi and none of them comprise a majority of the population" (Kalipeni, 2002; 2). Perhaps because of the multifaceted nature of tribal cleavages in Malawi there is little tribal rivalry as no one group has enough power to dominate the others. Even in recent political elections Deborah Kaspin found no correlation between ethnic groups but more of a correlation between communities that guided voting behavior (1995: 598).

The colonial time period for Malawi lasted from the establishment of the region as a protectorate in 1891 to independence in 1964. There are three main pieces in this time period that appear to have affected future terrorism: economic stability, rule by the colonial government, and the transition to an independent government. Historical economic stability in Malawi began with the state's ability to feed itself. Early Portuguese explorers traveling though the area between the 1600s and 1800s brought with them and helped introduce crops like maize, cassava, and sweet potatoes (Kalipeni, 2002: 2). The introduction of these crops and the later establishment of plantations provided the local population with ample food. In later years, during the droughts in the 1980s, Malawi was able to export food to help neighboring states (Levy, 1985). Added to this economic base was the influence of European settlers and a large Indian population. These settlers helped establish an infrastructure for an evolving state. At the time of independence, most of the service industry was still run by expatriates (Roberts, 1970: 60). Indians settled early in Malawi and established a major presence in the business community to a point where in 1992 they dominated the trading sector (Kalipeni, 1992: 4). By full independence, Malawi would not be the richest country in Sub-Saharan Africa, but with its European and Indian ties it certainly would have had fundamental trading links with the Western business community.

The establishment of colonial rule under the British protectorate was authoritative in nature. The system included a governor assisted by district commissioners with some positions help by local African chiefs (Kalipeni, 1992: 3). Integrated into this system was a rising African elite that was a result of the mission schools in northern Malawi. These elites formed the Native Association, which, for a period, gave "avenues of communication with the colonial government" (ibid.). As Malawi approached its end to colonial rule it did so without economic and political turmoil. The local population was not happy with its current status under colonialism, but with sufficient food, conditions were tolerable. Even when people are discontented, they are unlikely to take violent action. The price of rebelling against the established rule carried greater risks than remaining relatively docile under unfair colonial rule. Jack Goldstone found this to be a common outcome for discontented populations who were having basic needs met (1997: 112). Peasants rationally weighed the costs of revolt, which would most likely result in their death, against a meager existence. Almost always, poor, subjected populations refused to resort to violence until they were starving.

The move to independence was not without difficulty but was accomplished *sans* armed struggle. The movement to independence was accomplished by a group of young nationalists from the Nyasaland African Congress. In their quest for independence, they felt their movement needed the leadership of a mature figure (Kalipeni, 1992: 5). They found such a leader in a former native of Malawi, Dr. Hastings Kamuzu Banda, who had been practicing medicine in Ghana and Great Britain. As a result of some initial disturbances, the party was banned by the colonial government. In its place the Malawi Congress Party was formed. The key to this transition to independence was in the new political party. This nationalistic party transcended ethnicity, with members from various regions and ethnic groups (ibid.). This one-party movement had no opposition and moved into power with the support of the general populace.

The post-independence era for Malawi was a period when the newly independent government became a one-man-ruled party and state under Dr. Banda. In his initial years as president, he found opposition to his leadership. Through force he was able to solidify his position and, eventually, become president for life. These actions created opposition, but anyone who opposed President Banda did so from exile. His rise to power was accomplished with the support of loyal followers and the backing of the state's security forces.

Dr. Banda kept power by tapping into a local populace of unemployed young men in Malawi. The assumption by President Banda was that if the energy of young males could be channeled into productive means, then it was logical to assume a reduction in future problems. President Banda achieved this end through the development of the Young Pioneers, which was initially set up to give young males something to do so they would refrain from agitation against his dictatorial rule. As the Young Pioneers evolved over time, so did their activities. By 1980, the Young Pioneers had taken on a role as a paramilitary force loyal to President Banda. As this organization evolved further, it was able to collect intelligence and enforce the political will of President Banda (Phiri, 2000: 4), thus further preventing any terrorist activity and, indeed, preventing any violence at all from developing within the state. By 1992, this organization was estimated to have 6,000 armed members deployed throughout the state.

Another factor in a terrorism-free state is a professional military. For a small state, the Malawian military has a reputation of service to the people. From its beginning, it has maintained a standard of professional officers and noncommissioned officers. Many of the senior leaders of the state have attended U.S. military schools and have had an ongoing partnership in training with U.S. military personnel in the 1990s. The Malawian Army saw as its duty the defending of the state, rather than becoming involved in the internal politics of the nation. This forced the president to address political issues, rather than to crush opposition with military power, thus creating potential government-sponsored brutality. This underlying value was tested in 1992 at the end of President Banda's political reign. As opposition was growing to his thirty-year reign, several senior military officers informed President Banda that they were unwilling to perform policing duties against those calling for a multiparty constitution (Venter, 1995: 159). Additionally, a few months later, the military "showed signs of being ready to prevent the police launching a full-scale crackdown on opponents of the regime" (Venter, 1995: 162). The foundation for this potential insurgency was laid in 1993 with the elimination of the Young Pioneers by the Malawian military. This action left potential seeds for future terrorist action. The attack against the Young Pioneers was fully supported by the domestic population.

With the death of President Banda, new elections are scheduled in Malawi for 2009. Without President Banda and the Young Pioneers, the potential for a descent into violence becomes a real possibility. However, democracy seems to be growing in Malawi and without a recent history of chaos and violence, the prospects still look good.

Sub-Saharan Africa and Transitioning Terrorism

The cases examined from Sub-Saharan Africa closely resemble some of the cases found in South and Southeast Asia. Despite Sub-Saharan African states being some of the poorest, most chaotic, and most violent nations in the world, terrorism springs from multiple impetuses. To be sure, the chaos and poverty create a perfect backdrop of instability that can be exploited by terrorists, and in some cases terrorists use this instability to their advantage, but poverty alone is not the key determinant.

The LRA in Uganda is an interesting case of the chaotic, extremely violent, and poorly organized terrorism that can develop in an unstable atmosphere. The effectiveness of the LRA is in question due to the extremely poor organization of the group and its heavy reliance on children as perpetrators, but cross-border support from the Sudanese government (the same government that harbored Osama bin Laden and Al-Qaeda for many years) keeps the LRA afloat.

In both Angola and South Africa, terrorism faded due to a multifaceted approach toward dealing with the terror threat. Leaders were targeted for assassination or imprisonment, while more moderate elements in the terror movement were enticed into peaceful activism through the political system. In both cases, this approach was successful.

In Kenya, there are no domestic impetuses for terror groups, but its key location and friendly relations with the West make this state a target for international terrorism. Freedom of movement, a downside to democracy and capitalism, has helped terror perpetrators complete some devastating attacks.

Poverty and instability are key components in fomenting terrorism in Sub-Saharan Africa, and in several cases there is a Clash of Civilizations component. Having said this, most terrorism that does occur in this region is homegrown. There is little linkage with larger movements like Al-Qaeda, with the exception of spectacular attacks on U.S. interests like the twin Al-Qaeda bombings of U.S. embassies in Kenya and Tanzania. Each state's problems are different, and most African states seem on the verge of wider terrorism-related problems. The United States might expend some counterterrorism resources here simply to ensure that local terror problems do not become regional or international ones.

References

Boehmer, Elleke. (2005). "Postcolonial Terrorist. The Example of Nelson Mandela." *Parallax*. Volume 11, Number 4: 46–55.

Brittain, Victoria. (8 October 2001). "What You Get for Backing a Tyrant." *New Statesman*. Volume 130, Issue 4558: 24–25.

Byrnes, Rita M. (December 1992). *Uganda, a State Study*. Washington, D.C: U.S. Government Printing Office.

Davis, Steven M. (1987). *Apartheid's Rebels: Inside South Africa's Hidden War*. Craighall, Johannesburg: AD Donker.

Gettleman, Jeffrey. (01 January 2008). "As Kenya Bleeds, Tourism Also Suffers in a Land of Safaris." *New York Times*: 6.

Gettleman, Jeffrey. (28 February 2008b). "Kenya." *New York Times Online*. (http//topics.nytimes.com/top/news/international/countries and territories/Kenya/index.html). Accessed 5 May 2008.

Goldstone, Jack A. (1997). "Population Growth and Revolutionary Crisis." In *Theorizing Revolutions*. John Foran, Editor. London and New York: Routledge.

Hammer, Joshua. (23 December 2007). "The African Front." *New York Times*: 48.

Helling, Eric Robert, LRC, MC, USA. (November 2004). "Otologic Blast Injuries Due to the Kenya Embassy Bombing." *Military Medicine*. Volume 169, Number 11: 872–76.

"How to Save the World." (30 October 2004). *Economist*. Volume 373, Issue 8399: 80.

Kalipeni, Ezekial. (Spring 1992). "Political Development and the Prospects for Democracy in Malawi." *Transafrica Forum*. Volume 9, Issue 1: 27–40.

Kaspin, Debora. (December 1995). "The Politics of Ethnicity in Malawi's Democratic Transition." *The Journal of Modern African Studies*. Volume 33, Number 4: 595–620.

Lamb, David. (1987). *The Africans*. New York: Vintage Books Edition, Random House.

Leach, Graham. (1986). *South Africa. No Easy Path to Peace*. London and New York: Routledge and Kegan Paul.

Levy, Sam. (15 May 1985). "Malawi: Oasis in a Continent's Agricultural Desert." *The Wall Street Journal*: 1.

Lipton, Eric, and Benjamin Weiser. (5 August 2004). "Threats and Response: The Plots, Al-Qaeda Strategy Cause For New Alarm." *New York Times*: 1.

Malaquias, Assis. (December 2001). "Making War & Lots of Money: The Political Economy of Protracted Conflict in Angola." *Review of African Political Economy*. Volume 28, Number 90: 521–36.

Mandela, Nelson. (1986). *The Struggle Is My Life*.

McKay, Susan. (2005). "Girls as 'Weapons of Terror' in Northern Uganda and Sierra Leonean Rebel Fighting Forces." *Studies in Conflict and Terrorism*. Volume 28, Number 5: 385–97.

Melady, Thomas Patrick, and Margaret Badum Melady. (1977). *Idi Amin Dada: Hitler in Africa*. Riverside, N.J.: Sheed, Andrews, and McMeel.

Morris, Daniel. (June 2006). "The Chance to Go Deep: U. S. Energy Interests in West Africa." *American Foreign Policy Interests*. Volume 28, Issue 3: 225–38.

Ndumbe, J. Anyu, and Barbara Cole. (Spring 2005). "The Illicit Diamond Trade, Civil Conflicts, and Terrorism in Africa." *Mediterranean Quarterly*. Volume 16, Issue 2: 52–65.

Ousman, Abdelkerim. (Fall 2004). "The Potential of Islamist Terrorism in Sub-Saharan Africa." *International Journal of Politics, Culture and Society*. Volume 18, Number 1: 65–105.

Phiri, Kings M. (March 2000). "A Case of Revolutionary Change in Contemporary Malawi: The Malawi Army and the Disarming of the Malawi

Young Pioneers." *Journal of Peace, Conflict and Military Studies*. University of Zimbabwe Center for Defense Studies. (www.uz.ac.zw/units/cos/journals/volume1/number1/article3.html). Accessed 22 April 2008.

Quaranto, Peter J. (January/March 2006). "Ending the Real Nightmares of Northern Uganda." *Peace Review*. Volume 18, Issue 1: 137–44.

Roberts, Bryan. (January 1970). "Malawi Progress and Problems Since Independence." *African Affairs*. Volume 69, Number 274: 60–64.

Snow, Donald. (1998). *National Security: Defense Policy in a Changed International Order*. New York: St. Martin's Press.

"UNITA Attacks Civilian Train." (December 2001). *UN Chronicle*. Volume 38, Issue 4: 69.

"UNITA – Down but Not Out." (18 August 2001). *Economist*. Volume 360, Issue 8235: 35.

Venter, Dennis. (1995). "Malawi: The Transition to Multi-Party Politics." In *Democracy and Political Change in Sub-Saharan Africa*. John A. Wiseman, editor. London: Routledge: 152–92.

CHAPTER 13

Conclusion and Policy Prescriptions

Instability is the Key to Understanding Terrorism

WHILE THE U.S. GOVERNMENT HAS only recently and fervently joined the global war on terror, many states in Asia and Africa have been fighting their own terror demons for decades. This places the U.S. counterterrorism strategy at a disadvantage, as it is essentially embryonic in its development. What the U.S. government and policymakers should have considered is engaging state experts and scholars in rigorous study before any bold policy was enacted. Unfortunately, the U.S. government decided to leap before looking, and we believe U.S. resources may need to shift quickly to deal with new terror threats emanating from Central, South, and Southeast Asia as well as northern Africa.

One point becomes clear after our exploration of domestic and international terrorism in Asia and Africa: terrorism and instability go hand in hand. We set out to examine possible links of democracy, or lack thereof, civilizational differences, and poverty with terrorism. What we ended up concluding is that no single factor adequately explains all, or even most, of the terror events and campaigns on these two continents. However, each of these three factors do play a role in specific states' and specific terror groups' motivations. The key ingredient seems to be the instability these factors produce, which, in turn, provides chaos that terror groups can exploit to recruit members and community support.

Also, we have found that one of the worst actions a government can take is oppressing a minority group within society. In many cases, civilizational differences play an added role in this situation, as terror groups can lay reasonable claim to the fact that the central government has picked the minority for reasons of racism or religious persecution. This situation creates a higher probability of widespread support for the terror campaign.

This is seen clearly in the case of the government mistreatment of the Uygur minority in China, the Aceh minority in Indonesia, the Tamil minority in Sri Lanka, and the Muslim minority in the Philippines.

This chapter presents our conclusions drawn from both the statistical and case study analyses of terrorism in Asia and Africa. First, we examine the definitional problem once again. This is followed by an examination of the roles that democracy, civilizational and cultural differences, and poverty play in the fomentation of terror campaigns and events. We conclude by prescribing some suggestions for state leaders regarding counterterrorism tactics and strategies.

The Continuing Problem of Definition and Case Selection

The problem of defining terrorism goes far beyond the definitional debate highlighted in Chapter 2. Even when there is some agreement on a terror definition, or at least the acceptance of core tenants, or when scholars consciously decide to diligently apply one definition in identifying terror cases, it remains extremely difficult to discern terrorism from other forms of violence.

It becomes even more difficult in mixed cases of violence, as in Japan and the Philippines. Communist terrorist groups in Japan often robbed, kidnapped, and murdered for profit in order to fund their terrorist and political campaigns aimed at overthrowing the democratically elected government and replacing it with a communist regime. Should these acts, which are supportive of a larger terror campaign, be labeled terrorism? This is a very tough call. Further, these same groups sometimes kidnapped and murdered solely for political reasons, and those acts would clearly fall under the rubric of terrorism.

The same problem arises on the southern island of Mindanao in the Philippines. While a large portion of the populace supports an Islamic succession of Mindanao from the Philippine state, the terror groups, like ASG and MNLF, often fund their terror campaign through robberies, kidnappings, and murder. These same groups do engage in prolonged terror campaigns aimed at civilians and governmental officials, but it is, again, debatable whether the criminal acts supporting the terror campaign should be labeled terrorist.

There is a larger definitional problem regarding domestic versus international terrorism. As far as we are able to discern, this is the first study that attempts to examine both domestic and international terrorism separately. We believe this is extremely important, as it appears there is a wide motivational and attitudinal difference between international and domestic terror groups. But determining whether an attack is inspired or supported by an international or regional terror group, as opposed to strictly being home-grown terrorism, is very difficult.

In India's Kashmir region, the terror campaign did not really begin in earnest until after Al-Qaeda's success in Afghanistan. Further, Pakistani governmental support was also needed before terrorism became a huge problem in Kashmir for the Indian government. All of the terror events occur in Jammu and Kashmir, but some of the terror groups operate cross-border raids, returning to the safety and protection of Pakistan after a raid or series of raids. Some of the most heavily supported terror groups in Kashmir stay in Kashmir. From this example, it becomes readily apparent how difficult it is to discern domestic from international terror attacks.

In Indonesia, JI styles itself as a regional terror group hoping to install a caliphate stretching from Indonesia to Thailand. This group was founded in Malaysia by exiled extremists and expatriate Indonesians, yet JI has only successfully carried out attacks in Indonesia. Again, it is hard to discern whether JI is a regional group, making the attacks in Indonesia international terrorism, or whether it is a domestic group with regional aspirations.

These types of debates need to be held in earnest between scholars or studies of terrorism will become a jumbled mess. We are hopeful that our initial cut at these problems will allow for future scholarship in this area.

Democracy and Terrorism

We found no evidence supporting the assertion that democracy mitigates terrorism. Specifically, there was no statistical correlation between democracy and international terrorism. In terms of domestic terrorism, there was a weak positive relationship between democracy and such events. We think we understand this correlation better through our case studies. What seems to be happening is that states transitioning to democracy are extremely vulnerable and unstable, and this instability provides the perfect opportunity for terror groups.

In fledgling democracies, as in Indonesia, terror groups are able to operate fairly easily before the government can legitimize itself in the eyes of the people and consolidate power. In nations that have failed to transition to a fully stable democratic form of governance, like the Philippines and Thailand, opportunities still abound for terror groups. In fact, in all three of these cases, democratically elected governments have mistreated minority groups under their control. The same is true for Indian governmental mistreatment of the Sikhs and Muslims within their borders. Democracy, unfortunately, does not provide instant stability to a state, nor does it create immediate tolerance between cultural groups or cessation of historical mistreatment of these groups.

Democracy provides for ease of movement within the state as well, and hinders or prohibits intrusive spying on citizens. This also creates an atmosphere in which terrorists and terror groups have an easier time operating. Additionally, democratic citizens are less tolerant of harsh tactics when dealing with terrorists, which can also hinder effective counterterrorism strategy.

We do not want to leave the impression, however, that democracy always produces terrorism. Both the statistical findings and the case studies paint a picture of democracy offering greater ease to terror movements, while fledgling or transitional democracies are the most highly correlated with terrorism.

Finally, there is growing evidence that democracy is neither a guarantee of friendliness to Western nations nor an assurance that a democratically elected government will refrain from supporting terrorism. Recent democratic elections in Egypt, Lebanon, Palestine, and Iraq have produced anti-Western, anti-American legislative bodies and executive leaders (Fattah, 2007: A4). The U.S. foreign policy presumption is that all democratic governments and polities will be friendly toward the United States, and their initiatives are quickly proving to be mistaken.

The Role of Clashing Civilizations

Samuel Huntington stunned the discipline of political science with his articles and books on clashing civilizations. He was initially dismissed, but growing animosity between different ethnicities, religions, and cultures has brought his work back to the forefront of discussion. We found mixed evidence for his assertions and offer a modified "Clash of Civilizations" Thesis here.

Our statistical findings were interesting. It appears that states with one or two large minorities or religions had more of a predisposition toward high levels of terrorism. We also found an apparent diversity dividend for states with three or more ethnicities or religions. Malawi is a great example of this diversity dividend. In a continent of chaos, Malawi, a very multi-ethnic nation with a significant Muslim minority, has experienced no terrorism and virtually no violence. We want to be clear there is not a one-to-one correlation in either direction, but these preliminary findings certainly deserve further examination.

Our case studies again help to flesh out the statistical findings. At first glance, it does appear that civilizations are clashing across both Asia and Africa; to some extent, they are. But our deeper examination of states and regions paints a more nuanced picture. It is not the case, for example, that Muslims and Christians cannot get along. What is happening more often than not is that the ethnicity or religion that dominates government is mistreating cultures different from its own.

There are numerous reasons why this occurs. In Africa, there is a long history of tribal/ethnic rivalry and hatred. There is also a long history of economic deprivation and dictatorship. Dictators often retain power in economically distressed states by finding scapegoats in society. In South Asia, British colonization created ethnic rivalry through favoritism of Tamils in Sri Lanka, poorly drawn borders in Pakistan and India (including the failed attempt to create East Pakistan out of the Bengali people and lands), and an ill-conceived Partition Plan that created an unruly exodus of Muslims to Pakistan and Hindus to India and, in turn, resulted in massive death and long-term hatred. In Indonesia, the central government has for years, both through Sukarno's and Suharto's dictatorship and through the early democratically elected presidents, mistreated indigenous groups like the Acehenese in Northern Sumatra. China has historically mistreated the Uygur population, creating a terror problem that need not exist.

So it appears that civilizations are not preordained to "clash" as Huntington asserts. Instead, mistreatment of minority ethnicities and religions by the central government creates separatist movements that lack the power to confront the military directly; hence they choose asymmetrical warfare, especially terror tactics. The terrorists and the central governments do use racist and inflammatory language to create support and hatred for the other side and, eventually, this does turn into a clash of cultures or civilizations. But the sad fact is that many of these domestic clashes of civilization could have been avoided and are more easily dealt with once both sides agree to ceasing the abuse.

Conversely, in terms of international terrorism, there does appear to be a strong civilizational component. The two main international terror groups in our study are Al-Qaeda and JI. Al-Qaeda is fighting a global jihad against Western states, capitalism, modernization, and Western intervention into Muslim lands. JI is a regional group with the express goal of establishing a Salafist Islamic caliphate in Southeast Asia. Interestingly, these two groups are now working closely together to achieve their goals. Both of these groups are fundamentalist Islamic in nature and both are unwilling to concede or negotiate anything. Seemingly, Huntington's assertion that Islam and Western Christianity will clash is true in part at the international level, but at the domestic level there are numerous cases of Christians and Muslims co-existing peacefully for decades.

The Poverty–Terrorism Nexus

Our statistical analysis found no correlation between poverty and terrorism. Our case studies also support this finding for the most part. There is some terrorism in the second and third largest economies in the world—China and Japan, respectively—and no terrorism in some of the poorest states in the world, Malawi and Mongolia, for example. The Indonesian and Thai economies are rapidly increasing and yet so are the incidence and severity of terrorism. From a macro point of view, there is no correlation between a nation's economic standing and terrorism.

Having said this, it is far easier to recruit members in a state experiencing severe economic deprivation. It is also easier to find local support when many people cannot find work, feel the government is failing to meet their needs, or there is inadequate food to go around.

But what really stands out from our case studies is the link between poverty and cultural oppression. When governments intentionally, or through omission, allow minority religions or ethnicities to suffer economic deprivation, especially denying these groups access to adequate education or bureaucratic positions, terror groups exploit this abuse by the government very effectively. In Sri Lanka, historical economic oppression by the Sinhalese majority against the Tamil minority produced a particularly brutal terror campaign. Economic deprivation of indigenous Africans by Dutch colonial, apartheid rulers produced terrorism by ANC. Economic deprivation of Eritreans in Ethiopia caused Eritrean separatist terrorism and, eventually, a separate Eritrean state.

But where everyone suffers together under a fair and stable system, as in in Malawi and Mongolia, terrorism does not arise. Even in Malawi, where there is a Christian majority and a significant Muslim minority, economic deprivation alone is not causing a violent terrorist response.

Commerce also produces access to the state. States that have relied heavily on tourism, like Egypt, Indonesia, and Kenya, find themselves more vulnerable to attack. These states have been especially vulnerable to international terrorism because the tourism contained in these states drew in Western civilians. The ease of movement required for successful tourism makes it easier for foreign terrorists and domestic terrorists to case potential sites and execute extremely damaging attacks.

Understanding Domestic and International Terrorism and Crafting a Nuanced and Multifaceted Counterterrorism Strategy

One of the main purposes of this book was to examine terrorism in Asia and Africa and draw conclusions that could be used by policymakers to craft an effective counterterrorism strategy. Unlike most previous examinations of terrorism, we feel that lessons can be learned from both states experiencing terrorism and those that have avoided it.

Our success stories are few, as most states have dealt with terrorism on a significant scale. What do the states that have completely avoided or have experienced very little terrorism, like China, Malaysia, Malawi, Mongolia, Taiwan, and Singapore, have in common? The answer is not democracy, wealth, or a homogeneous population. The answer is decades-long stability. One of the core tenets of an effective domestic and international effort to quell terrorism must be creating stability in unstable states. This is no easy task, nor is it something that can be solved with the introduction of just one variable, such as democracy or capitalism. What has to occur is a concerted effort to build stable governance, humanitarian treatment by the government of all groups, a stable economy, and overall legitimacy. These are not easy tasks to accomplish, but it does appear that they are necessary if a long-term solution to terrorism is sought.

Unfortunately, forcing democracy upon states that have had a history of authoritarian rule will most likely be counterproductive. In Central Asia, Afghanistan had virtually no history of domestic terrorism until the U.S. coalition attacked and removed the Islamic Taliban government and occupied the state. We are not arguing that the Taliban government was benign. This fundamental Islamic government abused human rights, especially the rights of women, destroyed economic progress, allowed opium production to flourish, harbored Al-Qaeda, and destroyed priceless Buddhist shrines and statues. But in terms of counterterrorism, forcing democracy on Afghanistan has produced more terror than it has prevented. In fact, Al-Qaeda is argued to be stronger today than prior to the occupation.

Why is this so? War and occupation create two key ingredients for terror organizations. First, war and occupation, no matter how noble the end goal, create a massive amount of chaos, instability, and general malaise among the local populace. Second, occupation provokes nationalism. Even citizens that might have been tolerant or sympathetic toward Western nations and initiatives can become stalwart enemies once their state is occupied. The goals of the occupation—democracy, capitalism, and so on—can become meaningless when these ideals are forced upon people through the barrel of a gun.

Western powers are also missing the opportunity to help states that are stable now but are facing serious terrorist threats. Malaysia, Singapore, and South Korea are currently terrorism free but all three states face significant threats. Malaysia was the starting home of JI and has an organization, KMM, that is supporting terrorist activity elsewhere (although it has not yet perpetrated terror acts of its own). Singapore recently thwarted a JI terror plot and sent key leaders of JI Singapore to prison. South Korea is increasingly worried about Al-Qaeda's open insistence that it is a prime target due to the South Korean government's close relationship with the United States and the government's support of the invasions in Iraq and Afghanistan. These are stable states that need to remain stable and terror free.

But fledgling democracies need the most support. If Western nations want to effectively spread democracy throughout the world, then more attention and resources must be invested in transitioning democracies. Not only do these transitioning democracies need foreign investment and grants for infrastructure and manufacturing development, but they also need mentoring. The West needs to monitor fledgling governmental treatment of minority groups within these states. Nothing sparks and sustains terrorism like governmental mistreatment.

"Carrots" are not the only effective counterterrorism measure, though. "Sticks" have worked well for several states in this study. In Singapore, intelligence provided information that allowed law enforcement to arrest key plotters in a series of terrorist strikes there, all but eliminating, for the time being, the JI terror threat there. Poorly organized terrorist organizations, like the LRA in Uganda, are more easily thwarted by the targeting of key leaders for arrest or assassination, especially as the rank-and-file members of LRA are often children or very young men. Law enforcement worked exceedingly well in disrupting and, ultimately, destroying the communist terror threat in Japan as well.

These tactics are most appropriate for terror groups that are irrational or unwilling to engage in fair negotiation. Secessionist groups with a legitimate complaint about past and present unfair treatment are less likely to be dissuaded through military or law enforcement initiatives.

What is interesting is that the two international terror campaigns, Al-Qaeda and JI, fall under the irrational category. It seems that international terror movements have broad, even grandiose, complaints and plans to change the world or regional system. True believers in such campaigns have gone beyond simple complaints of governmental mistreatment to complaints that the whole world is in error. These groups will most likely not respond well to carrots or negotiation. Unfortunately, our study leads us to believe that these groups will have to be disrupted and destroyed.

This is a particularly difficult case as Al-Qaeda digs into southeast Asia and northern Africa while building a very safe base in Pakistan. Pakistan is the key to the future of international terrorism. The U.S. relationship with President Musharraf ended with his ousting in the summer of 2008. Pakistan is heading toward a more fundamental Islamic governance. While Al-Qaeda was easier to uproot in Sudan and Afghanistan, a fundamental Islamic government in Pakistan will be all but impossible to topple. No wonder, as Al-Qaeda expands its operations in Asia and northern Africa while fortifying its headquarters in Pakistan, intelligence reports are beginning to determine that Al-Qaeda is stronger than ever.

In the end, the counterterrorism strategies that work for states are multifaceted, fluid, and do exclude options, even if one of the options is negotiating with the more rational members and factions within terror organizations. Following the current path of placing all the eggs into the democracy basket will fail in the long run and might even strengthen our enemies. This book is a call to policymakers to consider alternatives when dealing with terrorists and terror organizations and to begin placing more emphasis on training state experts in order that the most efficacious counterterrorism strategy can be determined. The age of terrorism is only beginning, but much of the current terrorism in the world could have likely been avoided and, at the very least, appears open to mitigation.

Reference

Fattah, Hassan M. (10 August 2007). "U.S. Backs Free Elections, Only to See Allies Lose." *New York Times*: A4.

Index

domestic terrorism (*continued*)
in Kenya, 194; in North Africa, 168;
poverty and, 56; regime instability and,
82–83, 202; religions and, 79–80, 81–82
Dravida Munnetra Kazhagam (DMK),
140
drug trafficking, 162, 164
Dutch colonization, 190, 207
Dying to Win (Pape), 29–30, 33

East Pakistan. *See* Bangladesh
Egypt, 56, 57, 167, 191, 205; domestic
terrorism incidents, 171; international
terrorism, 170–74; regime stability
and democracy in, 173; tourism and
terrorism in, 172, 208
11 September 2001 attacks, 1–2, 15, 27,
68, 85, 102, 132; Indonesia survey on,
89; OIC stance on, 18; religious
motivation for, 29–30; South Korea
and, 120–21
enclave(s), 96, 139
Eritrea, 174
Eritrean Islamic Jihad (Ethiopia), 179
Eritrean People's Liberation Front
(EPLF), 174, 180
Ethiopia, 58, 167, 192; domestic
terrorism in, 77; minorities
mistreated in, 180, 207; separatist
movements in, 174–75, 207
ethnicity / ethnic division(s), 62–63,
130–32, 183, 184. *See also* diversity;
minority group(s); in Bangladesh,
126–27; in China, 109–12; Malawi's
diversity, 195–96, 197; in Nepal, 130;
in South Asia, 178, 206; in Sudan,
178; terrorism and, 80–82, 205–7;
United States and, 198
ethnocide, 11
Eubank, William, 32
"extrajudicial killings," 98, 103, 129, 132,
143

Fearon, James, 33, 35
Fergana Valley (Tajikistan /
Uzbekistan), 159, 160, 164, 165
foreign occupation. *See* occupation,
foreign

"fragmented states," 46
Free Aceh Movement. *See* Gerakan
Aceh Merdeka (GAM)
Freedman, Lawrence, 19
Free Kashmir, 150
Free Papua Movement (OPM), 91–92
French revolution, 9–10, 16

GAM. *See* Gerakan Aceh Merdeka
(GAM)
Gama'a al-Islamiyya, al- (Egyptian
Islamist group), 171, 172
Gandhi, Mahatma, 139, 147
Gandhi, Prime Minister Indira (India),
140–41, 142–43
Gandhi, Prime Minister Rajiv (India),
137, 141–42
Geneva Conventions, 11, 19
genocide, 11, 23–24n5, 168
Gerakan Aceh Merdeka (GAM), 91–92
Germany, 1
Gini coefficient: domestic terrorism
and, 77–78
glasnost, 160
globalization, 27
Goldberg, Joseph, 9
Goldstein, Baruch, 28
Goldstone, Jack, 196–97
Gross Domestic Product Per Capita
Purchasing Power Parity
(GDPpcPPP), 44–45, 56–57, 66, 175;
domestic terrorism and, 74–78
"Group of 272," 90
guerilla warfare, 10–11
Gyanendra, King (Nepal), 132

Hahashin, 10
Haleem, Irm, 33–34
Hamas, 31, 36, 173
Hambali, 92, 93, 101
Hamilton, James, 31
Hamilton, Lawrence, 31
Han Dynasty. *See* Western Han
Dynasty (China)
Han people (Chinese ethnic group),
109, 110
Haq, General Zia-ul, 148
Harkat ul-Mujahideen (HUM), 145